Praise for
The Async-First Playbook

"Async is the superpower the most successf... ...realized, so understanding the playbook for implementing a... ...-do for any leader moving into this type of operating system. Sumeet ha... ...enal job outlining that here."

—Chase Warrington, Head of Remote, Doist

"Collaboration is going async. The advantages are just too great: global reach—which enables more inclusion—and time zone immunity. Sumeet excellently decomposes the issues. And by zeroing in on async leadership, he tackles the elephant in the async room: leadership. Yes, you can be an effective leader, asynchronously."

—Cliff Berg, Co-Founder and Managing Partner, Agile 2 Academy

"*The Async-First Playbook* is a must-read for anyone part of agile teams in today's fast-paced and distributed work environment. This insightful book shows how adopting an async-first approach can transform the way teams collaborate. The result—higher productivity, better inclusion, and most importantly, fun! The future of work is remote, and async-first collaboration is the key to unlocking its potential. Through concrete examples, this book provides a roadmap for embracing asynchronous communication, enabling teams to focus on deep work and stay in a state of flow. I recommend this book to anyone seeking to unlock the full potential of remote collaboration and achieve better outcomes for their team."

—Iwo Szapar, Co-founder & Head of Remote,
Remote-First Institute

"Asynchronous work, when implemented well, can help create a sustainable and calm way of working. It enables individuals to design their days around productivity and priorities, creating a happier and more human-centric workplace. *The Async-First Playbook* thoroughly examines effective asynchronous work practices' benefits (and the challenges, too). This playbook discusses fundamental prerequisites that should be in place before transitioning to an async-first approach, including leadership practices, potential challenges, and a starter kit to help you determine your next steps. If you seek to alleviate information overload and minimize meetings, *The Async-First Playbook* is a valuable resource."

—Lisette Sutherland, Director of Collaboration Superpowers
https://www.collaborationsuperpowers.com/

"At a time when organisations are experimenting with how to make the most out of remote work, Sumeet offers a step-by-step approach on how to make software development practices more inclusive and future-proof. Furthermore, the section aimed directly at managers and leaders also turns the book into a strong advocacy-tool for sustainable remote collaboration."

—Pilar Orti, Director of Virtual not Distant

"*The Async-First Playbook* is a comprehensive guide for teams and leaders looking to optimize their remote work practices for a distributed world. The pandemic helped us see that knowledge work really shouldn't have a place, and now it's time to recognize and embrace that this work can be better accomplished asynchronously, too. Location-independent work? That's the first step in the transformation. Have you tried time-independent work? Sumeet shows us how."

—Tyler Sellhorn, host, *The Remote Show* podcast

"*The Async-First Playbook* is not just another book on Agile practices. It's a game-changer for teams looking to optimize their collaboration through asynchronous communication. In this comprehensive guide, you'll find everything you need to know about the principles, frameworks, tools, workflows, and cultural changes necessary to embrace an async-first approach. Even though I've been working in a remote setup with an async-first approach for many years, I still found improvements that I'll implement with my team. I found especially valuable the chapter on "The Async-First Leadership Mindset," and I can't wait to share this book with my team."

—Oana Calugar, Collaboration Consultant, Mural

"Every software company has recently been forced to adapt to remote work, and subsequently workers have awakened to the possibilities afforded by more flexible working. Companies have been experimenting and iterating to find a new equilibrium between in-office, hybrid, and fully remote work, and there have been many fits and starts. What's been missing is a practical guide on how to make the most of this newly popular work style so that both employees and employers win. Sumeet's book perfectly fills the void, giving teams and leaders the tools they need to escape the trap of synchronicity and make the most of their newfound asynchronous flexibility."

—Patrick Sarnacke, Managing Director, Thoughtworks UK

"The COVID-19 pandemic has provoked many publications about remote and hybrid work models. While benefits such as improved work-life balance and diversity have been praised, concerns about weakened personal relationships and burnout are also significant. One crucial element is that, too often, the cons result from companies attempting to put in place novel models while retaining old office-centric practices. That is why I like this book. In *The Async-First Playbook*, Sumeet Gayathri Moghe offers a practical, hands-on approach to making remote work effective for software development businesses. He emphasizes defaulting to action and provides actionable recommendations for optimizing distributed work arrangements. As someone who has led an organization through a similar journey and had valuable conversations with Sumeet while doing that, I can attest that this book packages knowledge from real-world techniques with a successful track record."

—Matheus Tait, Managing Director, Thoughtworks Spain

"Building on commonly established working patterns that have been adopted by many in the agile software development movement, Sumeet deftly re-examines the goals of these practices, and identifies remote-friendly alternatives that can lead your team to new heights. Of particular note is the emphasis on honing both writing and reading skills, and on guarding the time to use them both effectively. Those looking to navigate this new frontier would be well advised to set some time aside and read this first!"

—Andy Yates, Head of Technology,
Corporate Strategy, Thoughtworks

"The pandemic forced the tech workforce all over the world to work remotely. And since then, the focus has been on overcoming the challenges of remote working. Sumeet argues that the opportunity is bigger—to work differently, adopting async-first approaches and practices, to increase productivity and creativity by creating space for deep work and better collaboration amongst teams. *The Async-First Playbook* is a complete practitioner's guide to learn and implement async ways of working for yourself, your team, and your organization. In a new distributed and remote working world, this book has the potential to unlock productivity, better teamwork, and allow for improved work-life balance. A total must-read for technology or knowledge workers."

—Sameer Soman, Managing Director, Thoughtworks India

"Want to boost productivity and cut costs in your engineering organization? Sumeet's new book offers practical, actionable recommendations for optimizing team performance and streamlining processes via asynchronous ways of working. In today's digital-first world, boards are taking notice of the skyrocketing cost of engineering. Sumeet's book provides a valuable perspective on this issue, offering strategies for achieving better results in less time and at a lower cost. Whether you're a seasoned engineering leader or just starting out, this is a must-read for anyone looking to drive change and improve their organization's performance in a highly remote setting."

—Sagar Paul, Head of Global Solutions, Thoughtworks

"*The Async-First Playbook* is the book that the distributed agile world has been eagerly awaiting for years! Sumeet's direct and to-the-point writing style hits hard and very convincingly challenges our traditional norms. The book stays true to the format of a playbook by providing recommendations that are highly actionable and will enable the stated impact. An amazing must-read for software professionals."

—Santosh Mahale, Director, Engineering Group | e4r
(Engineering for research)

"The COVID-19 pandemic has accelerated the adoption of remote work, and it is now here to stay. However, many companies are still struggling to adapt to this new reality. This is where *The Async-First Playbook* comes in. In this book, the author makes a compelling argument for why async-first practices are essential for modern knowledge work. He guides the reader through the foundational elements needed to create an async-first culture, from individual and team practices to leadership and management styles. The author also highlights the challenges that come with remote work and provides readers with practical advice on how to avoid common pitfalls. Whether you're a developer, manager, or senior leader, this book will provide you with the tools you need to succeed in the new world of work."

—Sunil Mundra, Org. Change and Transformation Leader,
CXO Advisor, Thoughtworks

THE ASYNC-FIRST PLAYBOOK

THE ASYNC-FIRST PLAYBOOK

REMOTE COLLABORATION TECHNIQUES FOR AGILE SOFTWARE TEAMS

Sumeet Gayathri Moghe

✦ Addison-Wesley

Hoboken, New Jersey

Cover image: Mr Aesthetics/Shutterstock
Chapters 4, 9: Various emojis, Carboxylase/Shutterstock
Figure 4.2: Screen capture, Microsoft
Figures 6.1, 10.2, 23.1: Screen captures, Atlassian
Figures 9.1, 9.2, 29.3: Screen captures, Google
Figures 11.1-11.4, 12.1, 12.3: Screen captures, Slack Technologies, LLC
Table 15.1: Based on Gayathri Mohan, *Full Stack Testing: A Practical Guide for Delivering High Quality Software*, O'Reilly Media, Inc., 2022
Figure 18.2: Screen capture, ADR-Manager
Figure 20.2: Screen capture, Readme.so
Chapter 22, page 203: Definition of *busywork* courtesy of Pearson Education, Longman Dictionary of Contemporary English, 6th Edition, (c) 2014. Reprinted by permission of Pearson Education Limited.
Figure 21.3: Screen captures, Thoughtworks, Inc.
Table 24.1: Based on Nicole Forsgren, Margaret-Anne Storey, Chandra Maddila, Thomas Zimmermann, Brian Houck, and Jenna Butler, "The SPACE of Developer Productivity," *Queue*, Vol. 19, issue 1, ACM, 2021
Figures 29.1, 29.2, 29.4-29.7: Screen captures, Mural

For information about buying this title in bulk quantities, or for special sales opportunities (which may include electronic versions; custom cover designs; and content particular to your business, training goals, marketing focus, or branding interests), please contact our corporate sales department at corpsales@pearsoned.com or (800) 382-3419.

For government sales inquiries, please contact governmentsales@pearsoned.com.

For questions about sales outside the U.S., please contact intlcs@pearson.com.

Visit us on the Web: informit.com/aw

Library of Congress Control Number: 2023940413

ISBN-13: 978-0-13-818753-8
ISBN-10: 0-13-818753-3

1 2023

Pearson's Commitment to Diversity, Equity, and Inclusion

Pearson is dedicated to creating bias-free content that reflects the diversity of all learners. We embrace the many dimensions of diversity, including but not limited to race, ethnicity, gender, socioeconomic status, ability, age, sexual orientation, and religious or political beliefs.

Education is a powerful force for equity and change in our world. It has the potential to deliver opportunities that improve lives and enable economic mobility. As we work with authors to create content for every product and service, we acknowledge our responsibility to demonstrate inclusivity and incorporate diverse scholarship so that everyone can achieve their potential through learning. As the world's leading learning company, we have a duty to help drive change and live up to our purpose to help more people create a better life for themselves and to create a better world.

Our ambition is to purposefully contribute to a world where:

- Everyone has an equitable and lifelong opportunity to succeed through learning.
- Our educational products and services are inclusive and represent the rich diversity of learners.
- Our educational content accurately reflects the histories and experiences of the learners we serve.
- Our educational content prompts deeper discussions with learners and motivates them to expand their own learning (and worldview).

While we work hard to present unbiased content, we want to hear from you about any concerns or needs with this Pearson product so that we can investigate and address them.

- Please contact us with concerns about any potential bias at https://www.pearson.com/report-bias.html.

To every worker who's had joy sucked out of their life by a pointless meeting.

CONTENTS

Foreword   xxi
Preface   xxv
Acknowledgments   xxix
About the Author   xxxiii

PART I   ADAPTING TO THE NEW NORMAL   I

Chapter I   **There's Got to Be a Better Way to Work   3**
Work Deserves a New Look   5
   Complex Problems Need Smarter Collaboration   6
   The Promise of Flexibility   6
   Escaping the Shallows   7
   A More Inclusive Workplace   9
   Defaulting to Action   9
   Improved Knowledge Sharing and Communication   10
A Better Work Environment for All of Us   11

Chapter 2   **Foster a Mindset for Change   13**
Four Simple Ideas   13
   Focus on Value   13
   Visualize Change on a Spectrum   14

Make a Ulysses Pact   17
Appreciate the Balance   17
Go Far, Go Together   19
Ready for the First Steps   19

PART II   PREPARE TO GO ASYNC-FIRST   **21**

Chapter 3   **The Tools You Need**   **23**
With Tools, Less Is More   23
Tools Are Everything; Tools Are Nothing   27

Chapter 4   **The Biggest Async-First Superpower**   **29**
Writing Is a Practice; Documentation a Product   30
Why Meetings Are the Last Resort, Not the First Option   30
The Benefits of Writing   31
What About the Agile Manifesto?   33
How Do We Write Better?   34
How Much More Effective Is Face-to-Face Communication?   40
The Manifesto Deserves the Benefit of Doubt   40
To Work Async-First, We Must Write   41

Chapter 5   **Three More Async-First Superpowers**   **43**
What an Async-First Superhero Looks Like   43
Block Distractions   44
Read and Comprehend   45
Work Independently   46
Personal Productivity Leads to Team Productivity   47

Chapter 6   **Calm Things Down with Collaboration Protocols**   **49**
Work Execution vs. Workflow   49
Revisit Your Workflow Statuses and Transitions   50
Make Email and IM Secondary Communication Tools   52
Streamline Your Decision-Making Process   53
Identify Channels and Their Response Times   55
Fundamentals, Fundamentals, Fundamentals   56

PART III	THE PRACTITIONER'S GUIDE	57
Chapter 7	Meetings as the Last Resort	59
	Just. Too Many. Meetings.	59
	The ConveRel Quadrants	61
	When You Meet, Make It Count	63
	Account for Costs of Frequent Cross–Time Zone Meetings	64
	Stay Human	66
	Async-First, with Small Shifts	66
Chapter 8	The Value of Being Face to Face	69
	From URL to IRL	69
	The Time-Zone Question	69
	Face-to-Face Collaboration Isn't Free	70
	The True Value of Being in Person	71
	Camaraderie Has Dollar Value	72
	Rethink the Onsite-Offsite	73
	Be Conscious About Building Relationships	74
	So Much for Meetings	75
Chapter 9	Micro-Moves to Shift Left	77
	Small Shifts, Easy Wins	77
	Personal Shifts: Broadcast Your Commitment	77
	Team Shifts: Accelerate Leftward	81
	Build Async-First Behavioral Cues	85
Chapter 10	Write a Team Handbook	87
	Distributed Teams Need a Single Source of Truth	87
	By Default, Start with Your Team	88
	What Goes into a Handbook?	89
	Tools You Can Use	92
	Start Small, Own Collectively, Be Iterative	93
	Go Deep with Your Documentation Triggers	94
	Aim for a Shared Reality	95

Chapter 11   **Tame the "Instant" in Instant Messaging**   **97**
              Make Messaging Productive   97
                   If It's Urgent, Use a Suitable Medium   98
                   Choose Intuitive Names for Channels and Rooms   99
                   Show Your Status, Respect Others' Statuses   99
                   Limit the Number of Messages   100
                   Get to the Point   102
                   Target Your Conversations   102
                   React, Don't Respond   103
                   Use Threads: One per Topic   104
                   Slow Things Down, and Don't Argue on Chat   104
                   Make Your IM Guidelines Visible   105
              Messaging: Just Not Instant   105

Chapter 12   **Standup Meetings: An Easy Shift Left**   **107**
              Distributed Standups Can Be Painful   108
                   Use the Project Management Tool's Features   109
                   Automate the Ritual   113
                   Keep It Relevant   115
                   Make Peace with Lag   115
              Standups = Conveyance/Strong Relationships   116

Chapter 13   **Take Charge of Your Development Cycles**   **117**
              Sprint Ceremonies Can Hinder Async Work   117
                   Approach 1: Embrace Continuous Flow   118
                   Approach 2: Use "Shape Up" Cycles   122
              The Key to Asynchrony Is a Strong Process   125

Chapter 14   **Run Meaningful Retrospectives**   **127**
              Infrequent Retros Lead to Poor Team Health   127
                   View Retrospectives as a Process and Not an Event   128
                   Collect Inputs in Safety   130
                   Voting Synchronously vs. Asynchronously   131
                   Setting Up the Retrospective Environment   131
                   Retros as a Process, Not an Event   134
              Scrum for the 2020s   135

Chapter 15   Kickoffs and Desk Checks: Reduce Ritualized Interruptions   137
How to Maintain Quality with Fewer Meetings?   138
Approach 1: Go Async with Kickoffs and Desk Checks   138
Approach 2: Keep the Sync Practices and Plan for Them   144
Make Your Feedback Loops "Remote Native"   145

Chapter 16   Questions to Reimagine Your Tech Huddles   147
The What and the Why   148
How Much Autonomy Exists in Your Teams?   148
How Necessary Is the "Sync Up"?   150
What If You Defaulted to Action?   150
If You Must Huddle, How Do You Make the Meeting Effective?   151
Oh, and About the Regular, Scheduled Huddles...   152
Not a Zero-Sum Game   153

Chapter 17   Pair Programming: The Elephant in the Room   155
A Polarizing Topic   155
Let's Start with Why   156
Design for Flexibility   157
Use the Right Tools   158
Encourage Personal Discipline   158
Mix Pairing and Solo Work   160
If It's Fun for You, Pair by All Means   161

Chapter 18   Audit Trails from the Flow of Your Work   163
The "Just Ask" Pattern Breaks Down   163
Meeting Notes   164
Business Decision Records   166
Architectural Decision Records   166
Commit Messages   168
Pull Requests   169
Trails as the Most Frequent Form of Documentation   171

Chapter 19	Communicate Tech and Functional Design	173
	An Agile Approach to Design	173
	Idea Papers	174
	Feature Breakdown Documents	175
	Technical Design Documents	176
	Simplify Communication Complexity	178
Chapter 20	Two Stable Pieces of Handbook Documentation	181
	Being Agile About Documentation	181
	Your Ways of Working	182
	Codebase README Files	184
	Documenting Code? Think Twice	185
	Good Documents Reduce Guesswork	186
Chapter 21	Craft an Efficient Onboarding Process	189
	Write Once, Run Many Times	189
	Preserve the Dumb Questions Budget with an FAQ	190
	Build an Onboarding Checklist	191
	Focus on Automation and Reusability	193
	Find the New Hire a Buddy	194
	Foster Strong Relationships	195
	Onboarding Efficiency = Team Efficiency	195
PART IV	ASYNC-FIRST LEADERSHIP	197
Chapter 22	The Async Leadership Mindset	199
	The Tyranny of "The Way"	199
	How Can You Get the Most Out of Yourself?	200
	How Can You Be an Example, Not a Bottleneck?	202
	How Can You Avoid Busywork?	203
	How Can You Champion Inclusion?	204
	How Can You Make Your Team Resilient?	205
	Make Time for the Essential Stuff	206

Chapter 23   **Manage Your People with Care**   **209**
Corrections in the Right Direction   209
    Manage Your Own Workload   210
    Meet People One-on-One   211
    Practice Radical Candor   213
Be the Bridge Between Your Team and Your Company's Culture   216

Chapter 24   **Set Up Your Team for Success**   **217**
Design for Success   217
    Manage Team Cognitive Load Through Team Topologies   218
    Revisit Your Team's Internal Structure   219
    Reduce Pressure, Create Calm   221
    Consciously Build a Team Culture   223
    Align on a Common Purpose   226
Your Virtual Workplace Needs Configuring   227

Chapter 25   **Farm Tacit Knowledge in Your Company**   **229**
Beyond Handbooks: Into Communities   229
    Create Porous Walls   230
    Facilitate Flows While You Manage Stocks   234
From Team Knowledge to Company Knowledge   238

PART V   **NAVIGATE THE PITFALLS**   **241**

Chapter 26   **The Great Hybrid Kerfuffle**   **243**
People's Preferences Are Heading Remote   243
    Hybrid Organization, Not Hybrid Employees   244
    Avoid a Move Backward   245
    Avoid New Costs for All Stakeholders   246
    Embrace Science, Not Superstition   249
    Don't Create a Perception of Asymmetry   251
    Treat Everyone as "Remote"   251
Choice and Autonomy Are the Key Words   253

Chapter 27   **The Async Island**   **255**
Unpacking Organizational Inertia   255
    Forces for and Against Change   255
    Async Work Is a New Sport   258

	Help Your System Get Better	259
	Protect and Extend the Island	260
	While Being a Guerilla, Don't Forget Advocacy	265
Chapter 28	**Toxicity in the Virtual Workplace**	**267**
	Toxicity Builds: One Benign Step at a Time	267
	Celebrating the Hard Worker	267
	Digital Presenteeism	268
	Talking to the Document	269
	Not Investing in Meaningful Synchrony	270
	As a Leader, Stay Vigilant	271
PART VI	**BRING IT ALL TOGETHER**	**273**
Chapter 29	**The Async-First Starter Kit**	**275**
	Five Stages of Sensible Defaults	275
	Stage 1: Align on Goals	276
	Stage 2: Tabulate Baseline Data	278
	Stage 3: Agree on the Fundamentals	280
	Stage 4: Clean Up Your Calendars	282
	Stage 5: Build the 30-Day Program and Beyond	283
	A Team Shift, Owned by the Team	285
Chapter 30	**A Brave New World of Work**	**287**
	Another World of Work Is Possible	289
	Flexibility as a Desire and a Right	289
	A Skills Economy	290
	Digital Nomadism	291
	The Four-Day Workweek	292
	Gen Z and Their Sensibilities	294
	A Shift for Autonomy	295
	It's Time to Sign Off	295
	Endnotes	**297**
	Index	**321**

FOREWORD

Two decades ago in a workshop, we looked for a name for a new approach to software development. We settled on "agile," but one of the suggestions was "conversational." What I liked about "conversational" was that it emphasized how we were advocating a more collaborative approach to building software. Instead of tasks carved out by managers and architects, delivered by (usually poorly written) documents, we wanted people to talk to each other. Database engineers could collaborate with those coding business logic using that data. Programmers should talk to their users about what software would be most valuable for their work. Communication is the bloodstream of a software effort, and we wanted to recognize that and increase its flow.

A few years later, Thoughtworks, my employer, opened offices in India. We had embraced and pioneered this agile approach to software development, and it was showing great success. But how could this work with a development center in India? The close collaboration we were encouraging was one thing when it was just a walk down a hall to talk to someone; what did it mean when separated by thousands of miles and a dozen time zones?

We found ways to make things work, and in time, technology came to assist us further. By the early 2010s, we were making heavy use of video-call technologies for our meetings (a habit that served us well when COVID-19 hit in 2020).

Sumeet Gayathri Moghe has seen this activity first-hand, working with us in India through most of this time. He's managed several teams working across space and time zones in highly collaborative ways. As he's done this work, he's been reflecting on how effective our techniques are and how to improve them.

The video call has helped meetings work better when people are sitting far from each other, but even when in the same room, meetings aren't always the best way to collaborate. Questions that come up are often not best answered off the cuff—people need time to reflect. I like writing not just to communicate, but as a tool to arrange my thinking into a coherent structure, even for something as simple as this Foreword. When working across time zones, asynchronous activities become even more valuable, as they reduce the necessity to work at inconvenient hours.

It's a common slogan to hear "meetings are bad—get rid of them." But that's a simplistic reaction to the frustration of meetings that are badly run or inappropriately used. Sumeet has reflected on what situations require meetings and when they can (and should) be replaced by asynchronous techniques. This book sets out what he's learned and is a guide to improving our collaboration even as we sit further apart.

—Martin Fowler

FOREWORD

We've come a long way. Pioneers like GitLab wrote the playbook for remote work over a decade ago, yet it took a global pandemic to open the world's eyes to the possibilities of remote work. Today, many organizations embrace what we call "location independence." This encapsulates the magic that happens when a business decouples results from physical geography. While this has transformed millions of lives and enterprises, it's only the start of an even greater revolution.

The future of remote work—or, dare I say, the future of work—is time independence. Since at least the advent of the internet, the majority of knowledge workers have remained bound to time. The way we design our lives and the dreams we allow ourselves to contemplate are constrained by a fixed reality: the rigidity of a workday.

What happens when we shake off that rigidity? What design principles can humans apply to their own lives when we leverage tools, software, AI, and workflows to achieve professional goals outside the strict bounds of time?

We begin to optimize for what matters most. We reprioritize our individual identity stacks—the layers that make us individually *us*. Businesses become stronger and more resilient to crises. They become magnets for the most talented people, those who value flexibility over all else and who generate otherworldly results as a measure of their gratitude.

The "async-first" mindset is indeed what powers this time-independent way of working.

It's the key to saying "yes" to more midday adventures with my toddler. It's the cornerstone of the nonlinear workday—a concept I detailed in my own book, *Living the Remote Dream*. At the same time, it's a way to drive high-performing teams—something we've espoused for years as part of the "TeamOps" philosophy at GitLab.

Change, however, is hard. Concrete, tangible advice is tough to come by. We need frameworks and recipes to ensure that the asynchronous collaboration movement takes hold and scales to the ends of the earth.

The Async-First Playbook is one such resource. This book is the bridge between principle and execution. As opposed to being everything to everyone, Sumeet has focused this book on teams that build software. This, I'm sure you'll notice, makes much of the advice in the book immediately actionable for you, the reader. The focus by no means alienates other readers, though. Technologist or not, everyone can learn something about working asynchronously from this book.

There's a lot at stake. If workplace leaders get this right, we'll create a more flexible, inclusive, connected planet. This is where this book shines. Sumeet doesn't just focus on the everyday tasks that such teams perform, but he also sheds light on the responsibilities of effective managers and leaders in an async-first environment. His part-guerrilla, part-advocate approach is a great way for the intrepid yet enlightened leader to drive change in their realm of influence while they gather evidence and arguments for broader organizational change. And all the advice in the book comes to life with tool suggestions, examples, and resources for your team.

To be successful at asynchronous ways of working is to discover more of what makes work great—flexibility, space for deep work, frictionless knowledge-sharing, a bias for action, diversity, inclusion, and the ability to scale. By removing constraints through the power of technology, we empower society to put its focus on areas like community, service, and progress.

The plays in this playbook will empower you to lead and build differently. All that you need is an open mind and a belief that the status quo isn't worthy of defining the future.

—Darren Murph, Future of Work Architect and VP,
Workplace Design & Remote Experience at Andela

PREFACE

Welcome!

In March 2020, the world of work was in a frenzy. The pandemic had pushed everyone back to the safety of their homes, and it felt like our jobs and work were at risk. In the knowledge working and consulting industry, we were fortunate to have a higher exposure to modern collaboration tools. So, we coped better than some other industries that weren't as sophisticated with tool usage. As the months rolled on, our comfort with remote work grew to where we are today—most knowledge workers want to work remotely most of the time.

My path to remote work was slightly different from that of my colleagues. In the years preceding the pandemic, I had played several roles where remote work was the norm. For example, with one of my clients, I was the only Indian consultant in a group of 50-odd technologists, most of whom worked across Central and Eastern Europe on a suite of different products. It made more sense for me to work from my home office in Pune, India, than to commute to my company office several kilometers away. Through sheer coincidence, I became proficient with remote work well before most of my company colleagues.

As you can imagine, my clients, colleagues, and I had different pathways to the remote software development experience. With trial and error and some dumb luck, I'd realized well before the pandemic that a meeting-centric approach to remote work is unsustainable in the long run. Of course, the ability to jump into conversations and to tap each other on the shoulder models the office environment that we're all used to, but the office was no paragon of productivity. Mimicking the "office on the cloud" with modern tools re-creates the problems of the office at a much higher rate than earlier. The casualties? Our sense of satisfaction with work and our productivity.

Yet, it wasn't until I switched to part of the company serving North American clients from India that I could see the full extent of this "office in the cloud" dysfunction. For those of you in other countries, I want you to think of winter in the northern hemisphere. It's a 13.5-hour time difference between India and the West Coast of the United States! There's no overlap during standard office hours between these time zones. Even the East Coast of the United States isn't much better. But to this day, many of my colleagues in the tech industry straddle opposing time zones to collaborate with each other. The casualty? Our work–life balance.

But we needn't normalize these casualties. It doesn't have to be crazy at work. The tech industry will continue to grow. And at its heart, tech needs access to talented people. And those people won't always be in the same time zone as us. So, I believe distributed working is an inevitable part of the future of work. In recognition of that inevitability, this book aims to help software development practitioners build high-performing, distributed teams. Along the way, I hope I can show you how to make your processes less stressful, more efficient, more fun, more inclusive, and more thoughtful.

WHO SHOULD READ THIS BOOK

I've written this book for practitioners and leaders with a basic understanding of agile software development. If you're already working on a distributed or remote team, you'll recognize many of the challenges I describe in the book. You'll also see how going "async-first" can address many of those challenges. You may also be a manager or a leader who wants to guide their team or organization to a remote-native way of building software. In this case, this book will provide you with a blueprint to organize your teams. If successful, your experiments may catalyze broader change for your companies and clients.

People who've read early drafts of this book have told me it could be useful for a wider audience as well. Many chapters of the book that deal with collaboration and management practices are domain-agnostic. Indeed, if you're a curious knowledge worker, you needn't be a technologist to get value out of the book. I leave it to you to find your adventure with the table of contents!

HOW I'VE STRUCTURED THIS BOOK

As the name suggests, I've written this book as a practical guide to remote-native software development. Asynchronous collaboration is a means to that end. However, if you care about being agile and not just doing agile, you may not follow every practice I describe in this book. So, it's perfectly fine to read only the chapters that apply to your work. This isn't a book that I expect you to read from cover to cover.

To present the plays of this playbook, I've organized them into six different parts.

- Part I, "Adapting to the New Normal," introduces the value of asynchronous collaboration in our day and age and teaches you how to prepare your team to shift to an async-first way of working.
- Part II, "Prepare to Go Async-First," addresses the basics you need in place through tools, skills, and protocols before you tinker with your work practices.
- Part III, "The Practitioner's Guide," is the chunkiest section of this playbook. It aligns techniques for remote software development, with chapters that map to common software development practices. You can read every chapter if you're curious. But first, read the chapters that relate to practices you already follow.
- Part IV, "Async-First Leadership," teaches you how to be a supportive leader for your async-first team. The techniques in this part of the book will apply to people who are already in management or leadership roles or those who aspire to play such roles.
- Part V, "Navigate the Pitfalls," recognizes a few common traps when working async-first. No team is immune to these, so the mitigating techniques I describe in these chapters should interest every reader.
- Part VI, "Bring It All Together," closes out the book with a set of tools that'll help you guide your async-first shift.

So, dip in and dip out of the book as you shift yourself to an async-first way of working. Keep it close at hand so that when you're ready to introduce a practice to your team, you can refer to the plays relevant to it.

THE COMPANION SITE

Writing this book began by sharing some of my ideas with a broad audience. The companion website for this book, https://www.asyncagile.org, will continue to be the place where I'll share and discuss future musings related to this topic. As I learn, I want to learn aloud with you.

In many of the chapters, you'll see references to resources, examples, and templates that I've created for you. You'll find them all at https://www.asyncagile .org/book-resources. I encourage you to bookmark this page, so you always have the link handy.

With all that said, welcome, thank you for joining me, and let's get started!

ACKNOWLEDGMENTS

As a first-time author, I have many people to thank for bringing this book to life. First, I must thank the OGs, particularly pioneers such as Jason Fried and David Heinemeier Hansson and companies such as GitLab, which have been passionate advocates of remote and async work. I stand on the shoulders of such intellectual giants. Of them, there are many.

Closer to home, I consider myself fortunate to have worked at Thoughtworks, a pioneer of agile software development, particularly in IT consulting. To be perfectly honest, most of the ideas in this book stem from my experiences in working at Thoughtworks. I've curated several techniques in this book that I learned only because other colleagues at the company took the pains to teach me.

I must reserve a special word of thanks to colleagues like Santosh Mahale, Sagar Paul, Sameer Soman, and Thoughtworks India's Engineering Group, who afforded me the time to work on this book. Their support represents why Thoughtworks is such a welcome environment for sharing what we learn.

I wouldn't have started on the journey of creating this book had it not been for the guidance and advice I received from Martin Fowler. Not only did he help me validate the ideas for this book, but he also took time out of his busy schedule to read my rather messy manuscript. I'll always value the feedback he shared with me. The book is richer for it. Martin has also written a foreword for this book, which I consider a massive endorsement. Speaking of forewords, this book has two. The other one is from Darren Murph, one of the most popular remote-work leaders out there. Even while settling into a new role, Darren took the time to write a thoughtful note about the book. I can't thank him enough for it.

I also received tons of advice and encouragement from Gayathri Mohan, Paulo Caroli, Sunil Mundra, Vinod Sankaranarayanan, and Mangalam Nandakumar. As published authors, they were generous enough to share their experiences with me, so I had a frame of reference for what writing a book is like.

Sachin Dharmapurikar, Vijay Raghavan Aravamudhan, Sunita Venkatachalam, and Allison MacQueen gave me feedback on several pieces of writing. They've enriched the ideas in this book with their input. And how can I forget Dr. James Stanier? He was the technical reviewer for this book, and his candid, point-by-point feedback has helped me sharpen the book into the product you see today.

When ideas collide, new ideas emerge. Amy Luckey, Daniel Pupius, Mohammed Najiullah, and Priya Darshini M G helped me out by writing about their ideas and experiences of working and leading remotely. Their thoughts have inspired a lot of the content you see in the book.

Greg Doench, my editor at Pearson, was one of the first individuals to believe in the concept of this book, demonstrating unwavering faith from the start. His contagious enthusiasm has been a driving force throughout this project. Menka Mehta from Pearson India has been my go-to person throughout the development of this book. If I had a question, she always had an answer. Dr. Chris Zahn, the developmental editor for this book, offered me insightful written feedback that deepened my understanding of style guides and the process of crafting a polished manuscript. My copy editor, Kim Wimpsett, went through my manuscript with a fine-toothed comb. Her attention to detail helped me uncover many blind spots in my writing style. Julie Nahil and Charlotte Kughen guided me through production and design activities that I'd never experienced before writing this book. Without them and the entire Pearson brigade, this book wouldn't be in your hands.

As I take these ideas to more people, I must acknowledge the role of colleagues such as Pranav Shah, Ashwin Lal, Avneesh Chandhok, Ming Linsley, Shipra Shandilya, Jem Elias, and Jaydeep Chakrabarty for creating consulting and speaking opportunities for me. Even the idea of async-first work sometimes needs synchronous storytelling!

The last few years have taught me how valuable friends and family are. I must acknowledge those people in my life. Nagarjun Kandukuru has been a friend for the last decade and a half at Thoughtworks and an advocate for asynchronous collaboration. His support for my work has been heartwarming. My close friends, Anuroop Krishnan, Manish Vaidya, Chetna Soni, and Surali Vaidya, have been among my biggest cheerleaders. And my lovely wife, Gayathri, has always been my first sounding board. She must be tired of listening to my ideas and reading every first draft of what I write, and yet she humors me. If you enjoy reading the book, it's because it first passed through her filters. My kids—Avni and Vihaan—don't know yet that this book was a labor of love for their dad. But they were understanding enough to leave me alone when I was writing. They'll know how much that has meant to me when they grow up. For now, I put my gratitude in writing. I promise to make up for any time I lost with them.

Finally, a big shout-out to everyone who followed and supported Asyncagile.org in its infancy. You know who you are. You needn't have patronized me at the time. And yet, you took the time to read what I had to say, and you spread the word around. Without you, I'd have never had the confidence to write this book. Thank you, whoever you are, and wherever you are.

ABOUT THE AUTHOR

Sumeet Gayathri Moghe is an agile enthusiast, product manager, and design nerd at Thoughtworks. He's worked with a variety of clients over the last few decades, building software products and helping them improve their engineering effectiveness. During his time as a consultant, Sumeet has exposed himself to various domains such as retail, travel, telecom, payments, healthcare technology, education, and more. That, in turn, has helped him generalize his experience across industries. What you see in this book stands for what he's learned from his colleagues, their successes, and their occasional misadventures.

Sumeet now lives in Pune, India, with his wife and two kids. When he's not at work building software, you'll probably see him looking through a camera's eyepiece, photographing wildlife or a scene in the wilderness.

To get in touch, find him on Linkedin (@sumeetmoghe) or visit asyncagile.org where he blogs almost every week. If you're curious about his photography work, check out www.sumeetmoghe.com.

Part I

ADAPTING TO THE NEW NORMAL

The COVID-19 pandemic forced the knowledge work industry into remote work. Today several companies and teams continue to work remotely, though they still follow office-centric work practices. In this part of the book, I argue that these ways of working must change so we can take advantage of our new, distributed work arrangements.

- **Chapter 1**, "There's Got to Be a Better Way to Work," sets the scene for how asynchronous work has the potential to transform distributed software development so it's fun, sustainable, inclusive, and scalable.
- **Chapter 2**, "Foster a Mindset for Change," teaches you how to prime your team for a shift to an async-first way of working. Before you explore the playbook, the ideas from this chapter will help you create a framework to align your colleagues to the change.

THERE'S GOT TO BE A BETTER WAY TO WORK

6:25 am	Nita pulls herself out of bed, having pushed snooze on her alarm five times already. Oh boy, she's late! She shakes her son, Abin, awake. They barely have 30-odd minutes before they drive to school. Dang it—she has to drive. She'd much prefer to take the scooter, but it's pouring outside. If only she could control the Indian monsoon.
	Okay, 30 minutes. Freshen up, make some coffee, and get Abin's lunchbox ready. Drat! She forgot to order a milk delivery. Thank heavens she has some milk powder. She hustles to get a couple of sandwiches ready as she fries some eggs so Abin can have breakfast.
7:45 am	That wasn't the start Nita was hoping for. Life as a single mom is hard. She barely got her son to school on time. She'd have liked to wake up early and stay on top of things, but she went to bed late and didn't get a good night's sleep. Work doesn't begin till noon. Maybe she can sleep now? Or maybe not. She's got to cook, get ready, take out the trash, and put away the dishes. That won't happen by itself, will it?
12:00 pm	Nita works a midday shift. Work at home in Bangalore begins at 12 pm and, with an hour's break thrown in, ends at 10 pm. She works for a client in Boulder, Colorado, and some of her American teammates are based out of Boise, Idaho. This is the only way she gets an hour to overlap with them for meetings. She tried getting 30 minutes of shut-eye before starting work, but she ended up just tossing and turning in bed. The day has barely begun, and she already feels tired.

2:30 pm   Time to pick up Abin. There goes 40 minutes of her break time. Lunch was already at breakneck speed—coffees and dinners will probably need to be at the worktable. Sigh.

5:00 pm   As a designer, Nita is trying to build some wireframes for a new feature the team is scheduled to deliver in an upcoming sprint. But she has a meeting with the team's business analyst in 15 minutes. On some days, Nita wonders if she's getting any work done at all. The last four hours consisted of two hours of meetings—one meeting to onboard a new team member and another meeting to discuss the sprint planning meeting later this evening. She tried to make some progress independently, but there wasn't enough contiguous time or enough available information for her to start.

9:00 pm   Abin got back from cricket coaching, showered, and warmed up dinner. He's a good kid. Before heading to bed, he hugged Nita and kissed her goodnight. "Tomorrow will be an on-time start," he promised. Nita's been powering her day with coffee. The team is now in a sprint planning meeting with the folks in Boise and the client in Boulder. One more hour to motor through. Thank heavens for that coffee.

10:00 pm   Aargh! She's not done yet. The client asked for some changes to the proposed iteration plan. Nita now has to finalize wireframes for user stories that are kind of ready but not quite. The team huddle is in 15 minutes.

11:00 pm   Finally, time to get some sleep. Uh-oh! Hold on. She's got to put the milk bag out and double-check the milk order. Abin wasn't as good a boy as she thought, either. He didn't clean the kitchen before heading to sleep. Time to roll up her sleeves and clean up.

She gets the job done, changes, brushes, flosses, and gets into bed. Try as she might, she just can't sleep. Too much caffeine in the system? Too much of that bright screen? Who knows? Her attention shifts to her phone. The team is discussing the change in sprint plans. Maybe she should tune in until she feels sleepy.

WORK DESERVES A NEW LOOK

Phew! That day, unreal as it may be, is commonplace for many remote-working technologists operating across continents. Nita's character is fictional, but I know plenty of people who live and work like her. Of course, work hours can differ depending on the time zones the team is distributed across. But context-switching and highly interrupted days are common regardless of time zones.

In 2020, the global pandemic sped up the shift to remote work. To be sure, that was a change in the right direction. In a time of powerful computers in our pockets, great tools for online collaboration, and reasonably good internet connectivity in most places, it was strange to make people go through hours of commuting just to be in a noisy office every day. People made considerable sacrifices in their personal lives to have a career. For those with a single-minded devotion to that career, it was fine—but there were others who were looking for balance in their lives. And so, remote work came with the promise of restoring that balance. It gave organizations a way to tap into talent pools they hadn't considered before, simply because they didn't have offices in that area.

If you can now work from anywhere, an organization can employ you from anywhere. Knowledge workers are always more in demand than the supply, so being able to widen the talent pool gives employers a way to scale despite the constraints.

The purpose of this book isn't to extol remote work, though. There are plenty of other books to do just that. The question I like to ask is about Nita—is there a better way to work? The shift to remote work in 2020 was so abrupt that many organizations never had the time to consider if the same work practices that felt effective in an office are also relevant for remote work. As a result, you see many individuals, such as Nita, continue to make compromises to their work–life balance, their mental and physical health, and their ability to do deep, meaningful work. There's got to be a better way to work.

This book articulates a new way of working, especially for software development teams. That way is to embrace *asynchronous collaboration*. "What is that?" you may ask. The best way to define it is to combine a few definitions I've derived from Catherine Tansey and Marcelo Lebre.*

---

* Citations of facts and sources appear at the end of the book. A page number and a phrase identify the passage.

Asynchronous work is the practice of working on a team that doesn't require multiple people to be online simultaneously. You do as much as you can with what you have, write things up clearly, transfer ownership of the work to whomever needs to pick it up next, and then work on something else.

If that sounds quite different from the way you collaborate with your team today, let me explain why you should consider making the shift to this way of working.

COMPLEX PROBLEMS NEED SMARTER COLLABORATION

When I started my career in IT, the problems we solved for clients differed greatly from the problems we solve today. For example, few clients expect us to build simple create, read, update, delete (CRUD) applications—low code platforms have disrupted that space. How about simple storefronts? Services like Shopify have disrupted that space by simplifying it for noncoders. With services such as managing large data centers, the hyper scalers such as Azure, GCP, and AWS have made it easy for in-house IT teams to manage infrastructure.

The work we do today is far more complex—we build platforms and data meshes and deep learning and neural networks. We modernize decades-old legacy systems to give incumbents a way to compete with digital native disruptors. We explore new ways to develop the human–machine experience. It's impossible to run these kinds of projects with any of the following problems:

- An overdependence on meetings, conversations, and tribal knowledge
- A lack of good written communication
- No commitment to deep, uninterrupted work

Asynchronous collaboration comes with the promise to meet only when necessary, to make conversations productive, and to give people time so they can actually work.

THE PROMISE OF FLEXIBILITY

In April 2022, I surveyed more than 450 Indian employees in a leading software development unit of a global IT firm. I asked them what they dislike about their work. These were the top two responses from more than 50 percent of the respondents:

- Long contiguous hours
- Late hours

This is almost antithetical to the promise of remote work. Luke Thomas and Aisha Samake, in their book *The Anywhere Operating System*, outline this promise:

> When coworkers say, 'I love working from home,' it's about when they work instead of only thinking about where they work from. That's the secret hiding in plain sight!

Indeed, less than 5 percent of the people I surveyed recently want to go into an office every day. Sixty percent of the respondents preferred to work "regular, daylight hours," i.e., nine to five. Twenty-eight percent wanted a flexible schedule where they could do their eight hours, their way. And these expectations are changing. This observation bears itself out in Future Forum's research, which surveys a broader audience than my own:

> Knowledge workers who say they have little to no ability to set their own hours are 2.6x as likely to "definitely" look for a new job in the next year (compared to those with moderate schedule flexibility).

While the job market and economic conditions at any point may or may not afford such opportunities, it's clear where people's preferences are. Asynchronous work allows people the autonomy and flexibility they desire by allowing them to work during the hours that are most productive for them. More important, it lets managers and employers project a shared sense of trust and empowerment.

ESCAPING THE SHALLOWS

As a product manager and an aspiring designer, I was always at sea in an open office. If the constant white noise wasn't bad enough, the fact that I was "right there" implicitly meant that I was available to be interrupted. I got little joy out of my working day, especially when I needed to get work done for the team and needed time with my head down. I craved what Cal Newport terms *deep work*— the ability to concentrate without distraction on a cognitively demanding task.

When we started working remotely, though, I could cut out the white noise. Suddenly, I had my corner office. Except, of course, it was a room in my house. What didn't change were the interruptions. The across-the-table interruptions now became video meetings and all-day back-and-forth messages on our instant messaging platform. Like Nita, I've struggled to get time to do deep work because my day would get cut up into little one-hour chunks. Paul Graham noted this eloquently in his 2009 essay "Maker's Schedule, Manager's Schedule":

When you're operating on the maker's schedule, meetings are a disaster. A single meeting can blow a whole afternoon, by breaking it into two pieces, each too small to do anything hard in.

Asynchronous collaboration advocates for "meetings as the last resort, not the first option." If your current collaboration practices need loads of meetings, I understand this sounds radical. Asynchronous collaboration advocates for using communication tools thoughtfully. The sentiment I'd like you to empathize with is that interruptions have a cost—not just in terms of the time spent in the interruption but also as a fallout impact on productivity. Mihaly Czikszentmihaly, in his bestselling book *Flow: The Psychology of Optimal Experience*, speaks of a state that most of us want to get to at work:

> ... a state in which people are so involved in an activity that nothing else seems to matter; the experience is so enjoyable that people will continue to do it even at great cost, for the sheer sake of doing it.

Here's the killer, though: while 97 percent of the 450-odd people I surveyed claimed to care about "flow," only 12.5 percent—i.e., one in eight people—claimed to achieve it with regularity. Asynchronous work promises to give people a better chance at achieving flow.

The other benefit of deep work is the ability to have deep interactions with co-workers. In his landmark book *Thinking, Fast and Slow*, Daniel Kahneman outlines two systems of thinking. System 1 is an intuitive and fast way of thinking. You call on System 1 for the answer to your parents' names, for the result of 2+2, and for how you navigate your own home. Anything that needs slightly deep thought—double-digit multiplication, for example—needs slower thinking. Kahneman calls that kind of thinking System 2. System 1, being as instinctive as it is, can help us decide at speed but is also prone to biases and errors. An effective approach to work should combine both System 1 and System 2 thinking.

A culture that defaults to meetings as a way of working lives in the realm of System 1. There's barely enough time to slow down, go a few levels deep, and analyze things. You lionize responsiveness and presence, but deep work becomes the casualty. Asynchronous work prioritizes good analysis and thinking. When you do meet, people have given enough thought to a topic and are meeting for a specific time-boxed purpose that needs intense collaboration. You can now make the deep work you've done so far deeper.

A MORE INCLUSIVE WORKPLACE

The people I surveyed were in offshore development teams in India. Their unit served clients in North America. Many people were straddling time zones with up to a 13-hour time difference. You don't need me to tell you that this is hard. And if something is hard for most people, it's usually harder for historically under-represented groups such as women in IT. (Even after years of conversations about the topic, women's representation in IT was just 33 percent in 2022. In technical roles, that goes down to 25 percent.)

For example, a tight schedule with loads of meetings isn't easy for anyone, but it's especially hard for women, who bear a disproportionate burden of household and childcare responsibilities in most societies. Now let's imagine a workplace without arbitrary start and end times, where people work in schedules that make sense for them and when we don't have the pressure to cram all communication into those specific eight hours. Getting rid of those constraints can help more under-represented groups find a way into the workplace. We can't change society overnight. What we can change is the workplace—and that's the promise of being asynchronous.

While we're on the topic, consider the diverse personalities in the workplace. There are introverts who will rarely be the first to voice their opinions on a topic. There are people who are non-native English speakers who may be deep thinkers but lack the confidence to articulate themselves. Asynchronous communication allows them to have the space to share their thoughts and ideas at a pace convenient for them. Modern writing tools allow non-native English speakers to correct their spelling and grammar. Introverts now don't have to be the loudest voice in the room. If diversity is being invited to the party and inclusion is being asked to dance, asynchronous work helps that inclusion.

DEFAULTING TO ACTION

In software engineering, there's always a choice between waiting to be perfect and being wrong at speed. When everyone was in one office, sitting at one large table, people could ask for or offer help by just tapping someone on the shoulder and talking to them. Never mind the fact that the person who needed to help you might have lost their own flow. Still, you were one step closer to being perfect. Using the same approach in a remote setup creates many problems. It's hard to keep track of who is free, who is busy, and who you're interrupting when you're giving each other a shout. Remote.com speaks of the concept of "defaulting to action" in such a situation. Sure, interrupting someone can help get your work closer to perfection, but you can't overlook the impact it has on the person who is unblocking you. Instead, you choose to be wrong at speed. It's okay, if you have to backtrack at a later point, but it's better than waiting to be unblocked.

> *There are many times when work isn't ready for us to tackle, tasks aren't planned, decision makers aren't online, etc. In these times, successful teams execute, even if they later have to refactor and adapt, they don't waste time "waiting."*
>
> —Marcelo Lebre

Defaulting to action optimizes for speed and throughput, but it also encourages thoughtful communication. For example, a well-written requirement may preempt the need for a ceremonial kickoff, where a developer, product owner, and tester discuss its implementation and testing approach. A simple screen recording attached to such a requirement can allow a developer to continue development while giving the product owner and the tester a way to review the implementation, without interrupting what those two might be up to. Sure, the trio may meet up to iron out some sticking points, but the mantra of "meetings as the last resort, not the first option" works well here. If the developer does have to backtrack, it's also feedback for the user story. The product owner can incorporate this learning into the next set of user stories they write. When in doubt, teams that adopt asynchronous communication just execute.

IMPROVED KNOWLEDGE SHARING AND COMMUNICATION

Asynchronous collaboration isn't black magic. Getting time back to do deep work isn't a freebie. In return, people must be clear communicators—mostly through writing.

Many of us find it daunting to write. I admit we all must get better at this skill, but for now let's focus on the potential benefits. Daily writing brings with it many advantages, including the following ones:

- A regular record of project decisions that helps anyone understand your project's current state effectively.
- Easier knowledge sharing and project ownership transfer.
- Reducing fear of missing out (FOMO) because everyone can now know what's happening in any part of the project. There's no need to attend a meeting to learn what happened in the last meeting!

As projects and organizations scale, tribal knowledge and a system of "he said, she said" don't scale. Effective writing and thoughtful curation have a better chance at helping you scale, even as tenured people leave and new people join your team.

A BETTER WORK ENVIRONMENT FOR ALL OF US

Like most practices, asynchronous collaboration isn't a silver bullet. It won't solve all your problems. Regardless, it's safe to assume that every team that does any creative work will benefit from embracing asynchronous practices. Figure 1.1 summarizes the benefits we've discussed in this chapter.

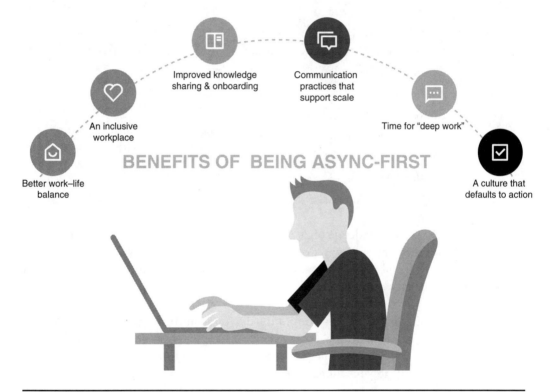

Improved knowledge sharing & onboarding

Communication practices that support scale

An inclusive workplace

Time for "deep work"

BENEFITS OF BEING ASYNC-FIRST

Better work–life balance

A culture that defaults to action

Figure 1.1 Benefits of an async-first work culture.

CHAPTER SUMMARY

The world of work has changed considerably since the start of the global pandemic, as many of our teams are now highly distributed and remote.

- Remote and distributed teams can experience burnout if they operate in primarily a synchronous manner.
- If you're building software or doing knowledge work in today's day and age, you limit your productivity if you depend too much on meetings and tribal knowledge. You need effective written communication and the ability to do deep work.
- The ability to work asynchronously, where people don't have to be in the same physical or virtual space simultaneously, has several benefits:
  - Better work–life balance
  - Higher inclusion
  - Improved knowledge sharing
  - Communication practices that support scale
  - Time for "deep work"
  - A culture that defaults to action

While the global pandemic of 2020 was a time of great pain for many of us, it also fast-tracked us into a new set of possibilities for how we work together in teams. How far you embrace these possibilities will depend on your appetite for change and your team's context.

Throughout the rest of this book, I'll help you identify asynchronous work techniques for your team. But before you try to change anything, you must enlist your team's support. So, in the next chapter, I'll describe how you can introduce this async-first shift to your immediate colleagues.

FOSTER A MINDSET FOR CHANGE

I started this book outlining the value of asynchronous work to remote and distributed teams. Your appetite and ability to introduce this shift may vary depending on the influence you wield in your organization. Having said that, it's safe to assume that for most readers of this book, the most sensible place to begin introducing async-first practices is with your immediate team.

FOUR SIMPLE IDEAS

In this relatively short chapter, I share with you four ideas that'll help you prime both your broader organization and your team for change. We're not yet at the step of an implementation checklist and a playbook. We'll get there in Parts III, IV, and VI of the book. Consider this as a four-part framework to help align your team to the need for change.

FOCUS ON VALUE

Like anything else we do in agile software development, the notion of "value" is at the center of this shift to asynchronous work. Let's get one thing straight: being async-first is not the goal. It's a means to an end—an end that overly synchronous ways of working cannot achieve. At the risk of repeating myself, let's take the benefits we discussed in the previous chapter and expand them in Table 2.1.

Table 2.1 The Benefits of Asynchronous Ways of Working

Benefit	How Asynchronous Work Helps
Better work–life balance	When people don't have to collaborate synchronously with each other, they can choose the work hours that work best for them. That way they get to give their life the time it deserves.

Benefit	How Asynchronous Work Helps
Higher inclusion	You don't have to worry about someone's location or their time zone. Introverts and non-native English speakers can use the safety of tools and writing to communicate freely. Flexible hours allow people with various personal situations to become part of your team.
Improved onboarding and knowledge sharing	A discipline to communicate clearly in writing reduces FOMO on teams. Regular writing and curation also help build referenceable team knowledge that you can use for knowledge sharing and onboarding.
Communication practices that support scale	Everyone cannot be in every meeting. People read faster (200–400 words per minute) than they can listen (140–160 words per minute). People don't remember every piece of information they see, read, or hear. This makes referenceability essential. The practice of writing allows your team to share information at scale. It's referenceable and fast to consume.
Time for deep work	When you don't have unnecessary meetings on your calendar, you can free up large chunks of time to do deep, complex work without interruptions.
A culture that defaults to action	Whenever we face a choice between waiting to be perfect and being wrong at speed, we choose the latter. The focus is on getting things done. If something is wrong, we choose to refactor and adapt.

The first step in introducing change on your team will be to align on these elements of value. The more of these benefits the team cares about, the more they'll be open to change. In Part VI of the book, I'll share a kit to help you surface how your team can improve the way they collaborate and which of these benefits they care about.

VISUALIZE CHANGE ON A SPECTRUM

Even when I'm consulting professionally, I fall into the trap of making binary judgments. You may identify with this tendency—something is either perfect or rotten. There's nothing in between those two extremes. As we embark on any journey of change, it's important to acknowledge that we may never be perfect. This is life in perpetual beta—you and your team will get better with time. Asynchronous work that's judgmental and unkind somehow belies its central intentions, which are to build flexible, inclusive teams that value deep work.

The key to plotting this change is to think of it as a spectrum, as you see in Figure 2.1. Thankfully, James Stanier did all the hard work of defining this spectrum in his book *Effective Remote Work*. I've just flipped the direction of his original diagram. You see, agile teams value the approach of "shifting left" when testing. The idea is to catch defects earlier in the development process. It can confuse teams to shift left for one thing and right for another. So, I prefer this direction of the spectrum.

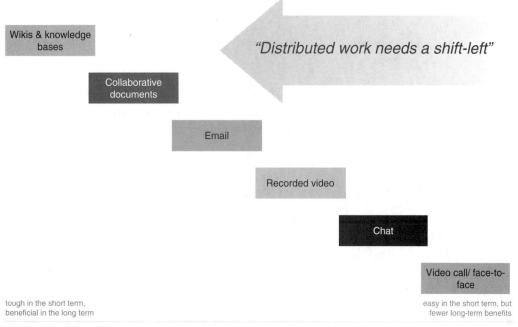

tough in the short term,
beneficial in the long term

easy in the short term, but
fewer long-term benefits

THE SPECTRUM OF SYNCHRONOUSNESS

Figure 2.1 The spectrum of synchronousness by James Stanier. (Source: Adapted from James Stanier, *Effective Remote Work*. The Pragmatic Programmers, LLC, 2022)

Here are a few things to note about the spectrum:

- As you go from right to left, you go from a fully synchronous medium to a fully asynchronous medium.
- Just as you don't want to run an entire project just on a wiki, you don't want to communicate only on video calls all the time.
- Communication methods on the right side of the spectrum are easy in the short term but may have fewer long-term benefits.
- As you traverse left, communications get relatively tougher in the short term but have longer-term benefits (the kind we discussed earlier).

To quote James Stanier:

> To fully embrace remote work, we need to shift our mindset and habits (on) the spectrum. Instead of choosing the convenient option, we need to choose to communicate in a way that enables an equal level of contribution from anyone, regardless of where they are in the world.
>
> …
>
> That's the habit that you need to promote within yourself and with your colleagues. Every time you communicate, can you purposefully shift further along the spectrum?

Using the spectrum as a reference will help your team co-own the change as you integrate asynchronous ways of working into your software development process. Coupled with the benefits you're looking to achieve, this gives you a sense of direction.

A Visual Depiction of Async-First

I've often encountered a common misunderstanding of the term *async-first*. People often misunderstand it as "async only" or "no synchronous collaboration." Since the more asynchronous channels start at the left and become more synchronous as you traverse right, the spectrum helps clarify the idea of async-first. Here are a few ways I've seen the image in Figure 2.1 help:

- It guides conversations. For example, before organizing a video conference, we ask, "Can we go async-first by sharing an artifact with some prep work?"

- Synchronous collaboration remains part of how we work, but by starting from the left, the spectrum encourages us to default to async-first mechanisms.

- By visually listing all means of communication before synchronous messaging and meetings, it helps the team consider if a meeting is indeed necessary for the problem we're trying to solve.

- Even when a meeting is necessary, recognizing all the communication channels available to us helps illustrate an "async-first, sync-next" mindset.

MAKE A ULYSSES PACT

There's a story in Greek mythology about the Sirens—a band of women singers sitting somewhere out on the sea. No sailor could resist the temptation of getting close to the Siren's rocks once they'd heard them singing. Of course, rocks and old wooden ships were never a fortunate combination, so the next thing to happen was a shipwreck.

Ulysses wanted to listen to the Sirens but didn't want a shipwreck. He made an ingenious plan. He stuffed his sailors' ears with wax and asked them to bind him to the mast as they approached the Sirens. Easy did it—not only did Ulysses enjoy the show but his sailors also steered the ship to safety.

A *Ulysses pact* is used to describe commitment strategies. By binding himself to the mast, Ulysses prevented self-destruction. Consider what the Ulysses pact for your team is. I recommend instituting a simple principle everyone can hold each other accountable to.

> *Meetings are the last resort, not the first option.*
>
> —37signals

The biggest obstacle to asynchronous work is meetings, which are synchronous. By agreeing to this basic pact, you can consciously avoid being trigger-happy with meetings. It also helps the team think hard about the meetings that are essential and find ways to make them effective. Through this conscious behavior, the Ulysses pact embodies the async-first mindset.

APPRECIATE THE BALANCE

All said and done, you can't be a zealot. Imagine a system in perfect balance. On one end, you have asynchronous collaboration with a certain value that it brings. On the other hand, you have synchronous interactions and their value. As we've discussed with the spectrum of synchronousness, this isn't a zero-sum game. You choose a certain interaction by assessing the value you're looking to get out of it. My argument for asynchronous agile stems from the fact that most teams are too far on the right of the spectrum. That doesn't mean I see no value in being on the right sometimes!

There are a few trade-offs you make when you decide the nature of your interaction.

- **Thoughtfulness versus spontaneity.** Writing up a document is slower than brainstorming on Zoom. Waiting for people to think things through and comment on your document slows things down even further. In addition, people with flexible hours may not optimize for speed or spontaneous ideation. In return for slowing things down, you optimize for thoughtfulness instead.

- **Depth versus breadth.** A side effect of speed is that you cover more ground in a brief period. Taking that metaphor further, it's easier to cover several miles in an hour than it is to dig a few feet at the same time. Similarly, synchronous interactions allow you to quickly cover a wide range of topics. If you want depth, though, you'll need to be more asynchronous.

- **Focus versus connectedness.** Even the most ardent advocate of asynchronous work will tell you that while you'll find more focus and flow when working by yourself, it can get isolating after a while. You don't need to kid yourself. We're all human, and we want contact with our friends and colleagues from time to time. Synchronous interactions offer that connectedness.

- **The future versus the moment.** Last, there's the value that James Stanier calls *permanence*. With the focus on writing things up, asynchronous work helps you create assets and artifacts for the future—be it for reference-ability or for onboarding. Synchronous work, on the other hand, is all about the present moment. If you need an instant solution or urgent help, you'll need to be synchronous! The persistent artifacts from an asynchronous way of working also help make transient communication more effective.

Anyone who's watched *The Karate Kid* can't forget the lovable Mr. Miyagi. There's a quote of his from the movie that I love.

> "Lesson not just karate only. Lesson for whole life! Whole life have a balance, everything be better."

In a comparable way, I encourage you to think about synchronous versus asynchronous interactions as the balance of trade-offs I just described. Figure 2.2 summarizes those trade-offs. You can't do without synchronous events. The idea is to get the most out of such communication. You do so by being intentional.

Figure 2.2 Asynchronous versus synchronous communication—the balance of values.

GO FAR, GO TOGETHER

If you want to go fast, go alone. If you want to go far, go together.
—African proverb

Without buy-in from your team, any change you try to introduce won't last long. So, I urge you to spend time aligning with your team to agree on the value you'll get from being more asynchronous. Any change that looks too daunting won't go too far either. Think of small steps and quick wins to get you started. Commitment strategies will help, and so will a pragmatic, balanced approach.

Whatever you do, don't be a hard-nosed zealot. Remember, you are *part-guerrilla, part-advocate*. Be a guerrilla to change the things you have influence over. Every little win will help you justify later experiments. Use those wins to be an advocate to make your case with bosses and co-workers. This will help you garner the support you need.

Most important, be ready to move from the whiteboard to the trenches. A successful async-first team doesn't need hand-waving leaders. You'll be valuable to your team when you can get into the details and help your colleagues out when necessary. Show them how to execute a practice in an asynchronous fashion. Create an environment conducive for change. Be a role model with your own way of working. Don't worry; we'll address all this in Parts III and IV of the book.

READY FOR THE FIRST STEPS

This chapter brings us to a logical point where we can start thinking about ways to be more asynchronous on distributed software development teams.

CHAPTER SUMMARY

Your immediate team is a logical place to introduce async-first practices. Here's how to go about it:

- Focus on the value your team expects to get out of this shift. The more aligned they are to the benefits, the more they'll warm up to the change.
- Make the change small. Use the spectrum of synchronousness to guide the shift-left to a more asynchronous way of working. Every win counts.

- Make a Ulysses pact—"Meetings are the last resort, not the first option." By making this basic commitment, the team makes conscious shifts to reduce unnecessary meetings.
- Appreciate that you need a balance of both sync and async communication. Both modes have their benefits. When you understand these benefits, you can choose the right communication patterns for the problems you're solving.

In the next part of the book, I'll describe how to lay the scaffold for change. We'll explore the tools, skills, and protocols that are essential to move to an async-first way of working.

Part II

PREPARE TO GO ASYNC-FIRST

Now that we understand the need for change and are prepared for some challenges we may face, it's time to lay down the foundational elements for an async-first way of working. This part of the book addresses the fundamentals you must have in place before you address any of your team's development, communication, and collaboration practices.

- **Chapter 3**, "The Tools You'll Need," will address the categories of collaborative tools most software development teams need. This will help you identify any gaps in your collaboration stack.

- **Chapter 4**, "The Biggest Async-First Superpower," and **Chapter 5**, "Three More Async-First Superpowers," address four important skills and behaviors for asynchronous collaboration. We'll call them *superpowers*, particularly because they're fundamental to an async-first way of working. Not only is it important to recognize these skills, but the team must hone these abilities to collaborate efficiently.

- In **Chapter 6**, "Calm Things Down with Collaboration Protocols," you'll take away another set of sensible defaults. This time you'll learn about how to structure your workflow, how to make most decisions, and how to use the different communication media you have at your disposal.

3

THE TOOLS YOU NEED

When describing an async-first way of working, I assume a high level of distribution with the locations your team works out of. This is not to say that you can't work asynchronously if you're all in the same space. In this book, however, we'll consider co-location as an exception and not the norm.

To work remotely and asynchronously, you need effective tools. Since a large part of this book will assume the presence of some such tools, I want to introduce you to the essential applications you'll need to go async-first.

The good news for us all is that most of our employers have some version of these tools already in place. Even the companies that were originally slow to adopt collaborative tools had to make these investments during the pandemic. Use this chapter to assess your collaboration tool stack and to identify any gaps you see in it.

WITH TOOLS, LESS IS MORE

For tool junkies like me, it's tempting to introduce our colleagues to every promising new tool we find. The true cost of a tool, however, isn't the licensing fees you pay. And the true value doesn't come from just its feature set.

All new tools have a cost of onboarding your team, a cost of checking several compliance parameters, and, of course, a cost of confusion. If you have several tools that have only minor differences among them, the cost of choosing the right tool for the right interaction can add up fast.

The value of the tool, on the other hand, is in how it simplifies your work and saves you time. You must navigate this tension carefully. For instance, the design of an instant messaging platform seeks to increase engagement and time spent on the platform. In contrast, we want to reduce interruptions and give people time for deep work. So, you don't want your tool choices to defeat your cause.

I recommend a "less is more" approach to crafting your collaboration stack. With that sentiment, I've divided the various tool categories into prioritized lists.

- **Must haves**: The essential set (Table 3.1)
- **Good to haves**: The productivity boosters (Table 3.2)
- **Optional extras**: Unique and useful, but could be more useful to some teams than others (Table 3.3)

Many of these will seem familiar to you already. That's a good thing. You just need to use the tools effectively.

BEST PRACTICE

Work with Your Team to Identify the Tool Set You Need

The tables that follow represent broad suggestions that'll apply to most teams. That said, not all companies can have all the tools you see here, so use the priorities I've mentioned (must have, good to have, optional extras) to guide what you need in your context. I suggest examining these tool categories with your team to see if you have an immediate or foreseeable need for them and then take things from there.

Table 3.1 The Must Haves: Essential Collaboration Tools

Tool Category	Examples	Notes
Email	Outlook, Hey!, Gmail	The OG of written communication. Particularly useful when communicating with clients and between teams.
Videoconferencing	Zoom, Fuze, Blue Jeans, Microsoft Teams	Async-first teams need some synchronous communication, and a video tool is the best way to do it.
Instant messaging	Slack, Google Spaces, Microsoft Teams, Twist	Instant messaging can disrupt asynchronous work, but when used effectively, it can also help teams coordinate themselves in a timely manner.

Tool Category	Examples	Notes
Collaborative documents	Google Workspace, Office 365, iWork, Almanac, Dropbox Paper	These are the most common tools to build up ideas in depth, either individually or collaboratively. They lend themselves to inline commenting, suggestions, version control—features that help you track how you build a concept.
Collaborative diagramming	Google Drawings, Excalidraw, Draw.io	These are specialized tools that you can use to create architectural and other diagrams.
Collaborative whiteboard	Mural, Miro, Jamboard, Apple Freeform	These tools allow you to work synchronously and asynchronously, just the way you'd use a whiteboard in a physical space. They just have many more powerful features. In an async-first setup, any meeting you organize should be active. Having a shared whiteboard can help facilitate those interactions.
Knowledge base	Confluence, Notion, SharePoint, Mediawiki	Every team should have a place to host their onboarding information, project documentation, team social contract, ways of working, and other artifacts. These tools make it easy to construct that knowledge base.
Code repository	GitHub, GitLab, Bitbucket	All modern-day software development teams already use a Git-based code repository and version control system. These tools also have issue tracking and features such as pull requests or merge requests that facilitate code reviews.
Task board or project backlog	Jira, Pivotal tracker, Trello, Kanbanize	Agile teams need a shared view of progress and what their backlog looks like. This is also where you have in-context discussions about individual pieces of work.
Password manager	1Password Teams, Zoho Vault, LastPass	You need a secure way to share secrets—common credentials, code signing certificates, SSH keys, and the like. Vaults and password managers offer you that functionality.

Table 3.2 The Good to Have: Productivity Boosting Tools

Tool Category	Examples	Notes
Asynchronous video	Loom	These tools give you the ability to record short videos to do a demo, describe an issue, or communicate an update. You can even use videoconferencing tools to do recordings, but specialized tools make the whole process of sharing, collaborating, and commenting much easier.
Asynchronous audio	Yac	Audio is arguably easier to consume than video. I understand it's less popular, but with tools that transcribe speech well, audio can be a powerful communication tool.
Collaborative design	Figma, Invision, Axure RP	These tools help simplify conversations and collaboration about visual design and user experience.

Table 3.3 The Optional Extras: Tools That May Be Useful in Specific Contexts

Tool Category	Examples	Notes
Pair programming* tools	Tuple, Pop, Live Share	Pair programming by definition is a synchronous activity, but I also consider it as "deep work." So if your team "pairs," you should continue to do so but find a way to bring in specialized tools to do this well.
Task automation	Zapier, IFTTT, Trello Butler	If you have access to any of these tools, you can automate several mundane tasks—e.g., check-ins, standups, status updates, reports, and the like. That can free up a lot of time to work asynchronously.
Team hubs	Confluence, Basecamp, ClickUp, Asana	These modern tools combine functionality from multiple different tools that you see in the must-have toolset into a rule-them-all package. The challenge? Companies already have several other tools that offer similar functionality, albeit in a piecemeal manner.
Automated documentation tools	CodeSee, Scribe, tl;dv, Otter assistant	The explicit act of creating documentation is no fun. On the other hand, if the act of documenting is frictionless and can become part of our day-to-day work, it doesn't feel daunting anymore.

Tool Category	Examples	Notes
Enterprise search	Glean, Elastic, Google Cloud Search, Coveo	In an ideal world, you'd like it to be just as easy to find information inside the company or team as it is to find things on the internet. Enterprise search is often a companywide decision. With the right tools in place, you can save people a lot of time by making search and discovery efficient.
Meeting facilitation	Hugo, Fellow	These modern tools make it easy to create collaborative meeting agendas, document meetings, and then share and access these notes at a later time.

* Pair programming is an agile software development technique in which two programmers work together at the same computer, on the same coding problem. We discuss this practice in Part III of the book.

TOOLS ARE EVERYTHING; TOOLS ARE NOTHING

There you go! That's the tools question done and dusted. You should now be able to assess your own toolset using the lists in this chapter and figure out what your team needs.

CHAPTER SUMMARY

Tools enable remote and async work, so it's worth spending some time figuring out which tools you need.

- Adopt a "less is more" approach to tool selection. Balance the incremental benefits of introducing new tools with the costs you incur. Onboarding, compliance, and the cost of confusion can set you back.
- Evaluate tools based on the capabilities you need. Use the must-have, good-to-have, and optional extras lists to help you think through what your team needs to be effective.

I must end this chapter with a couple of caveats. Tool recommendations are always tricky. The lists you see in this chapter represent the tools I have experience with. They also represent a snapshot in time.

Inevitably, some of these tools will become obsolete, and new ones will replace them. So, look at the examples in this chapter for what they are: indicators of capability. Years after this book hits the market, you may find new tools that provide you the same capability, albeit in a more sophisticated manner.

Now that we've got tools out of the way, we can discuss how we use them. The first step is to focus on the skills and superpowers you and your team will need to be async-first. That's up next.

4

THE BIGGEST ASYNC-FIRST SUPERPOWER

Okay, I'm going to say it. I know you may not want me to, but I have to. It's the dreaded *D* word. Oh boy, didn't you know this was coming? Let me spell it out for you. *D-o-c-u-m-e-n-t-a-t-i-o-n*. All right, that's done now. Let's move on.

As I discussed in Chapter 1, I understand that the thought of documentation may make you uncomfortable. Let's get this absolutely straight, though.

There's no asynchronous work without written communication.

Notice that I say "written communication" and not "documentation." There's a subtle difference between those two, isn't there? Table 4.1 explains what I mean by each word.

Table 4.1 Written Communication vs. Documentation

	Written Communication	**Documentation**
What is it?	A practice.	An output or a product.
Definition	The practice of communicating in long or short form with text as the primary medium. Visuals and other media help enrich the message if and where necessary.	An umbrella term that encompasses all written documents and materials related to the project. Documents differ by use case and are a by-product of written communication.

WRITING IS A PRACTICE; DOCUMENTATION A PRODUCT

Many agile teams have trouble creating documentation. One of the root causes is infrequent written communication. And while easier documentation is one benefit of communicating in text, it's hardly the only one. This chapter is all about writing as the fundamental practice for being async-first. Let me tell you how this humble practice can be a superpower for remote and distributed teams.

WHY MEETINGS ARE THE LAST RESORT, NOT THE FIRST OPTION

What the Research Tells Us

In a delightful summary of existing research, Atlassian, the company that makes team collaboration tools such as Trello and Confluence, noted a few stunning insights:

- The average employee attends *62 meetings per month.*
- These employees consider *half those meetings a waste of time.*
- They face *56 interruptions each day.*
- They spend 2 hours each day recovering from these distractions.

Almost every hero needs a villain. If our hero is asynchronous work, then by definition, *pointless synchrony* is the villain. Let me stress the "pointless." I accept the need for occasional synchronous collaboration, especially for low-latency, high-bandwidth conversations and decision-making. If emotions are high, you will need to see each other and diffuse tensions. It just can't be your primary way to collaborate. Otherwise, as you notice from the data in the "What the Research Tells Us" note, you'll have a productivity nightmare on hand. Couple this with the difficulty of working across time zones. Not only will you frustrate and burn out your team, but you'll exclude some people from being part of your group.

So if you aren't always meeting and aren't constantly interrupting each other, how do you communicate? Well, the quickest and lowest-tech approach is to just write—clearly, precisely, and, if necessary, in long form.

THE BENEFITS OF WRITING

Not all of us are writers. I get that. Business communication, however, differs greatly from creative writing. You don't have to be a best-selling author to communicate with your teammates. Before we get into how you can hone your writing skills, let's discuss some benefits of writing.

Inclusive by Default

Non-native English speakers often struggle to keep up with a fast-paced conversation. Introverts frequently hold back during a charged discussion. Not everyone can comfortably attend a synchronous conversation, especially when you throw time zones into the mix.

- Writing allows non-native English speakers to construct their thoughts and use the help of tools, such as spell checkers and grammar plugins. They can use a translator to convert text into a language they understand.
- Introverts get the space to express themselves without the pressure that a group setting creates for them.
- People with disabilities can use speech recognition or screen readers to create or consume writing.
- People can write at whatever time they are working. And others can respond at a time convenient to them.

Thoughtful and Deliberate

In meetings, there's not enough time to slow down and examine topics in detail or to analyze them threadbare. Offering ourselves the space to study problems, to structure our thinking, and to write things down makes communication more thoughtful and deliberate.

The side effect of this is that it also makes synchronous communication more productive. If people have given thought to a topic beforehand and everyone has consumed each other's thoughts before a meeting, the meeting itself can focus on using that information to make decisions.

Gonçalo Silva (CTO, Doist), in the InfoQ podcast, explains why slowing things down is a feature, not a bug:

> It's always long form, always thought out, and this is 99% of the conversations we have about everything. I understand why we can be skeptical about this. For example, decision-making is delayed, because most things will take at least

24 hours to move ahead. The truth is…this leads to better discussion…thoughtful ways of approaching a problem, which in the end leads to better decisions.

So, we can take the hit on decision speed because we gain on decision quality.

When we place too much emphasis on a meeting-driven culture, we're implicitly optimizing for speed. The casualty of speed, as every technologist will know, is often quality. When you slow decisions down to let everyone "write things up," you'll have a better chance of making excellent decisions.

Indexable and Searchable

Text is the easiest kind of content to index. Whether it's search on your email, your task boards, your instant messaging platform, your wiki, or your repositories, text search is a common feature. It's also easier to query text inline, for example, when you're looking for a specific word within a piece of content.

It's Easy to Structure, Change, and Interact With

Most tools allow you to create a structure using headers and formatting and allow you to bring in multimedia and images where necessary. In a synchronous conversation, you'd do something similar with a presentation, and your spoken words would substitute for the text. Writing has an advantage, though. You can develop your thoughts iteratively and modify them as you receive feedback, at a low cost.

Moreover, it's easier for people to interact with what you've written than it is for them to interrupt you when you're speaking synchronously. They can comment inline—a feature most wikis and word processors afford—and give you feedback for a specific point. You can have intricate, threaded discussions—a feature of most wikis, task boards, and forums. It's an infinitely more interactive approach if you look at it this way.

A Longer Shelf Life

Conversations are ephemeral. Written communication has a long shelf life. It's referenceable in the future and can help create an audit trail on your teams. Frequent, well-thought-out written communication can lead to easier documentation. Whether it is to onboard people to your team or to explain your product to your customers, the practice of writing has a high payoff.

WHAT ABOUT THE AGILE MANIFESTO?

These days, most software development teams follow some version of agile development. The Manifesto for Agile Software Development includes 12 principles. Most of them are relevant even today, but there's one in particular that may seem at odds with asynchronous work:

> The most efficient and effective method of conveying information to and within a development team is face-to-face conversation.

I've found that many of us have a simplistic understanding of this principle. So, it's worth examining this principle in our current context. Let's first understand the argument in favor of this principle.

Face-to-Face Communication Wins on Speed and Fidelity

Sidu Ponappa is an ex-colleague and one of the superstar tech leaders of our time. He made some interesting points about the effectiveness of face-to-face communication in an early 2022 podcast. I'll leave you to listen from the 64th minute onward, but let me paraphrase his arguments.

Sidu compares communication efficiency between humans to the efficiency of a network:

> You increase the latency, increase the error rate, reduce the throughput, and there are direct consequences on the quality of the processing that the network carries on.

He expands his argument to compare human communication to how computers communicate. The sender serializes, compresses, and transmits data. The receiver then reverses the process to interpret the data. In the context of team communication, Sidu argues that the act of serializing a concept into English language or a diagram, compressing it for brevity or efficiency, and then transmitting it over your communication channels is lossy and error prone. The act of decompressing and interpreting information is equally, if not more, error prone.

In contrast, he explains, face-to-face communication has higher fidelity due to body language and nonverbal communication. Sidu also adds that you can make decisions faster in a face-to-face setting than in a remote setup. This explanation summarizes why the Manifesto for Agile Software Development advocated for face-to-face communication. Sidu is right, of course, but I'd like to add some nuance to his argument.

Effective Communication Has Some Nonobvious Parameters

So yes, face-to-face communication is faster and has higher fidelity. But are those the only parameters that make communication effective? In a fast-talking, primarily English-speaking setup, whose points of view usually make it to the top? You know this already. It's the extroverts, people who speak English fluently, and people who are neurotypical who dominate. In a business, we want the best ideas to win, not the loudest voices. Inclusion is a key parameter for decision hygiene. Here's what Sarvenaz Mysilicki, VP of Technology at American Express, has to say about inclusive communication:

> Anyone who has a say in how they run brainstorming sessions or idea gathering sessions [should] embrace the fact that everyone has different styles and try to accommodate them. So instead of getting everyone together for a one-hour brainstorm where they're constantly talking over each other, maybe do an offline document where people contribute all their ideas, not just their best one that they can get in during the time allotted. It's all about inclusivity.

Context is another parameter for communication effectiveness. If a group of people must make the right decision, it helps if they're all acting on the same information. This information serves as context. The more loaded the context, the less effective an impromptu side-of-desk conversation. Complex topics need structure. Writing helps create structure and share context at scale. Once everyone has shared context, a face-to-face or synchronous conversation can help them arrive at a decision. Consider this point made in the article "A Problem with the Agile Manifesto" on the *Remote Java Dev* blog:

> You could listen to a podcast at 10x speed, and it would be far more efficient than listening at 1x speed. Yet if you can't digest the information at 10x speed, then it's not effective, is it? While a synchronous exchange can certainly be beneficial, it's usually best when it occurs after an asynchronous one. And synchronous should certainly not be used in isolation regarding topics of any complexity.

Communication is rarely a one-and-done event. It's a process. A solely synchronous, or face-to-face, communication event can be useful if the topic is simple and has zero context. For almost every other type of communication, you need an artifact to reference, which in turn needs some deep thinking in advance. As Gonçalo said, sometimes you need to sacrifice decision speed for decision quality.

HOW DO WE WRITE BETTER?

At this point, you may think that writing is hard. Let me tell you what's harder: speaking. I'm Indian. I don't speak English as a first language. The first time I met native English speakers who spoke in their own accents, I froze. I'm more comfortable today, after many years of experience, but as an introvert, I still struggle to get my points across in meetings. And look, I'm an outlier. I had an English education. I've spent 15 years working at the same firm, so I've built enough social currency for people to listen to me. My consulting credentials allow me to have a voice. Not everyone has the same privilege. I agree, writing is hard, but speaking isn't much easier. And I think we all can get better at writing by doing a few simple things.

Ditch the Emotion; Be a Journalist

I often hear the criticism that people can misinterpret writing, especially when it comes to emotion and tone. We'll address that in a bit, but let's agree that a lot of business communication is factual, not emotional. You need to write like a journalist. Dry, straightforward, plain English. No fluff, no literary calisthenics, just get to the point.

A few years back I learned about the inverted pyramid of journalism, as you see in Figure 4.1. The most substantial information sits up top. As you go through the article, the information in it diminishes in importance. From a reader's perspective, this means you could just read the first parts of a story and get its gist. From an editor's standpoint, you can easily edit a story by "cutting from the bottom." This is useful if you're going to press soon and you have limited space to accommodate a story.

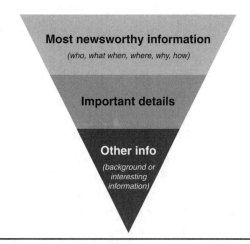

Figure 4.1 The inverted pyramid of journalism. (Source: Based on US Air Force, Shawn Air Force Base, *20th FW Editorial Policy & Submission Guidelines*, The Air Force Departmental Publishing Office, n.d.)

Writing at work isn't vastly different. You want to get to the point as quickly as possible and write with the assumption that people will read only the first few bits. This contrasts with editorial writing, which makes long-drawn, emotional points that can be open to interpretation depending on your background, personal beliefs, and political stance. By the way, this chapter is an example of editorial writing. I wouldn't write this way when I design a feature.

I'm not for a moment saying that journalistic writing is an easy skill. All I'm saying that journalistic writing is an effective way to share information at scale. I also think that with the writing tools we have at our disposal these days, it's easier to be a journalistic writer than it is to get out of your introverted skins or to become a fast-talking, fluent English speaker or to overcome your neurodiverse nature.

RESOURCE

Learn to Write Better

While there are several resources to help improve your writing, I have five recommendations that can help you elevate your skills in a short time.

- Tips for better writing by GitLab
- Technical writing courses by Google
- Technical writing fundamentals by GitLab
- *Smart Brevity* by VandeHei, Allen, Schwartz
- "How to Write in Plain English" by the Plain English Campaign

You can find more information about these resources on the book's companion site at https://www.asyncagile.org/book-resources.

Use Modern Ways to Emote and to Be Clear

Sometimes you must communicate emotion. This is where I agree that writing is difficult. I also agree that face-to-face communication, or even synchronous video communication, conveys emotional messages with a level of fidelity that most people struggle to convey through writing.

With that said, if you trust your writing skills, you should absolutely write away! Use emojis! They aren't just for millennials and Zoomers 😀. They can help you explicitly communicate emotion.

Editors like Hemingway and Microsoft Word have powerful tools to help you write clearly, concisely, and in an inclusive manner. The act of writing and then editing your thoughts helps you slow down so you can diffuse your emotions and focus on your message. I like using the Flesch-Kincaid reading tests (as in Figure 4.2) that are part of Microsoft Word to help me learn how difficult it may be to read what I've written. This is a bit like writing code. You must refactor your document till the point that an eighth-grade student can understand it. As I noted earlier, you can improve what you've written even after sharing it with people. If that isn't a superpower, what is?

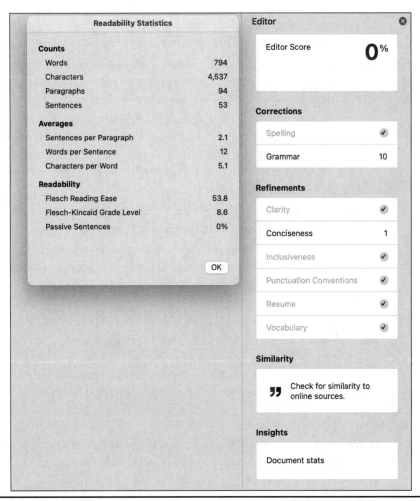

Figure 4.2 Readability statistics in Microsoft Word.

Use Asynchronous Video or Audio

Some pushback I've heard about writing comes from the fact that people don't consider themselves as capable writers. Social media has also killed people's attention spans for reading. People argue that recording audio or video is easier and we should use that instead of writing.

First things first, whether you write or record, you must structure your communication. So recording a well-thought-out audio or video isn't a freebie. Consider a few other disadvantages of videos and audios:

- Inline searchability of videos and audio clips is pretty low, even on the most sophisticated platforms. This, however, is getting better with time.
- Our ability to consume content is slower on videos and audio clips. Our listening speeds are about 140 words per minute (wpm) as compared to our reading speeds, which for most people are greater than 200 wpm.
- Writing is also more flexible to consume. If you see familiar content, you can easily skim it or skip to the next section. It's easy to jump back to a specific point as well. It's possible to do this with well-produced audio or video content that has built-in markers, but it takes more sophistication than adding headers and a table of contents to a document.
- The ability to comment inline is almost zero with video versus with text, unless you have a specialized platform for the purpose.
- And with non-native English speakers, comprehension breaks down considerably with video. In the first place, you may struggle to understand another person's accent. Even if you have captioning tools, the AI struggles to recognize every unique speaker's accent.
- It's difficult to edit audio clips and videos after the fact, and if you expect frequent iterations to the content, the cost of communication adds up quickly.

Those disadvantages aside, audio and video can be effective, especially to support written documents. There are also some use cases for which they're more effective than text.

- If you're creating **unidirectional content**, such as a demo, a screencast, or a video recording to describe product features, video is a great format.
- Content with a **short shelf life**, such as your CEO's message, can be an acceptable candidate for video, unless you're expecting people to interact with specific parts of the communication.

- Internal podcasts, which are all about listening to people in conversation, **without the need to interact with the content,** are another great candidate for audio. These are effective for passive listening, for example when driving or when working out.

┌─ BEST PRACTICE ──────────────────────────────

Short Videos Bring Documents Alive

To add some life to your writing, you could record yourself and do a short video presentation. If you trust your presentation skills, this is an effective way to create a short, referenceable, easy-to-consume artifact that can communicate emotion the way you intend. Figure 4.3 represents how a video can sit within the textual narrative of a document.

Figure 4.3 Inline videos can liven up your writing.

Whatever medium you choose, please don't lose empathy for the consumers of this content. Meeting recordings, for example, belie a low level of empathy for co-workers. What could otherwise be a single-page summary of meeting outcomes now becomes a long video for people to watch even at 2x speed. Multiply that across every member of the team, and you lose several hours of productive time because someone didn't bother to summarize in writing.

HOW MUCH MORE EFFECTIVE IS FACE-TO-FACE COMMUNICATION?

For a moment, let's accept the thesis that face-to-face communication is the best way to relay information in a development team. Now let's ask ourselves a few questions:

- How much more effective is it?
- In what contexts is it truly effective?
- What's the cost you incur for face-to-face communication?
- How do you weigh the benefits in comparison to those costs?

Here are a few questions for distributed teams that can't be face-to-face all the time even if they wanted to be:

- Is a 20-person Zoom call with video off and mics on mute the same thing as face-to-face communication?
- Does your message really need multiple people to interrupt their work so they can attend a conference call?

The unequivocal arguments in favor of face-to-face communication, especially in this era are superstitious at best. While I say this, I also believe that short bursts of face-to-face interactions are a terrific way to build relationships and camaraderie. We'll explore that dimension in Chapter 8, "The Value of Being Face-to-Face." When you stop being trigger happy about synchronous and in-person interactions, you can plow back the time savings to use these interactions in meaningful ways.

THE MANIFESTO DESERVES THE BENEFIT OF DOUBT

The agile manifesto is more than 20 years old at the time of writing this book. We have the benefit of that much more experience, advances in collaboration tools, and a global pandemic to guide our thinking. Think about it. There's so much that wasn't around in 2001: real-time, collaborative editing; videoconferencing with screen sharing; digital whiteboards; asynchronous audio and video; or platforms like YouTube or Spotify. Heck, even emojis became popular only after 2010!

Moreover, we didn't know at the time that our work could adapt to our life or that it was okay to hug our kids in the middle of a workday. In theory, we could connect to the internet and work from anywhere. It still took a pandemic to convince us that remote work is a sensible default for so many of us. The world has changed considerably since 2001 and more so since 2020. Our mindset about communication and collaboration needs to change as well. Thankfully, there's precedent in a familiar part of the knowledge work industry. Sidu tells us who should inspire us:

> Open-source projects are doing stuff for 40 years without any face-to-face meetings without conference calls. But they do it because they have exceptionally high adherence to the process. And frankly, the truth is, most companies can't even come within shouting distance.

TO WORK ASYNC-FIRST, WE MUST WRITE

So maybe, we in the corporate world can borrow from the volunteer world of open-source and improve our processes and communication. Writing is at the heart of that improvement.

CHAPTER SUMMARY

There's no asynchronous work without writing. It's a fundamental practice for going async-first.

- If we don't meet to communicate, then writing is the quickest and most cost-effective alternative. It has some clear benefits.
  - It's inclusive by default for non-native English speakers, introverts, and neurodiverse people.
  - It's thoughtful and deliberate. Slowing down allows us to study problems and structure our thinking around them.
  - Writing is indexable, searchable, easy to structure, change, and interact with.
  - Unlike conversations, written communication has a long shelf life. You can write once, run many times.
- We must acknowledge that face-to-face and even video communication win against writing on speed and fidelity. Writing, however, wins on inclusion and the ability to share context at speed. Even real-time communication benefits from an async-first approach, where you can reference a written artifact.
- Writing well is a skill we all can get better at. By applying the inverted pyramid of journalism, using readability tools, emojis, and async audio and video, you can guide yourself through the learning process.

All this said, writing is not the only superpower you'll need. I have three more async-first superpowers that I want to introduce you to. Let's look at those in the next chapter.

5

THREE MORE ASYNC-FIRST SUPERPOWERS

Writing is the number-one async-first superpower. In fact, I'll say that it's the number-one superpower for remote work. Period.

While this book assumes remote work as a default, I don't intend for it to be a remote-work playbook. That said, some remote-work skills become crucial when working asynchronously.

WHAT AN ASYNC-FIRST SUPERHERO LOOKS LIKE

In this chapter, I'll add three more superpowers to our list to go along with written communication. This quartet of abilities, which Figure 5.1 illustrates, will help you and your team enhance your individual and collective effectiveness. Here are the three other superpowers:

- Distraction blocking
- Reading and comprehension
- Working independently

Let's look at what each of these skills involves and how you can practice them. You can use the same ideas to help your colleagues pick up these skills.

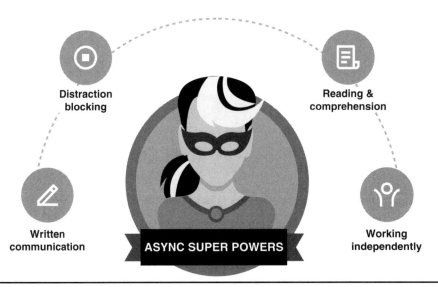

Figure 5.1 The four superpowers for asynchronous work.

BLOCK DISTRACTIONS

A key benefit of asynchronous work is that it reduces interruptions and gives you time back for deep work. But many of us have conditioned ourselves to seek distractions. This is a phenomenon that authors such as Cal Newport and Johann Hari have written about extensively. This is what Harvard University's SITN blog has to say about such constant distractions:

> Smartphones have provided us with a virtually unlimited supply of social stimuli, both positive and negative. Every notification, whether it's a text message, a "like" on Instagram, or a Facebook notification, has the potential to be a positive social stimulus and dopamine... influx.

We don't just seek dopamine hits from social media. Checking our email or Slack triggers a similar rush. However, if we give in to these temptations, then we erode the benefits of working asynchronously.

> *Efforts to deepen your focus will struggle if you don't simultaneously wean your mind from a dependence on distraction.*
>
> —Cal Newport

So, we all need the ability to block out distractions when we want to work deeply. Here are a few strategies that I suggest you start with:

- **Plan your week in advance**: Set up your days such that you have at least a couple of uninterrupted, three-hour work slots on your calendar every day. Be sure that no one can pull you in for a meeting during these times. Apps like Google Calendar allow you to define these as "focus time," so your deep work slots are visible to your colleagues. You'll must also learn how to decline avoidable meetings. Dropbox has some delightful suggestions on how to decline meetings tactfully:

  "Thanks for including me! I'm wondering if we could try to solve this over email instead?"

  "I've been in so many meetings lately, and I'm trying to be conscious of my schedule. Can we try to solve this without a meeting first?"

  "I'll be happy to give you feedback on that! Before we schedule a meeting, could I review it in Google Docs?"

- **Ration the distractions**: Your smartphones, laptops, and tablets all come with a "do not disturb" feature. Be sure to enable that when you're in a deep work session. On the Apple ecosystem, you can use Screen Time to control which apps you can use when and for how long. Android and Windows devices have similar features. It's amazing how much you can achieve by just introducing a little friction on your devices.

- **Use an app blocker**: While features such as Screen Time are fabulous, sometimes you need a heavy-handed, no-way-out solution. App blockers like Freedom allow you to define rules that apply to all your devices. When you begin a deep work session, any app or website in your block list becomes inaccessible. Even if you instinctively navigate to a distraction, you can't use it. Yet again, the friction is liberating.

READ AND COMPREHEND

This is a corollary to the first superpower, written communication. The most frustrating thing for any co-worker is when they write something up but the people who should have read it don't read it.

There's no asynchronous work without writing. And if no one's reading, the writing is pointless. So, you'll need to set aside time in the day not just to write stuff up but also to consume writing that someone intended for you. If you or your colleagues have lost the reading habit, then this may seem daunting to start with. I have some good news for you, though.

If you have already freed up your calendar, you're no longer under time pressure to finish reading before that next meeting. Breathe. Slow things down. Read. Take the time you need to grasp what your colleagues are saying.

Reducing distractions will help build your focus. If you're working in tech, it's likely you have latent reading skills from your years of formal education. At the base speed of 200 wpm, you can read a 10-page document in 15 minutes. Developing this habit will help you consume high densities of information in short periods of time.

Train yourself to read on the personal side as well. Set aside two slots of 10 uninterrupted minutes each day to read anything that you enjoy—a book, a magazine, articles on your favorite websites. The more you exercise the reading muscle, the stronger it gets and the more productive your asynchronous work experience will be.

Try building these habits as a team. Make a team commitment to set aside time each day for personal and professional reading. Book clubs are a wonderful way to build this habit. The entire team reads the same book for a specified duration and shares their reflection on a document, a wiki page, or even a synchronous call. How about starting with this book?

WORK INDEPENDENTLY

Last but not the least, you'll need to learn how to work independently. This doesn't mean you don't collaborate with others. It just means you can't be looking for someone to manage you. You should be able to default to action instead of waiting indefinitely. Above all, you must to respect your colleagues' autonomy and flexibility just as much as you crave it for yourself. In GitLab's terminology, the following is the idea of being a "manager of one":

> In an all-remote organization, we want each team member to be a manager of one. A manager of one is an attribute associated with our Efficiency value. To be successful at GitLab, team members need to develop their daily priorities to achieve goals. Managers of one set the tone for their work, assign items and determine what needs to get done. No matter what role you serve, self-leadership is an essential skill needed to be successful as a manager of one.

There are several strategies to achieve this, but here are a few I recommend you follow:

- **Practice self-sign-up**: Agile teams are by design management-light. So team members usually choose the tasks they work on. This is in contrast to traditional teams where a manager assigns work to people. When motivated individuals get together, they will autonomously figure out what they need to do. Waiting for someone to tell you what to do is an anti-pattern.

- **Analyze your tasks well and ask for help early**: This is key to asynchronous work. When you sign up for a task, you expect that the last person who worked on it left enough detail for you to pick it up. Not only must you analyze it well, but you must give others the time to help you if you need help. That way your colleagues can plan a convenient time to work with you.

- **Communicate progress proactively**: It can be annoying if people keep pinging you about the status of a task. Not only does it create interruptions for you, but it can also get frustrating for you to communicate the same thing repetitively. On the flip side, knowing your progress is important to the team. There may be downstream tasks that depend on the task you're working on. It's only fair that people responsible for those tasks know where you're at, with the work you're doing. On an async-first team, communicate progress at every logical juncture. That way, you don't just protect your sanity, you're also being empathetic of how interdependent work can be in a team. Don't be afraid to share work-in-progress. Use screen recordings where necessary to make your updates visual. Communicate early and often on your task board, in the task's context.

- **When in doubt, execute**: We've discussed this earlier. If you're in doubt, choose to be wrong at speed over being perfect. Asynchronous teams focus on getting things done. You'll inevitably make mistakes. Take that in your stride and use the learning to make your process more sophisticated the next time. And when something goes wrong, be sure to refactor and adapt.

PERSONAL PRODUCTIVITY LEADS TO TEAM PRODUCTIVITY

Your personal productivity affects how you work with others on a distributed, async-first team. As you drive change in your team or organization, you shouldn't just develop these superpowers for yourself. Coach others and help them gain these abilities.

CHAPTER SUMMARY

Aside from writing, you need three other superpowers to be an async-first knowledge worker:

- Distraction blocking helps us work uninterruptedly so we can immerse ourselves in the work at hand. What do you gain? Deep work and flow.
- Reading and comprehension complement a writing culture. There's no incentive for people to communicate in writing if no one will read. We all must build our reading muscles even if we've lost touch with the practice.
- To work asynchronously, we must learn to work independently as well. This is in line with the "manager of one" philosophy. Self-sign-up, proactive communication, and defaulting to action are by-products of being able to work independently.

While this chapter and the previous one focused on personal productivity, we must now shift focus to the team. Every sport has its rules, and every team has its norms and rituals. In the next chapter, let's explore how you can create a calm team atmosphere by introducing efficient protocols.

6

CALM THINGS DOWN WITH COLLABORATION PROTOCOLS

Our scaffold for change is taking shape. You understand the various collaboration tool categories, and I expect you're thinking about your own tool stack. We've also explored the four superpowers you need to be effective asynchronous workers. It's now time to zoom out and examine your team's work and communication protocols.

WORK EXECUTION VS. WORKFLOW

We all value "self-organizing teams" and "autonomy" at work. We also misunderstand these terms. You don't want to tell a skilled developer how to code a certain requirement. If two developers are pairing on a problem or a developer and designer are figuring out a solution, you want to trust their skills. Smart people expect that once they understand a problem, they'll have the freedom to figure out solutions. Cal Newport calls this *work execution*.

Newport distinguishes work execution from workflows. Workflows define how we do the following:

- Find and prioritize work
- Assign it to people
- Communicate about it

- Coordinate it
- Review it

Teams that don't agree on a workflow end up reinventing it each time they execute. This is not just wasteful, but it makes communication ineffective. Jason Fried mentions M&Ms—meetings and managers—as a reason why offices are ineffective. On the contrary, we need effective meetings, and we surely need proper managers. But as we've seen earlier in the book, our meetings aren't always effective or even necessary. And managers can often be more a hindrance than help.

Dig deep and you'll realize that the root cause for many such problems is a poorly designed workflow. Often the workflow is nonexistent. This leads to frequent, inefficient, back-and-forth communication. Such interruptions fragment your workday. Instead of fixing the workflow, teams find themselves with a bloated managerial layer. That way you at least have someone who can make sense of all this communication. And before you know it, you're in a "how many techies does it take to screw in a light bulb?" situation.

When teams go remote, they wade into another trap. I call this the "office on the cloud." This happens when you re-create the workflow of the office using communication tools such as email, instant messaging, and videoconferencing. These fast, inexpensive communication systems worsen all the problems I just mentioned. You become victims of what Newport calls the "hyperactive hive mind." Always connected, always interrupted.

Efficient teams need efficient workflows and protocols, so they collaborate and communicate predictably. So, in this chapter, I introduce you to the fundamentals you need in place to avoid the hyperactive hive mind.

REVIST YOUR WORKFLOW STATUSES AND TRANSITIONS

If you're working on a remote team, you most likely have a task board in a place like you see in Figure 6.1. It doesn't matter whether you use Jira, Trello, Asana, or another tool. Most project management tools allow you to define a workflow for your team.

Table 6.1 describes some typical workflow steps on software development teams.

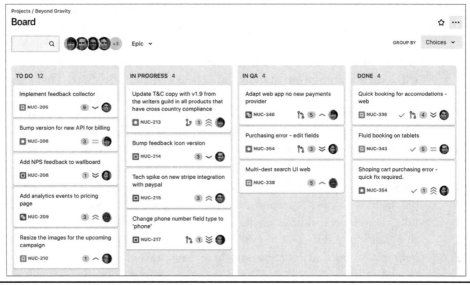

Figure 6.1 A task board on Jira (from *Atlassian*).

Table 6.1 A Simplified Workflow for Software Development Teams

Workflow Stage	Description
To do	The backlog of work; sorted in descending order of priority.
Analysis	Tasks that the product owner or business analyst is fleshing out so they're ready for a developer to pick up.
Dev	The list of tasks that developers are currently working on. This could include bug fixes, technical tasks, and new feature development.
Test	Tasks that developers have written code and unit tests for, which a quality assurance (QA) analyst runs exploratory and end-to-end tests on.
UAT	QA-tested functionality that internal users are testing.
Done	Tasks representing functionality that's in production and/or meets the definition of done.*

---

* These are a collection of criteria that the team must meet, so a task or software requirement is "done." This doesn't just include business logic or acceptance tests. Depending on the team, the definition of done (DoD) can include logging, monitoring, and even documentation. We discuss this further in Part III of the book.

Your workflow may look similar or different or even more complex. The number of stages doesn't matter as much as the principles of setting up the workflow.

1. **Represent every stage of your process on the task board:** Often, teams don't show their informal or shadow gate checks in the workflow. This creates a few problems. One, you can't tell what's happening with a task by just looking at the task board. Second, you can't gather data on where tasks get stuck. Imagine, for example, that undocumented desk checks cause stories to stay in development for too long. If you have no data about this, how will you make the process efficient?

2. **Define primary ownership for each stage:** For example, your product owner or business analyst is responsible for fleshing out the tasks in the "analysis" lane. Developers handle stories in the "dev" lane. Testers pick up items in the "test" lane. Of course, every team member can roll up their sleeves and help in case tasks are stuck somewhere. You must still be clear about primary responsibilities.

3. **Optionally, spell out the rules to transition between stages:** Not all tools allow you to do this. If your project management tool has such functionality, consider using it in the interest of a disciplined workflow. For example, you may want a tester to log all user feedback when transitioning tasks out of the UAT stage. In such cases, you can set up the workflow to remind them about this step. Effective processes help people avoid inadvertent errors. This isn't micromanagement. It's a helpful nudge.

When you revisit your workflow, be careful not to design for the exceptions and worst-case scenarios. Don't create unnecessary gate checks in your process to cover for rare occurrences. This is the risk aversion that makes a user story go through several different meetings before it hits production. Optimize your process for flow and avoid creating bottlenecks.

MAKE EMAIL AND IM SECONDARY COMMUNICATION TOOLS

Your task board should be the source of truth for all the work your team is up to. Most team communication should be about work in progress. For an agile team, that work is transparent on the task board. All conversations should be "in-context." Almost every task board allows you to have conversations inside a task. You can tag people on the team to get their attention on the task. If you're interested in updates about a specific task, most tools allow you to "watch" it.

When you make your task board the primary communication interface for the team, you'll gain two advantages.

- You have only **one place to track communication** about work in progress. The tools allow you to be specific in how you choose to communicate. For example, you can set up the tool to generate notifications only for the tasks you've signed up for and the tasks you're watching.
- The contextual conversations for a task card serve as its **audit log**. Anyone can look at a card, examine its details—i.e., the description, attachments, and comments—and know what's happening with it. You don't need a manager to keep asking people about updates.

What about email and instant messaging then? I suggest making them secondary tools. Use them for external or interdepartmental communication first and general internal communication next. If your chat conversations take more than five minutes or five back-and-forth messages, then you're probably using the tool for the wrong purpose. Some companies remove their entire IM history every few weeks. This discourages people from placing permanent, referenceable information there. Modern IM tools such as Twist do away with presence indicators and notifications. That way people can use it without feeling like they must respond ASAP.

Knowledge workers spend way too much time checking email and IM. The average worker can't go more than a few minutes before switching to one of these tools. Think about the cost of those interruptions and how deep work becomes a casualty. You don't have to change your entire toolset. Avoid the ASAP mindset these tools promote. Create safety in the team so it's okay to check email or IM once or twice daily.

STREAMLINE YOUR DECISION-MAKING PROCESS

When teams don't have a standard decision-making process, every decision can be chaotic. Everyone wants to be part of every decision. Work slows down. You end up with too many meetings and communication overload. Worse, the team ends up with a risk-averse attitude. This is what Seth Godin calls *thrashing*—i.e., "the apparently productive brainstorming and tweaking we do for a project as it develops."

Before I go on, I must admit that we sometimes need a democratic or consensus-based decision-making approach. However, as Aviva Pinchas of Parabol says, "All decisions are not spicy." Today, with the sophistication of continuous delivery, most decisions are reversible. While that's no reason to make poor decisions, it's certainly a good reason to simplify decision-making.

Instead of getting everyone to bless all decisions, adopt a consent-based decision-making process as your default. Consent implies "no objections." Figure 6.2 describes how an asynchronous, consent-based decision-making process could work:

1. A team member writes up a proposal in a shared document or a wiki page about the decision they want to make. They also write a time by which they expect to hear from everyone else. There shouldn't be a false urgency to this timeline.

2. If a decision seems irreversible, then the team or the team member proposing should attempt to make it reversible.

3. People have the chance to respond to the proposal. They do so through inline comments or questions. This is also the time to raise objections if any.

4. The proposer can then incorporate suggestions and amend the proposal if necessary.

5. If there are no major objections after this, the decision goes through; otherwise, people can get onto a meeting and sort things out.

6. The team should default to a meeting if, despite their efforts, a decision seems irreversible.

With a written, consent-based decision-making process, you avoid the endless loop of seeking perfection and settle for "good enough." You slow down everyone's thought process, so the proposer is deliberate about what they're suggesting.

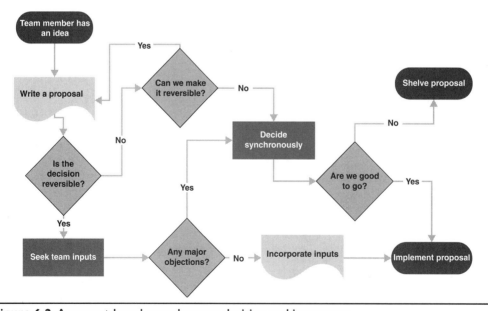

Figure 6.2 A consent-based, asynchronous decision-making process.

Everyone else needs to think about whether they have any objections or just suggestions. Here's what Jeff Bezos, founder of Amazon, says when warning us about heavyweight, risk-averse decision-making processes:

> Some decisions are consequential and irreversible or nearly irreversible one-way doors (Type 1 decisions). If you walk through and don't like what you see on the other side, you can't get back to where you were before. But most decisions are changeable, reversible—they're two-way doors (Type 2 decisions). You can reopen the door and go back through. As organizations get larger, there seems to be a tendency to use the heavyweight Type 1 decision-making process on most decisions, including many Type 2 decisions. The end result of this is slowness, unthoughtful risk aversion, failure to experiment sufficiently, and consequently diminished invention.

By taking a consent-based approach instead, you'll embrace a high decision velocity and a bias for action.

IDENTIFY CHANNELS AND THEIR RESPONSE TIMES

Last, but certainly not least, you must agree on response times for various collaboration tools and channels that you use. James Stanier provides us with a sensible default in his book *Effective Remote Work*, which I've reproduced in Table 6.1. Use your judgment when implementing these protocols on your team. Just be mindful of the following principle:

> *Only a few things can be "urgent." ASAP is toxic. Keeping someone blocked, though, is insensitive.*

Table 6.1 A Sensible Default for Communication Protocols on Various Channels

Medium	Length	Reply Expected	Reply Time	After Hours?
Phone call	Short	Yes	Immediate	Yes
Text message	Short	Mostly	Hours	No
Chat	Short	Mostly	Hours	No
Video call	Medium	Yes	Immediate	No
Email	Medium	Not always	Days	Np

Medium	Length	Reply Expected	Reply Time	After Hours?
Asynchronous audio/video	Medium	No	N/A	N/A
Written document	Long	Not always	Days	No
Task board	Variable	Not always	Variable	No
Wiki	Variable	N/A	N/A	N/A

FUNDAMENTALS, FUNDAMENTALS, FUNDAMENTALS

The work you put into setting up your workflow, decision-making process, and communication protocols may seem pedantic to start with. However, you'll see the payoff in a calmer, more thoughtful team environment. This serves as the foundation for every practice you tweak on your team.

CHAPTER SUMMARY

Before you start tweaking your team's practices to be more async, you must set up some fundamental processes and protocols for working in a distributed fashion.

- Show your workflow transparently on your task board. Everyone should know in a single view what the team is up to. Define ownership for each stage of the workflow and design for the best average cost and not the worst case.
- Make your task board the primary hub for communication. Email and IM should be for external and interdepartmental communication first, general team communication next, and task-based communication only as an exception.
- Adopt a consent-based decision-making process rather than a consensus-based or democratic decision-making approach every time. This will help you default to action while improving the overall pace and quality of decisions.
- Agree on response times and reply expectations for each channel. Without these expectations in place, people will suffer from FOMO, and you'll risk becoming an ASAP culture.

Take some time to think about how you'll align your team to these new protocols. Once you're done, head on to the next part of this book where I show you how to be async-first, practice by practice.

Part III

THE PRACTITIONER'S GUIDE

It's time to roll up your sleeves and examine the way you work. Each chapter in this part addresses specific collaboration practices that software development teams follow. You'll come away with ideas on how to execute these practices more efficiently with an async-first approach or how to improve them if they must remain synchronous.

- **Chapter 7**, "Meeting as the Last Resort," and **Chapter 8**, "The Value of Being Face to Face," unbundle the Ulysses pact of "meetings as the last resort." You'll learn about pragmatic ways to reduce the number of meetings, and you'll also learn why async-first teams must value in-person interactions. **Chapter 9**, "Micro-Moves to Shift Left," closes this discussion with simple ideas to reduce the number of meetings by employing individual or team plays.

- In **Chapter 10**, "Write a Team Handbook," you'll learn about the advantages of maintaining a team handbook as your primary knowledge base. The chapter will also describe a suggested structure for such a resource and how you can create and maintain it.

- **Chapter 11**, "Tame the 'Instant' in Instant Messaging," shines a light on a common communication tool—instant messaging. This chapter gives you tips and tricks to guide your team's usage of such tools so you can not just be productive but also reduce interruptions and noise.

- Across **Chapters 12**, "Standup Meetings: An Easy Shift Left," **Chapter 13**, "Take Charge of Your Development Cycles," and **Chapter 14**, "Run Meaningful Retrospectives," we focus on the common scrum ceremonies—standups, sprint planning, sprint reviews, and retrospectives. You'll learn how to make some of these rituals fully asynchronous or make them more effective by introducing asynchronous collaboration elements.

- **Chapter 15**, "Kickoffs and Desk Checks: Reduce Ritualized Interruptions," and **Chapter 16**, "Questions to Reimagine Your Tech Huddles," explore a few common activities that happen during sprints, such as kickoffs, desk checks, and huddles, and how you may be able to get similar value without meetings in an async-first work setup.

- In **Chapter 17**, "Pair Programming: The Elephant in the Room," we'll discuss pair programming, a common synchronous practice that has immense value. You'll learn ways to practice pairing while staying true to the async-first mindset.

- Across **Chapters 18**, "Audit Trails from the Flow of Your Work," **Chapter 19**, "Communicate Tech and Functional Design," and **Chapter 20**, "Two Stable Pieces of Handbook Documentation," we'll shift tracks to documentation and artifacts. A pragmatic documentation strategy helps distributed teams scale and move at speed. You'll learn about audit trails, which are the most frequent forms of documentation; design documentation, which is less frequent; and developer documentation, which is usually the most stable.

- Lastly, **Chapter 21**, "Craft an Efficient Onboarding Process," will show you how all the effort you put into an async-first way of working will help you onboard new team members efficiently. By the end of this chapter, you'll have actionable advice to leverage your handbook and other artifacts to craft the onboarding experience for your team.

7

MEETINGS AS THE LAST RESORT

In Chapter 2, I mentioned that to adopt a mindset for change, the team must agree to a Ulysses pact.

Meetings are the last resort, not the first option.

Following through on that pact may seem daunting. This is especially true for teams that have built meetings into all their work processes. How do you cut back on them, and why? These are questions to address as a team.

JUST. TOO MANY. MEETINGS.

The global pandemic of 2020 ushered in the remote-work revolution. There are indications that productivity goes up when people have the autonomy to work from anywhere. Between 2021 and 2022, I surveyed more than 1,800 technologists at a global IT services firm to understand the state of remote work in my country, India. The "Remote Work Statistics" note has some findings that you may relate to.

Remote Work Statistics

Here are some interesting remote-work statistics:

- 81 percent of people were just as satisfied or more satisfied with their jobs since they started working remotely.
- In the middle of the pandemic, 49 percent of these people believed they were more satisfied with their work as a result of being remote.
- 92 percent of people believed that the quality of their work had improved or remained the same because of remote work.
- In the middle of the pandemic, 53 percent of these people believed the quality of their work had improved because of remote work.
- 55 percent of people claimed to have a day that extended beyond nine hours on average.
- 66 percent of people believed they were working more than they were before the pandemic.
- 76 percent of people believed they were in more meetings as compared to before the pandemic.
- 14 hours was the average amount of time each person spent on meetings every week.
- 32 percent was the percentage of these meetings people claimed were ineffective.

I want to point something out from these statistics. Just for the 1,800-odd respondents I surveyed, having 32 percent ineffective meetings accounts for about $23 million wasted annually! If you extrapolate these costs to companies or the entire knowledge work industry, the impact on productivity is staggering.

You may remember me mentioning the concept of "flow" in Chapter 1:

> ... a state in which people are so involved in an activity that nothing else seems to matter; the experience is so enjoyable that people will continue to do it even at great cost, for the sheer sake of doing it.

You'll also remember that I quoted some stark results from my survey:

> While 97 percent of the people I surveyed claimed to care about flow, only 12.5 percent—i.e., one in eight people—claimed to achieve it with regularity.

And what was the number-one obstacle to achieving flow? One word: meetings.

So, it's clear that we need fewer meetings. This is step 1 to being asynchronous. I argue that it's also the most critical step to take if you want to be a productive, remote-first organization. Let's start by outlining a framework so you can figure out which meetings you need and which ones you can get rid of.

THE CONVEREL QUADRANTS

I adapted the framework shown in Figure 7.1 from *The Anywhere Operating System* by Luke Thomas and Aisha Samake. It's such a simple and powerful concept that I think it deserves a visual and a memorable name, so I call it the ConveRel quadrants. It's a classic 2 × 2 matrix, and the following sections explain the two axes.

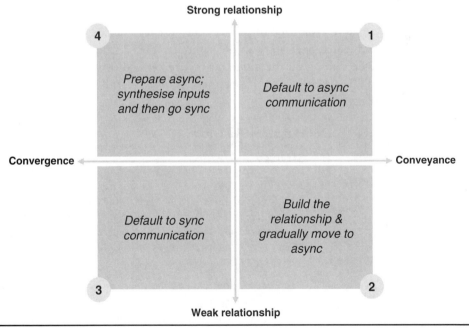

Figure 7.1 The ConveRel quadrants. (Source: Adapted from Luke Thomas and Aisha Samake, *The Anywhere Operating System*, Friday Feedback, Inc., 2021)

The "Conve" Axis

Thomas and Samake say that at a high level you can break communication down into two parts:

- **Conveyance.** As you may expect, this is mostly unidirectional information transfer. An example is a status update.
- **Convergence.** This happens when two or more people need a low-latency, high-bandwidth exchange of ideas to come to a shared understanding. An example is using available information to make a team decision.

The "Rel" Axis

This axis quantifies the strength of the relationship across a wide spectrum:

- **A weak relationship.** This is often the case between people who haven't worked with each other for very long, or even if they have, they haven't had the chance to agree on their ways of working.
- **A strong relationship.** Such relationships often exist between high-performing teams and individuals inside and across organizations who have built a deep camaraderie working together.

Now that you have visualized the matrix, let's use it to decide which meetings are necessary and which ones you can do without. Table 7.1 describes the strategies you can use depending on the quadrant your proposed or existing meeting falls in. There will be exceptions to these strategies, of course, but consider the advice as a sensible default.

Table 7.1 Strategies for Each ConveRel Quadrant

Quadrant	Strategy
1. Conveyance–strong relationship	*Default to async.* This is as straightforward as it gets. If the information is unidirectional, remember that people can read faster than they listen. Moreover, an asynchronous artifact is persistent, is editable, and allows for more in-depth, inline interactions—e.g., questions about the content.
2. Conveyance–weak relationship	*Build the relationship with the aim to move async.* While nothing changes with the information between quadrants 1 and 2, sharing information in a meeting is a contrivance to building a working relationship. As the relationship gets stronger, you shouldn't need these meetings anymore.

Quadrant	Strategy
3. Convergence–weak relationship	*Default to sync.*
	Without established ways of working, it's tough to enforce a diligent culture where people prepare for a meeting and make the most of synchronous time. Many work relationships will start here, and trying to rush through this stage may be counterproductive.
	So, it's okay to default to meetings here, if you also commit to improving the relationship as you go.
4. Convergence–strong relationship	*Prepare async, synthesize inputs, and then go sync.*
	While it's likely that these interactions will need a meeting, everyone must do some legwork to make that meeting effective. This means everyone who attends needs to study the relevant information. You may need conveyance leading up to the point of convergence. Sweat those details.

WHEN YOU MEET, MAKE IT COUNT

When you follow through with the rule of "meetings as the last resort," you'll reduce the number of meetings for your team in a big way. Your next task is to ensure that the meetings you do have are productive. While asynchronous communication has its own costs, it's usually inexpensive compared to equivalent meetings for the same purpose.

A one-hour meeting for eight people is not a one-hour meeting at all. It's an eight-hour meeting. Multiply that with salaries for internal employees or with opportunity costs to compute the full cost of meetings. We can't be trigger-happy with these expensive interactions. There are a few simple things you can do.

- **Answer the big questions.** What's the purpose of the meeting, and what will happen next? This should be clear on your meeting agenda. And yes, promise yourself never to set up meetings without an agenda. No agenda, no attenda!

─ BEST PRACTICE ─────────────

"No Agenda, no Attenda!"

Cameron Herold coined the phrase "no agenda, no attenda" to decline meetings without clear objectives. Such meetings are likely to be a waste of time. You can make "no agenda, no attenda" part of your team's collaboration charter so everyone feels safe to decline meetings without objectives.

- **Keep the size of the meeting down.** Choose the smallest group of people necessary for the meeting and eschew blanket invites. More than eight people, and your meeting is likely to be a waste of time. While there'll always be the exceptional meeting with more than eight people that is useful, use "less than 8 people" as a rule of thumb when inviting attendees to a meeting. The key is to add people by hand instead of inviting an entire mailing list.

- **Make it active.** Don't waste time with presentations. Share documents and videos in advance to save everyone time. If people don't have a reading habit, then set aside the first few minutes for people to consume the background information in silence.

- **Implement good decision hygiene.** Guard against the anti-patterns of meetings where groups succumb to groupthink and bias cascades. Allow everyone the time to silently write their points of view about the decision before diving into an intense discussion. Determine the factors that should influence the decision and the weightage each of them should carry. Delay intuition until you've allowed all the data and viewpoints to surface. Help each other avoid knee-jerk reactions and make deep thinking a team sport.

- **Document it for everyone else.** You can use automated tools or do it yourself, but whatever you do, show empathy for the people who weren't in the conversation. Make it easy for them to consume the outputs. Brevity, structure, and simplicity are important characteristics of meeting minutes as well. Just sending out a meeting recording is insensitive. It's an optional extra, but not a substitute for a succinct summary.

┌─ BEST PRACTICE ───

The Six-Page Memo Pattern

Jeff Bezos, founder and former CEO of Amazon, has a unique approach to meetings. Amazon employees create six-page, rich narratives around the topic of discussion for a meeting. The first few minutes of a meeting are silent. Everyone reads the document in a study hall session. You can implement a similar pattern in your team to promote an async-first mindset. Not only will this encourage preparation for meetings, but it'll also build the reading habit in teams.

ACCOUNT FOR COSTS OF FREQUENT CROSS–TIME ZONE MEETINGS

Remote work gives you the theoretical advantage of hiring people from anywhere. However, it helps to have a reasonable overlap across members of your development team if you expect daily synchronous communication in such teams. The best case is for everyone to be in the same time zone. In the worst-case scenario, *aim for at least a four-hour overlap.* There will be the odd time when people need to synchronize, and having any less than four hours of overlap is just impractical.

The exception to this rule is where a few stakeholders or clients are in a distant time zone. This is what we see in typical offshoring situations where a client may be in the United States and the development team is in India. You'll inevitably need some meetings to coordinate with such stakeholders, but if they're infrequent, you can work around the time zone problems. I still suggest *at least one or two hours of overlap* between the stakeholders and the development team so that no one has to work outside their regular daylight hours to accommodate the other party. If this isn't possible, there are three alternatives:

- **Alternate the inconvenience.** Don't leave the burden of staying back late or starting early only on people in one location. Take turns sharing the inconvenience. Not only is this an effective way to build a sense of "one team," it's also a way to ensure that one set of people don't burn out because of odd working hours.

- **Create a team in an intermediate time zone.** This situation, while less typical, is gaining popularity in recent years. If your clients are on the American West Coast and your main development team is in India, an intermediate team in Eastern Europe could help ease the communication. You can then orchestrate some synchronous communication through a baton pass from the United States to Eastern Europe to India and vice versa.

- **Internalize the costs.** If neither of these options is possible, then it means that some people must bear the cost of synchronous collaboration across time zones, by taking time away from their personal lives. At Thoughtworks, we've dealt with such situations by taking two key steps:

  - **Reduce this impact to the smallest number of team members possible.** This way you can protect most team members from having to work late hours. If the responsibility is possible to rotate, agree on that rotation mechanism in the team.

  - **Use your project budget to pay a shift allowance to people who are working odd hours for a prolonged duration of time.** The later the shift, the higher the allowance. This allowance will not make the work any easier, but it'll internalize the cost of working odd hours. By using the project budget to pay these allowances, you'll also encourage stakeholders to think about the impact of such a way of working. It'll also help you start conversations about changing the status quo.

Constant meetings across opposing time zones are hard to keep doing over a prolonged period. Please apply the strategies I've outlined, with the understanding that they're suboptimal and often unsustainable. Eventually, you must look to adopt an async-first approach and aim for a sustainable pace and schedule at work.

STAY HUMAN

While you work to reduce team meetings, don't lose sight of the fact that you're still human. We enjoy social interactions. Meeting people in person or online helps build the relationships that'll take you to the top of the ConveRel quadrants. So, there are some meetings that I think you should always have:

- **One-on-one catchups.** Use these to check in on each other, identify areas of common interest, support each other, and get to know each other. Gossip is fair game as well. Sure, you can talk about work too, but if you've been communicating asynchronously about that, then you can focus these conversations on your work relationship.
- **Team activities.** Now and then, consider getting together as a team to either play a game or do an activity like an Airbnb experience together. Discover each other's hidden talents. Shared experiences build team culture and bonding. Find opportunities to create different, fun experiences for the team. This is important for your company as well, so find a budget for it. That way, people don't have to pay out of their own pockets for such events. Also, be mindful that some people don't enjoy such activities. Don't force the issue. Be considerate about people's personal preferences.
- **Meet up in person.** When possible, meet your colleagues in person for coffees, lunches, dinners, sports games, movies, or other activities. If your company sponsors it, organize a meetup where you fly everyone to a specific location. Remember that you're doing this to build camaraderie, so don't stuff work into the meetup. If you're used to working remotely, this will just be inefficient. Instead, curate social experiences for the team. Who knows, you may find friends for life!

ASYNC-FIRST, WITH SMALL SHIFTS

If you've been working in a mostly synchronous environment, you won't be async-first overnight. Collaborate with your colleagues to make tiny shifts left along the spectrum of synchronousness. Every shift left is a win; plan and celebrate them all with your team.

CHAPTER SUMMARY

Meetings, while necessary to some extent, are the biggest blocker to asynchronous work. To be async-first, meetings should be the last resort, not the first option.

- Audit your existing and upcoming meetings using the ConveRel quadrants. Meetings for conveyance can generally move async. Convergence may need some real-time interaction.

- When you meet, follow the best practices we've discussed in this chapter to keep meetings effective.

- If you expect meetings to regularly cross time zones, aim for at least a four-hour overlap between all members of the development team. If your clients are in a distant time zone, it helps to have at least an hour or two of overlap.

- Connectedness is a feature of synchronous communication. This helps you navigate to the right of the ConveRel quadrants. So, don't lose your humanity. Make time for team bonding, in person or online.

Point out your wins in your weekly reflections or retrospectives and tag the cheerleaders for shifting left. You can also put some of your time savings into building relationships with your teammates. In fact, that's the topic of our next chapter.

8

THE VALUE OF BEING
FACE TO FACE

When we discussed writing as a superpower in Chapter 4, I addressed the Agile Manifesto's perspective about face-to-face communication. While face-to-face communication wins on speed and fidelity, written and other asynchronous forms of communication are more inclusive. Writing also helps share information and context at scale.

But then what is a face-to-face interaction (F2F) good for? In a world where you can work productively when you're remote, is there any value in being in the same physical space?

FROM URL TO IRL

Let's get a few things out of the way. Being on Zoom isn't the same thing as being F2F. At least not in 2023. We've also acknowledged in the previous chapter that you need meaningful, synchronous interactions to build relationships. An async-first approach to work balances the trade-offs between sync and async interactions, as we discussed in Chapter 2.

F2F meetings are a special kind of synchronous interaction. In this chapter, let's explore how you can get value from such events.

THE TIME-ZONE QUESTION

The beauty of asynchronous work is that it transcends time zones. As you perfect the baton pass with different people, it doesn't matter where they work from. That's for day-to-day work. It's when you decide you need to synchronize across time zones that you run into problems. The conspiracy of geography, physics, culture, and the limits of the human body means that finding a common time to work together can be difficult. Ask Indian consultants like me who collaborate primarily with clients in North America!

Traveling to the same time zone can make time-boxed, synchronous collaboration much easier than when everyone is working from their respective countries. Well, if you're already traveling, then why not work face to face? That brings me to my next point.

FACE-TO-FACE COLLABORATION ISN'T FREE

It should be obvious, but let me say it, anyway. There's a reason people don't want to commute to the office. Commuting represents a cost to our personal lives and a cost to productivity as well. So, just because people are in the same time zone doesn't mean you must uproot everyone and bring them F2F. Be intentional about this. What are you trying to achieve in person that you can't achieve otherwise?

Modern, collaborative whiteboards and videoconferencing tools make collaboration far more efficient than it would be in person. For example, I've run complex workshops for 100-odd people in an online setting, and there's no chance that I'll be able to do something similar in a F2F setup with such ease.

Productivity and efficiency are not good enough reasons to meet F2F. If you still want to try being productive in person, then let me throw one more thought your way. Meetings don't get a free pass just because you're F2F for a short while. They're still the last resort, and you must continue to follow best practices:

- Use the ConveRel quadrants.
- Prepare well.
- Limit the attendees at each meeting.
- Treat everyone as if they were remote. Don't disadvantage colleagues who have no option but to attend remotely.
- Use modern tools like collaborative whiteboards and collaborative editing, so you create artifacts in real time. This will also make it easy to share meeting outputs, after the fact.
- Summarize the meeting for everyone's benefit.

Be disciplined about these practices. Each time you make an exception, you'll inadvertently normalize future exceptions as well.

Hybrid Meetings: Why Treat Everyone as Remote?

When organizing F2F meetings, I've tried to get everyone in my remote team to the same location. However, despite everyone's best efforts, people often have personal commitments or other blockers such as immigration issues that prevent them from attending the F2F. In such circumstances, I err on the side of inclusion by leveling the playing field. I treat everyone as remote, for the duration of work activities, such as meetings.

Location-independent work is easy when everyone enjoys similar conditions when they collaborate. This is why all-remote and all-in-an-office type patterns work quite well. However, when meetings become hybrid, we must consciously think about inclusion by using the same tools for collaboration as we would when working remotely. Here are two practices I follow for my hybrid meetings:

- Everyone joins with a dedicated video feed, regardless of location. This allows remote attendees to see everyone clearly.
- Everyone has equal access to shared artifacts for a meeting, be it an online whiteboard, document, or presentation.

This doesn't mean people who are F2F can't enjoy the other benefits of being together, such as in-person team activities or lunches and dinners. When it comes to work, though, please be inclusive.

With all this said, let's get back to the key question. Why meet face to face?

THE TRUE VALUE OF BEING IN PERSON

You can build friendships and camaraderie online. I might give away my age as I write this, but many generations back when I was a kid, there was this concept of pen-pals. We'd forge friendships just on the strength of writing letters to unknown people in another part of the world. It was slow, but it worked. Remember the value of being synchronous, though? You can be "connected," and you can do that spontaneously. In-person interactions enhance that sense of connection in a way that Zoom camera feeds can't. The best way to characterize this is by using the term *simcha*, a word Rabbi Jonathan Sacks popularized. This is what he says:

> Simcha, by contrast, is not a private emotion. It means happiness shared. It is a social state, a predicate of "we," not "I." There is no such thing as feeling simcha alone.

If you dig deep down, think about the deepest relationships you have: your BFF, your mates on a sports team, the people you visited even when the pandemic was raging on. You forged these relationships face to face. There lies the power of such interactions. And yet, we undermine that power.

CAMARADERIE HAS DOLLAR VALUE

These days in-person interactions are so expensive in terms of relative dollar value (travel and hotels) and the clear cost to people's lives (commute, time away from family, stress) that there's an implicit need to make them seem "productive." What'll the bosses say? While we know that we need F2F interactions to build camaraderie, we create several obstacles to achieve that goal.

Before you know it, your face-to-face meeting becomes packed with presentations and workshops as if there's no tomorrow. You don't even stop to think if all this is at all necessary. You want to "make the most of our time together." Stop. Pause for a moment. You don't need to play to the galleries here. There's a dollar value to camaraderie. If your employers don't see it now, they'll suffer it in the future. Data from Gallup shows this clearly:

> Our research has repeatedly shown a concrete link between having a best friend at work and the amount of effort employees expend in their job. For example, women who strongly agree they have a best friend at work are more than twice as likely to be engaged (63%) compared with the women who say otherwise (29%).

We need to resist the urge to engage in "productivity theater." You can be far more productive when you're remote. Meet to build relationships instead. Whatever work you do is a contrivance to this end.

Keep Charging Your "Social Battery"

David Heinemeier Hansson (DHH) of 37signals speaks of the concept of a "social battery." A remote, async-first team is like an online community. DHH explains that the strength of an online community comes from the good faith of its participants.

After working apart for long, online communities and remote teams can experience an erosion of good faith. People's intellectual guards may go up, debate may become less constructive, and people may be less open to new perspectives. This is due to the social battery that's out of charge.

Meeting in-person helps rebuild that good faith by recharging the social battery. Little nuances such as a colleague's disarming smile, body language, or eye contact can help lower our guards. With short bursts of in-person interaction, you can go back to work remotely for weeks or months on a full social battery.

RETHINK THE ONSITE-OFFSITE

You may remember the term "offsite." We used it to refer to team gatherings outside the office. In recent months and years, because of budgetary constraints or to preserve the relevance of offices, I see these off-sites are now on-site, i.e., in the office. After all, if everyone works remotely, the office is technically offsite.

Some inspiration comes from the big Silicon Valley tech firms who've invested in many comforts to keep their employees at work for longer. Companies like Infosys own quasi-hotels to make the "onsite-offsite" work. I admit their campuses can feel like amusement parks after a while. Salesforce has built its own ranch in the redwoods to help employees discover the "spontaneity and joy" of in-person interactions.

If you're one of those companies, I'll grudgingly admit that you can plan your entire F2F at your company premises. However, if you're like the rest of us, think about the value you can get by separating your work and play environments. If you've planned to do some work together, then by all means, do it in the office. It'll give you a familiar, predictable work environment, and you'll probably be more effective. When you're done, how about shifting to another, more social space?

Find out what works for the group. Optimize for fun and bonding. Go camping together. Stay in a wildlife sanctuary for a night. Plan a hike for everyone. Go bowling or bungee jumping. Scratch that. Don't go bungee jumping. I'm sorry I suggested that. And yes, there's a dollar value to fun as well.

Even in those spells of in-office work, during the "offsite," leave some slack for social interactions. A long lunch conversation, time for walks together, or low-key, after-hours activities—these are all ways to get more value from your time together. By leaving slack in the schedule, you don't just get more value from the F2F. You also give people who've traveled a long way to get to the F2F time to recuperate.

BE CONSCIOUS ABOUT BUILDING RELATIONSHIPS

Organizations that pride themselves on remote work are conscious about meeting up regularly. Check out Doist or Automattic. GitLab works with the Cowork experience to organize their off-sites. Yours truly has organized two company-wide retreats for Thoughtworks.

You need face-to-face time to strengthen relationships and camaraderie in the team. If you're a manager or a leader, here are some suggestions for you to consciously build in-person interactions into your ways of working:

- Find a budget so people can meet their colleagues for activities or just a casual meal together. This is important and has value for your employers, so don't expect such interactions to happen only after hours.
- Explore if your employers will allow a co-working budget, where a few people who live in a certain neighborhood can rent a co-working space for a few hours before they head off to a lunch or a dinner. People who get energy from the feeling of working alongside colleagues from time to time may enjoy this option.
- If there's a budget for it, organize a team retreat every few months, where the entire team can get away from work for a day or two and just enjoy each other's company. Don't ask people to compensate for lost time at work. Remote and async-first work will improve productivity enough to compensate for any of those lost hours.

⎯ BEST PRACTICE ⎯⎯⎯⎯⎯⎯⎯⎯⎯⎯⎯⎯⎯⎯⎯⎯⎯⎯⎯

When Planning IRL Meetups, Keep Base Locations in Mind

When all your colleagues stay relatively close to each other—for example, in the same city—in real life (IRL) meetups will look different from those with people who live farther apart. If people live in the same city, you can organize IRL meetups at a higher frequency and at shorter notice. You may even be able to agree a cadence at the team level.

In contrast, when team members live in different cities, you must be more thoughtful when planning such interactions. These interactions most likely will be at a lower frequency, say once a month or once a quarter. It's also a clever idea to think of these as memorable events. Plan a few activities, spread across a few days. If you plan to do any collaborative work during this time, be sure to include only those activities that you believe will be more effective, face-to-face. Don't forget: the focus is on building relationships.

SO MUCH FOR MEETINGS

In the previous two chapters we've addressed online and face-to-face meetings. In this chapter, we covered the value of being in-person and how that's a special kind of synchronous interaction.

CHAPTER SUMMARY

Face-to-face meetings are a special kind of synchronous gathering. We must be thoughtful about the value we seek from such events.

- Overcoming time zones is a good reason to travel, but it can't be the only reason to meet F2F.
- There's a significant cost to F2F meetings. Productivity and efficiency aren't big enough reasons to justify this cost.
- The true value of F2F is in building strong, lasting relationships. You can also do this remotely, but it takes a long time.
- Avoid the trap of "looking productive" and making the office the sole venue for an otherwise vibrant purpose.
- Be conscious about building relationships through in-person interactions. This will mean setting aside time and discretionary budgets for the purpose.

You'll notice that my suggestions are team oriented and not org-wide. Part-guerrilla, part-advocate, remember? Try these experiments with your team first. If they work, you can advocate them to the rest of your company. It doesn't have to be all or nothing. Make the micro-moves. Speaking of micro-moves, the next chapter is all about them.

9

MICRO-MOVES TO SHIFT LEFT

You are what you do and not what you say you'll do. I'm going to adapt a James Clear quote, so I can make my point:

> *Every action you take is a vote for the type of team you want to become. No single instance will transform your beliefs, but as the votes build up, so does the evidence of your identity.*

The Ulysses pact of "meetings are the last resort" is the foundation of being an async-first team. We've got to get the fundamentals right. The entire team must vote with their behavior for that async-first work culture. Otherwise, it'll all feel like lip service.

SMALL SHIFTS, EASY WINS

Our goal is to shift left on the spectrum of synchronousness, in small steps. Some of these steps are personal, and some will be for the whole team. Scoring a few easy wins can help the team's morale when making this shift. That's what this chapter is all about: easy wins from small shifts. I have a grab-bag of eight ideas for you to implement: five for the individual and three for the team. Let's get into them now.

PERSONAL SHIFTS: BROADCAST YOUR COMMITMENT

As James Clear said, every behavior is a vote for your team's identity. The more consistently people practice a behavior, the more it becomes second nature. Activities that become second nature serve as evidence for the team's identity. Everyone broadcasts their commitment to the cause. The following are five simple things everyone on the team can do.

Change Your Chat Status

Regardless of the instant messaging tool you use, you can set your status. Set up your default status in a way that everyone knows you use the platform in an asynchronous manner. That way, you take the "instant" out of instant messaging. Here's an example:

 Deep work; will be slow to respond

The more people see this, the more they'll get the message. Combine this with the communication protocols we discussed in Chapter 6. That way, people will know when they should just pick up the phone and get your attention for something urgent.

Use a Pro-Async Email Signature

Many of us work in global teams, and even if we don't, we may have colleagues who work different hours from us. Being async-first is all about flexibility and autonomy after all. You don't want to inadvertently pressure people into responding to your email the moment they see it. To pre-empt an unnecessary sense of urgency, I use the following email signature:

PS: My work hours may not be your work hours. Please don't feel obliged to respond outside your normal schedule.

That way, even if people receive my email when they're getting on with their lives, they know I don't expect an immediate response.

Schedule Your Messages

Sometimes we have a brainwave in the middle of the night. You don't want to lose the thought, and you want to share it with someone right then. First things first, consider if you can make a note somewhere and follow up when it's a good time for other people. If you absolutely have to share immediately, then schedule the message to go out when you expect the recipients to be at work.

This approach comes in handy when you work across time zones. Your morning may mark the end of someone's day. Seeing a message at that time may keep them at work longer than is necessary. Since asynchronous communication can wait till their morning, schedule the message to go out at a reasonable time for them.

Most email and instant messaging tools provide this functionality, like Gmail does in Figure 9.1. So, you have no excuse. If you err on the side of thoughtfulness, your colleagues will appreciate you for it.

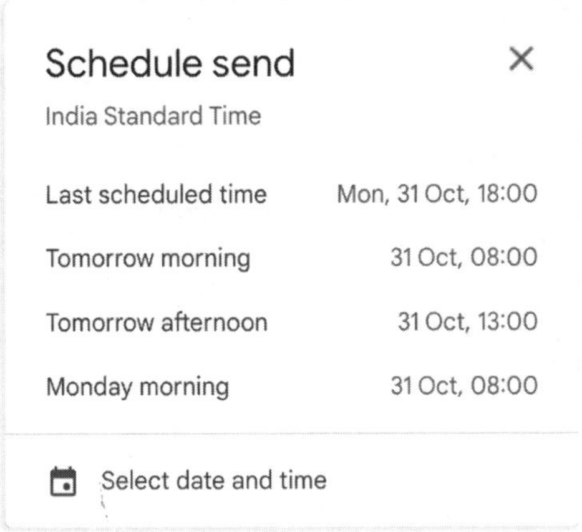

Schedule send   ✕

India Standard Time

Last scheduled time   Mon, 31 Oct, 18:00

Tomorrow morning   31 Oct, 08:00

Tomorrow afternoon   31 Oct, 13:00

Monday morning   31 Oct, 08:00

📅   Select date and time

Figure 9.1 Scheduling an email on Gmail.

Plan "Focus Time" for Deep Work

Both Outlook and Google Calendar (as in Figure 9.2) allow you to broadcast when you're in the middle of deep work, by helping you block out "focus time." The beauty of these calendar features is that they don't just visually show that you're "in the flow"; they also allow you to autodecline meetings during these times. Two benefits for the price of one—nifty, isn't it? If you use integrations like Clockwise, you can even sync your calendar availability onto instant messaging tools such as Slack so people know what you're up to.

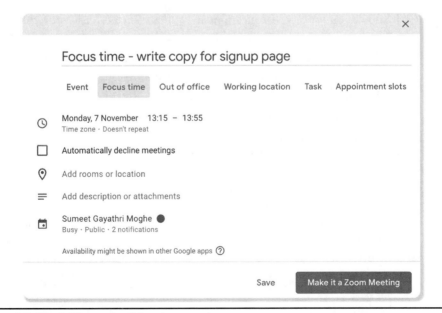

Figure 9.2 Block "focus time" for deep work.

Replace "Quick Syncs" with "Async"

I stole this one from Dropbox. How unoriginal! Let me explain why I added this to the list. Often, when you ask your colleague for a "quick sync," it's for what you think of as an immediate need. You and I can agree that in most cases it's not urgent. An answer to a set of questions, a search for a how-to, or someone's opinion on a certain idea—there are many such triggers. I empathize with that need. Now spare a thought for the person you interrupted. While you may get what you wanted by pulling them into a "quick sync" and you can just continue with what you were doing, the meeting you created interrupts their flow. Context switching comes at a cost to your colleagues, as Figure 9.3 illustrates.

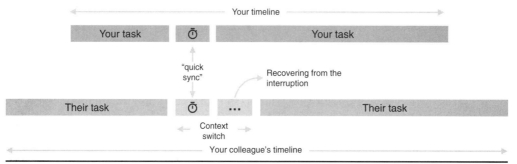

Figure 9.3 The quick sync may help you, but it interrupts your colleague.

Another world is possible.

- Why don't you write your questions in a document and ask your colleague to answer them inline, by a certain day or time?
- Why don't you record a video of where you're stuck and have your colleague comment on it to tell you what you may be doing wrong?
- Why don't you write up your idea in reasonable detail and give your colleague some time to process it and then give you feedback?
- Could a picture speak a thousand words? If a sketch or a diagram brings your questions to life, how about you add it for clarity?

Figure 9.4 illustrates this more deliberate approach. You won't get instant gratification, but in most cases, you'll get thoughtful inputs. Your colleagues will benefit from fewer interruptions, and you can perpetuate a virtuous cycle of deep work. The side effect? You also have a referenceable artifact for everyone else on the team. Remember, this advice is not for stuff that's truly urgent. If you need help to douse a fire or if you feel you're blocked for some reason, by all means get immediate help!

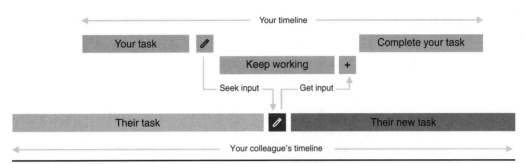

Figure 9.4 Slow down. Give your colleagues time for a thoughtful response.

How Much Do Context Switches Hurt Us?

A mere 20 minutes of interrupted performance can lead to higher stress, frustration, workload, effort, and pressure for individuals.

Asana's 2022 anatomy of work reports that we spend a lot of time context switching:

- 42 percent of people are spending more time on email than one year ago.
- 40 percent are spending more time on video calls than one year ago.
- 52 percent are multitasking during virtual meetings more than one year ago.
- 56 percent feel they need to respond immediately to notifications.

Add to this the staggering cost of ineffective meetings that we've addressed in Chapter 7.

TEAM SHIFTS: ACCELERATE LEFTWARD

Those first five ideas help you be a model asynchronous citizen at work. You can practice what you preach. The next three plays are for the whole team. I think of them as "gimmes"—things that are incredibly easy to do. The more you play these cards, though, the easier it is to keep the Ulysses pact.

Inviolate Half Days

You might remember Paul Graham's essay about a maker's schedule versus a manager's schedule from Chapter 1. Makers need long, uninterrupted blocks of time to achieve something meaningful.

> There's another way of using time that's common among people who make things, like programmers and writers. They generally prefer to use time in units of at least half a day. You can't write or program well in units of an hour. That's barely enough time to get started.

A straightforward way to give people a contiguous block of time back for work is to make one-half of the day "meeting free." For example, you could decide that from 9 a.m. to 1 p.m. there are no meetings. If you have recurring meetings, move them to the other half of the day so that there are no exceptions. Here are a few tips to make this tick:

- **Make it predictable.** Decide which block of four hours is meeting-free and stay consistent with that practice. This will help make things predictable for the team, and everyone can settle into a routine.

- **Encourage productive behaviors.** Having meeting-free time is all nice and dandy, but if people face interruptions from chat, email, social media, or phone calls, you won't get much benefit out of this. So, people will have to employ their own productivity habits—for example, distraction blocking—to make the most of this time.

- **Sync your calendars.** You can cut off distractions from within the team, but it's no fun if you have distractions from outside the team. Set up your calendars so it's clear to everyone in the organization that this time is interruption-free. That way, no one will block your time for an interview or other company commitments during these hours. You can even set up calendars to autodecline invites during these hours.

No-Meeting Fridays (Or Any Other Day)

A few teams I know have designated a day of the week as "no-meetings" day. I love Friday as a no-meeting day for a bunch of reasons. Let's start at the end. Having a clear Friday allows me to end the week with a sense of accomplishment. If I don't get work done that day, I know I have only myself to blame. I can't tell you how happy it makes me feel to go into the weekend with the recency bias of having achieved something. The other little benefit of no-meeting Fridays is that it's something you all can look forward to as a team—an eight-hour reward to end the workweek.

Your mileage could vary, so pick a Monday if that floats your boat. Remember, all the tips I mentioned for inviolate hours apply here as well.

┌─ **BEST PRACTICE** ──

Maker Weeks

If a few hours each day or one day each week feel like too little, try "maker weeks" or "focus weeks." The idea is simple. Cancel all meetings for a week or two every few months. You can decide how often you want to schedule such weeks. For example, Slack has experimented with maker weeks twice each quarter. Just be sure to get your stakeholders onboard if you make such a plan.

└──

Purge All Recurring Meetings

Is this one easy? Perhaps it isn't. I understand, but let me explain. In fact, let me have David Heinemeier Hanson of 37signals explain:

> How does your day accumulate mass? I have these three, four, five standup meetings. I check in one-on-one with these people every week. Before you know it, you've created entitlements around 30 hours of your week. That's just at the baseline. There's 10 hours left now to do things. Not that the other stuff isn't work, but that it's already accounted for. I loathe that sense. I get such an anxiety of feeling I'm being held down in such a way if my week is fully structured in a way that's just accounted for, that I can't get out of. No. Absolutely not.

You see what I mean? Recurring meetings are problematic for a few reasons:

- They're meetings without an agenda. You dream up an agenda because you have the meeting. How messed up is that?
- You usually mark them to the broadest audience possible because of FOMO.
- Many people don't engage in these meetings because most of them are about "conveyance." Remember the ConveRel spectrum? These should ideally be async.

This is not to say that recurring meetings have zero value. Some people enjoy these as a vehicle for team cohesion. After all, if you get a bunch of intelligent people together, you're likely to have some interesting conversations. However, the vast majority of recurring meetings lose their efficiency after the first few runs. The cost of the meeting far outweighs its marginal value. Before you know it, you see a majority of people attending these meetings with their mics and videos off, doing something else on the side. You can, of course, blame people for not running these meetings well. I suggest, instead, to fix the recurring nature of these meetings, which causes most of the problems. This is what Dropbox, Asana, and Shopify did in their respective meeting resets.

Hard as it may seem, get rid of all these recurring meetings except for one-on-ones. In a remote setting, one-on-ones are an effective way to build relationships and to learn from each other. So, don't lose them in the process of cleaning up your calendars.

If you're leading a team and taking responsibility to shift left, then you must inform stakeholders about this change with meetings. The "Keep Stakeholders Informed about No Recurring Meetings" box has an example of such an email.

— BEST PRACTICE —

Keep Stakeholders Informed About No Recurring Meetings

Hi [Stakeholder name],

As you may be aware, we are making some changes to our ways of working so the development team has fewer interruptions during the day and can be more productive. One action we're taking is to make our meetings more effective. We realize that our recurring meetings aren't as productive as we'd like them to be, so we're removing them from our calendars as the first step of our reboot.

I assure you that as and when we need a meeting, we'll set it up with a focused group and a clear agenda. Please expect us to prepare for these meetings and to share relevant materials ahead of time so you also have time to prepare. And yes, we'll check your calendar before we block your time.

Cheers,

[Your name]

Change that email to your context and set up the meetings you truly need on a case-by-case basis. If you need meetings for team cohesion, set them up with a purposeful design. Once you get accustomed to the time you buy back, you won't regret this at all.

BUILD ASYNC-FIRST BEHAVIORAL CUES

A small change in what you see can lead to a big shift in what you do. As a result, you can imagine how important it is to live and work in environments that are filled with productive cues and devoid of unproductive ones.

—James Clear

Our environment and its cues impact the way we act. In this chapter, we discussed behaviors that help us broadcast cues to each other, about the way we want to work.

CHAPTER SUMMARY

Small moves from individuals and teams can help us vote with our behavior for an async-first work culture.

- Personal plays help us broadcast our commitment to an async-first culture.
  - Set your chat message to broadcast that you're working asynchronously.
  - Write an email signature that tells people they can reply when they are back at work.
  - Schedule your messages and emails to go out at times when you expect your recipients to be at work.
  - Block out focus time on your calendars so it's clear you're in the middle of deep work.
  - Replace "quick syncs" with "async."
- Team plays help us accelerate our shift leftward.
  - Institute an inviolate four-hour block each day when there are no meetings and everyone actively avoids distractions.
  - Choose a day of the week to designate as a no-meeting day. I recommend Fridays.
  - Delete all recurring meetings and from that point on, set up purposeful meetings that follow best practice.

The strategies I've outlined shift you left on the spectrum of synchronousness so that you can gradually align your team and stakeholders to that principle. You won't get there on day one, and that's okay. Micro-moves matter!

As you implement these new ways of working on the team, you'll need a place to write up your learnings and team norms. This place will also be the home for team knowledge. Next up then is the team handbook.

10

WRITE A TEAM HANDBOOK

On remote teams, clear documentation is often the most direct way to share information at scale. Yet, many teams avoid this until the point that a lack of documentation starts hurting. Some of this stems from a misconception about agile software development. People believe that if you're working on an agile project, documentation is not necessary.

Martin Fowler says this:

> Agile methods downplay documentation from the observation that a large part of documentation effort is wasted. Documentation, however, becomes more important with offshore development since face-to-face communication is reduced.... As well as documents, you also have more need for more active collaboration tools: wikis, issue tracking tools and the like.

Across the IT industry, timely delivery matters. To support timely delivery, you need easy access to information. A team handbook catalogs the most important pieces of information related to a team.

DISTRIBUTED TEAMS NEED A SINGLE SOURCE OF TRUTH

A lack of documentation leads to communication overhead. There are too many meetings, closed email threads, and instant messaging discussions to disseminate information. This makes repeated activities, such as onboarding, inefficient. Knowledge sharing is slow, information moves in bits and bobs, and those inefficiencies cause interruptions galore.

As GitLab rightly says,

> As a team scales, the need for documentation increases in parallel with the cost of not doing it.

Writing a handbook that contains stable documentation about the team's work is a better alternative. Daunting as it may seem, a handbook-first approach has many advantages. Not only do you maintain a single source of truth for the team's knowledge; you also reduce the chaos and confusion from inefficient communication. In this chapter, I'll walk you through some ideas about what to include in such a resource and how you can create and maintain it.

BY DEFAULT, START WITH YOUR TEAM

The first question to answer is about the scope of your handbook. Who is it for? All-remote organizations such as GitLab document everything about their company in a handbook. Changing your whole company, however, will be hard even if you're influential. So, I suggest that you focus on your immediate team. Makers will experience immediate benefits from an asynchronous way of working, so it makes sense to start documenting your practices and team information with your immediate colleagues in mind.

The good news is that nothing succeeds like success itself. If you can implement this way of working successfully with your team, your handbook could become a blueprint for other teams in the organization.

Team Handbook vs. Company Handbook

In an ideal world, your team's handbook will sit on the same system as the company handbook. Several companies achieve this using systems such as Confluence, SharePoint, or Mediawiki, which allow different groups to organize their content into spaces or team sites.

However, it may not always be possible to set up a universal system such as this. For example, in professional services firms, team documentation usually rests in client-approved systems. In other kinds of firms, there may not be an org-wide system available yet. In such situations, teams must set up their handbook using a tool they agree on and can procure. It helps to also onboard adjacent teams to this tool so sharing information becomes easier.

Once you've had some success with your team's handbook, you can make a case for more org-wide tools if that makes sense for your business.

WHAT GOES INTO A HANDBOOK?

Imagine your dev team as a mini company. There are two critical parts of knowledge relevant to your work.

- The organizational *context* that lays down *how you work* together
- The *content* of *what you work on* together

You can use a similar model to structure your handbook. Figure 10.1 helps you visualize this content architecture. Let's dive into a little detail.

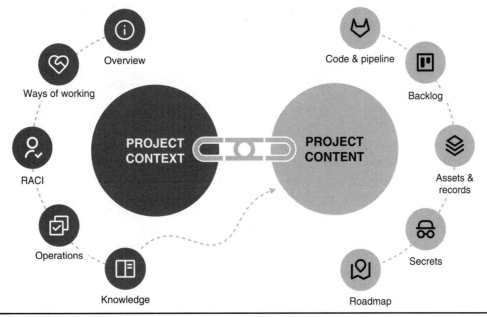

Figure 10.1 **The structure of a project handbook.**

Project Context

This part of your handbook derives from several topics we've addressed so far:

- **Overview.** The problem you're solving, with its industry context, stakeholder bios, and any background information that's useful for the team, goes here.
- **Ways of working.** Team values, guidelines, work agreements, and communication protocols and response times go here.
- **Responsible, accountable, consulted, informed (RACI).** As teams get larger and distributed, everyone can't possibly do everything. Clear roles and responsibilities on projects help avoid confusion. RACI charts are a succinct way to describe these roles and responsibilities. The chart clarifies roles using four labels.

- **Responsible (R):** The people who do the work
- **Accountable (A):** The person or group that all stakeholders will hold accountable for the task or deliverable
- **Consulted(C):** The people who give advice or input for the work
- **Informed (I):** The people who need to know what is happening with the work

Your RACI chart can help broadcast who does what and who they must collaborate with. I usually make it using a simple table with outputs in one column and a column each for the different roles on my team. The intersecting boxes describe how each role participates in delivering that output. Table 10.1 is an example RACI chart for a small development team. Your chart could look quite different based on your project context.

Table 10.1 An Example RACI Matrix

Outcome/ Output	Product Manager	Engineering Lead	Developers	Quality Assurance	Designer
User research	A	I	I	I	R
Product road map	RA	I	I	I	C
System requirements	RA	C	I	I	C
Site blueprint	C	I	I	I	RA
Design system	C	I	I	I	RA
Wireframes and mockups	C	I	I	I	RA
Architecture	I	RA	R	C	O
CI/CD and environments	I	RA	R	C	I
Code quality	I	A	R	I	I
Unit testing	I	A	R	I	I
Integration and automation tests	I	C	C	RA	I
UAT	C	I	I	RA	R
Team management and reporting	C	RA	I	C	I

- **Operations.** Depending on the team you are in, there will be operational information that everyone on the team should have. For example, people will need instructions on filling timecards; steps to get access to specific resources; or, for that matter, information about getting laptops serviced.
- **Knowledge.** Not only is this section useful for new members of the team, it's also important to existing team members. Everyone can't be familiar with every part of the project, and referencing the information in a structured fashion speeds up learning for the team. This section also links to your project content.

Project Content

Depending on the tools your team uses, these assets can exist across systems. Therefore, the knowledge section of your project context should provide a way to navigate across systems and provide your team with a bird's-eye view of your project's structure. The following are some of the most rudimentary components of your project content:

- **Codebases and pipelines.** Code is at the heart of your project. You should have an up-to-date catalog of your repositories, and it should be clear to your team how they can generate the application. In a Chapter 20, we'll discuss lightweight techniques to document your codebase.
- **Backlog.** The structured list of requirements your team is building should be here. It should be clear to the team how they can navigate this backlog and make sense of it.
- **Assets and records.** From design documents to prototypes to research or design sprint outputs—all these artifacts add up to the story of your product. Catalog these artifacts so your team can make sense of the part of the solution they're dealing with at any point in time. This is also the place where you should log all decision records and meeting notes.
- **Secrets.** You'll need access to SSH and API keys, passwords, and other sensitive information. It should be clear within the team how you will access these securely.
- **Roadmap.** If you've made commitments to stakeholders or the market about what functionality or capabilities you'll deliver in the immediate future, make these commitments visible to the team. Ideally, they should have provided input for this road map. Making the roadmap visible to the team allows everyone to own it.

Of course, you can think of other branches to this structure, and each level of this structure will have its own substructure as well. Much like someone must pave the road before others travel on it, some people on the team must structure version 1 of the handbook so others can benefit from it. This list is a starting point for that first version.

TOOLS YOU CAN USE

On tech teams, tools are a topic of endless discussion. I always suggest using the tools that your team already has access to. Even if there's a more efficient tool out there, you'll face trouble if your company doesn't already use it.

- Access control will be problematic. It's hard to keep information secure, and you'll end up taking on too much risk of inadvertent intellectual property leakage.
- Onboarding people will be difficult because your teammates may not know about this new tool.
- Off-boarding people is also tough. If you don't remove people when they leave the team, you'll risk unauthorized access to content, code, and credentials.
- You'll have to maintain tools yourself and manage subscriptions and licenses at the team level, which is unnecessary overhead.

If your company doesn't provide you with a basic set of documentation tools, start with a work-around and make a case to get the right tools in place. The due diligence and sign-up may take time, but once the new tools are in place, you'll be able to translate the benefits outside the team as well. You don't really need fancy software. GitLab, Confluence, SharePoint, Notion, Almanac, Mediawiki—these are all good starting points.

┌─ RESOURCE ─

Simplify Documentation with Modern Tools

Modern tools can help automate some of your documentation efforts.

- Qatalog can help set up a structure for your team's workspace using a simple prompt.
- Scribe can help create effective, visual how-to guides in a short time.
- Glean can enhance the discoverability of your content with its AI-powered search.

START SMALL, OWN COLLECTIVELY, BE ITERATIVE

If you look at the various elements of project context and content, you'll realize that putting together the first version of your handbook is about a week's effort. You don't have to be perfect. Just get it out there. Expect everyone in the team to update relevant sections of the handbook over time. I encourage my colleagues to build a habit of updating the handbook whenever they face a question and the answer isn't in there. Designate someone in the team as the handbook manager and, if it works for you, rotate the role. This will help build collective ownership, and people's trust in the system will improve as a consequence.

Let me also offer some advice on version control. Most documentation tools offer some level of versioning. Figure 10.2 illustrates versioning in Confluence. You can also "watch" pages for which you want the system to notify you, whenever there's a change. These features allow you to be a light touch with editorial control for your handbook.

- Make it easy for everyone to edit all pages. You can limit editing access for some pages only if the content is sensitive and if the cost of misinformation is high. Such content should be the exception, not the norm.
- Leave comments open on pages where you've restricted editing. This way, the team can still suggest changes to the page.
- Encourage people to summarize their changes using an edit summary. Most version-controlled documentation platforms offer this functionality. If the platform doesn't allow such a summary, they can report their change as a comment on the page.

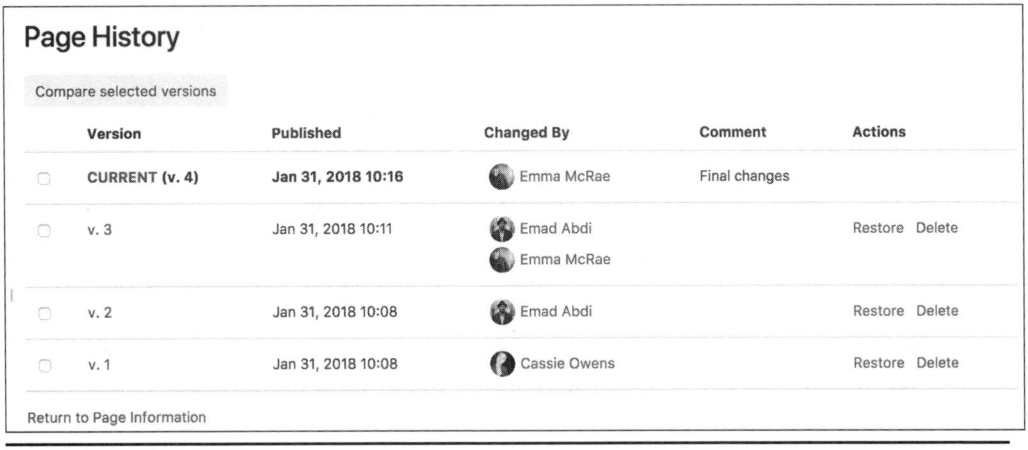

Page History

Compare selected versions

	Version	Published	Changed By	Comment	Actions
☐	CURRENT (v. 4)	Jan 31, 2018 10:16	Emma McRae	Final changes	
☐	v. 3	Jan 31, 2018 10:11	Emad Abdi Emma McRae		Restore Delete
☐	v. 2	Jan 31, 2018 10:08	Emad Abdi		Restore Delete
☐	v. 1	Jan 31, 2018 10:08	Cassie Owens		Restore Delete

Return to Page Information

Figure 10.2 Version control on *Confluence*.

- Page owners can watch their pages if they want to stay on top of all changes. Comparing versions will help them easily spot the change.

- If you notice a change that you must revert, use the versioning system to do so. Be sure to share feedback with the contributor so they know why you reverted their change.

Tools such as GitLab enable everyone to make changes using a system of merge requests. However, for an internal team handbook, where trust levels are high and the risk of vandalism is close to zero, I suggest taking the more permissive approach that I described.

GO DEEP WITH YOUR DOCUMENTATION TRIGGERS

Your handbook will need constant updates if it is to be useful. This means keeping old documents up-to-date and adding new ones when necessary.

On teams where a writing culture doesn't exist, you may need to remind yourself of triggers when documentation can help. I use the acronym DEEP to remind my colleagues about the opportunity to write or to create a referenceable artifact. Here's what the acronym stands for:

- **Decisions.** Teams make many decisions over their lifetime. Each time you decide something, document it in a way that someone who wasn't involved in the decision can understand its rationale.

- **Events.** Meetings, workshops, town halls—they're all events. By documenting these events, you persist the outcomes and knowledge from these interactions.

- **Explanations.** Every project has a body of knowledge, be it about the domain it operates in or how part of the system works. We often repeat these explanations verbally to each other. A written reference is easier to share and to improve as a team.

- **Proposals.** In the lifetime of a project, the team and its stakeholders will share many ideas and plans. Whether we implement these or not, it helps to document the thought process and the details of such proposals. Not only does it foster decision hygiene, it also helps build the collective memory of the team.

Each time there's an opportunity to document something that corresponds to the DEEP acronym, we remind each other to write things up. On one of my teams, we printed the DEEP acronym on coffee mugs to remind colleagues about these documentation triggers.

BEST PRACTICE

Learn to Respond with a Link

If you're writing things up regularly and referencing them in your team's hand-book, you can avoid redundant conversations by encouraging people to read. Just share the link and let them self-service. This will also improve adoption of your handbook and your asynchronous knowledge resources. This isn't rude. It's efficient.

Here's an example of how I'd respond with a link:

> **Co-worker:** Hey Sumeet, can you talk me through the requirements for the notifications service? I wanted to figure out what endpoints we need to build out to support the new functionality.
>
> **Me:** Hey, mate! I already wrote up the requirements as part of the proposal ([Insert link here]). Check it out. You'll find explanatory wireframes in there too. If something is not clear, just drop a comment and I'll address it pronto.

If you can't respond with a link, then it's a trigger to write things up. Help your colleague out, create the document, and then get their feedback to check whether it answers their original question. That way, you can respond with a link in the future.

AIM FOR A SHARED REALITY

For a distributed team, a single source of truth, such as a handbook, helps you build a shared reality. Without it, your team will be like the blindfolded people and the elephant that you see in Figure 10.3. Everyone will build their own mental model of the project, but the team will be none the wiser. Instead, create the handbook, figure out a way for people to contribute to its upkeep, and watch the blindfolds disappear. In this chapter, we've discussed a few ways to begin this iterative journey.

Figure 10.3 Without a single source of truth, everyone has their own truths.
(Source: mentalmind/Shutterstock)

CHAPTER SUMMARY

A team handbook helps make information about work explicit to existing and new team members. This is a critical asset for async-first work.

- Focus on writing things up for your team first. Don't worry about organizational knowledge at the start. If you're successful, your handbook can be a blueprint for the company.

- Divide your handbook information by project context and project content. *Context* lays down *how you work* together. *Content* describes *what you work on* together.

- Avoid being too fancy and use the tools your company already provides.

- Expect everyone to improve and update the handbook and designate editors on a rotational basis. Start small and iterate on the content and design.

- Use the DEEP acronym to remind each other about the triggers for documentation. Printing it on team merchandise is an effective way to make the triggers visible for remote colleagues.

Easily retrievable team knowledge will reduce communication churn on the team. You'll have fewer meetings and fewer interruptions from email and instant messaging. Speaking of instant messaging, let's talk about that next.

TAME THE "INSTANT" IN INSTANT MESSAGING

A lot of people mis-attribute productivity to speed.

—Justin Mitchell, CEO, Yac

There are many reasons to optimize for speed on teams. After all, many measures of productivity measure the rate of output, and speed enables such efficiency. That said, high productivity doesn't always need a frenetic process. Most of our work in software development teams is thoughtful and creative, be it design, coding, or testing. That kind of work benefits from slowing down.

An ASAP culture is toxic to work in. Asynchronous work is anything but "instant." There's value in "instant," but that's not what asynchronous work is for. So that begs the question—what about "instant" messaging?

MAKE MESSAGING PRODUCTIVE

Instant messaging tools are common in the workplace today. In fact, a lot of the marketing for these tools equates their speed of communication and the ubiquity of that interaction pattern with productivity. In certain cases, I don't disagree with their utility. Enterprise messaging software has its benefits:

- **A quick back and forth.** Sometimes people need to share a few messages between each other and get to a decision within minutes. Chat is a great tool for that.

- **Essential information, front and center.** Broadcast messages, overnight changes, production issues—these are great candidates to share in a chat group (among other places). Many tools offer the ability to "pin" messages. So, you can ensure that your valuable information is visible even when the activity stream keeps moving on.

- **Building connections.** Most of the communities in my company have their equivalent chat rooms. They're a terrific way to connect with people who have similar interests and to create a sense of belonging not just to the craft but to the company as well. The collegial nature of chat often flattens whatever hierarchy may exist in an organization.

- **Sharing and learning.** If you want to share something with a large group of people because you found it interesting, instant messaging is an effective mechanism to do that. In fact, that's a pattern most of us follow outside work as well, so there's a low learning curve in promoting such behaviors in the workplace.

- **Plain old fun.** At my employer, Thoughtworks, we have a forum called "Dad Jokes." It's a place where memes, puns, and odd internet humor come alive. You can always open that room and come away smiling. Even if your company doesn't have an equivalent, you can identify with the humor and fun associated with jokes on IM, GIFs, emojis, and stickers. And fun is a good thing!

Chat is indeed an essential part of your toolset, as I mentioned in Chapter 3. It finds mention on the spectrum of synchronousness as well.

The trouble, as I mentioned, is in the "instant" of instant messaging. To be "instant," you need to monitor chat all day. Not only does that build interruptions into your way of working, but it can also be mentally exhausting to keep up with all the channels your team and company have created. And when you use instant messaging ineffectively, it becomes, as 37signals says, an "all-day meeting." Since almost every team on the planet uses messaging tools of some kind, this chapter focuses on how to use them effectively so you can support a more productive, async-first way of working.

IF IT'S URGENT, USE A SUITABLE MEDIUM

If we can agree that people don't have to look at chat all day, then how do you get their attention for something urgent? My advice—use the phone or whatever medium you've chosen for urgent communication. Try your messaging app, by all means, but don't let an urgent situation get worse by expecting an immediate response on chat. This is where the communication protocols from Chapter 6 will come in handy. And remember—if you're interrupting a colleague, it better be urgent!

CHOOSE INTUITIVE NAMES FOR CHANNELS AND ROOMS

There are a few distinct kinds of chat channels.

- Internal that are only for your team.
- External facing that are for other teams and individuals to reach out to your team
- Departmental chat rooms that span multiple teams
- Community chat rooms that could span the entire company
- Official, companywide chat rooms for broadcast communication

You may already experience this at work—the bigger the organization, the more chat rooms. It can become difficult to find the right chat rooms to connect with a specific group of people. Matthew Skelton and Manuel Pais, in the *Remote Team Interactions Workbook*, recommend naming channels intuitively so they're easy to find. This is where it helps to agree on some conventions across the company. Here are some examples of intuitive, discoverable channel names:

- **#[client name]-platform-payments-internal**: Team chat room for the payments team, working in the platform group for [client name]
- **#[client name]-platform-payments**: Open channel to contact the payments team, working in the platform group for [client name]
- **#hr-benefits**: Open channel to contact the benefits team in the HR department
- **#community-design**: Community of practice for designers

It's possible that you can't drive consensus for these naming conventions for the entire company. In that case, limit the chaos in your own sphere of influence. Name the groups you interact with the most in an intuitive manner. Later, you can use your experience to influence others in the company.

SHOW YOUR STATUS, RESPECT OTHERS' STATUSES

Your personal boundaries are a good place to start. In Chapter 9, I explained how your chat status can broadcast that you're working asynchronously. In addition, you can set up statuses to show that you're at lunch, are in a meeting, or are pairing with a colleague. If you set up your calendar to reflect how you've planned your day, tools such as Clockwise can sync your calendar to your Slack status, as Figure 11.1 illustrates. That way, everyone knows when to expect a quick response and when they should wait.

Figure 11.1 Synchronize your calendar to your chat application's status.

The pay-it-forward side of this practice is that you must respect others' statuses as well. Don't get cross with a colleague who is busy coding and hasn't responded to your message in minutes.

LIMIT THE NUMBER OF MESSAGES

My surveys over the last few years reveal that more than 50 percent of the respondents identified chat messages as one of the biggest barriers to deep work. *Wired Magazine* quotes a 2021 survey by Cendex that shows how much time employees lose to communication tools:

> The average full-time member of staff in a medium to large business loses 9.3 hours per month, or 112 hours per year on digital communication programs, products, and tools.

Of course, communication is a part of our jobs, but there's a case for making it more effective. One fallout of the short messaging culture in our personal lives is that we communicate in short, and often incoherent, sentences. While those habits have their own fallout outside work, when we bring these behaviors to work, we end up creating loads of noise. Before you know it, you have 50 messages for what could have been an email or just a single, well-thought-out message.

It's okay to write longer chat messages! Save everyone the extra notifications. Use emojis and text formatting to make these messages easy to read, like you see in Figure 11.2. Not only will you save others from the interruptions, writing a single coherent message will allow you to go back to your own work quicker.

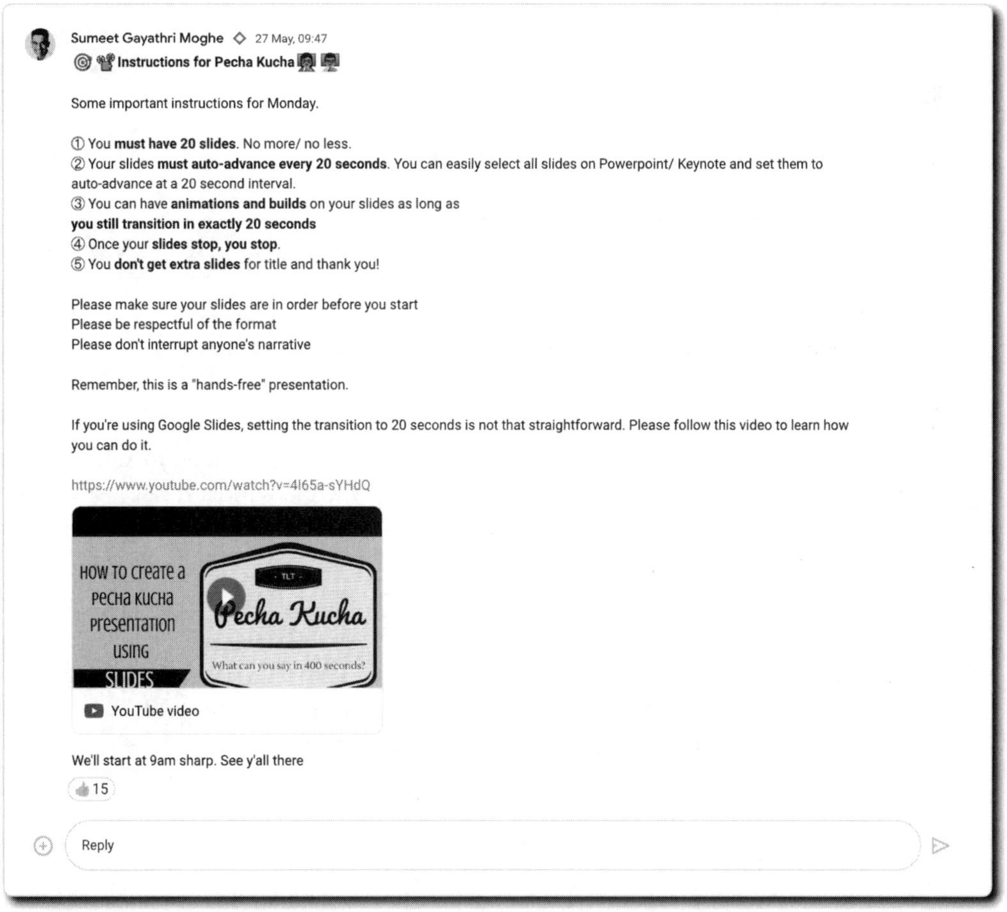

Figure 11.2 Consolidate what you want to share in a single message.

GET TO THE POINT

When we worked in the office, it was almost rude to get to the point. You couldn't just walk up to a teammate and ask a question. Invariably, you'd start with a greeting. For example, "Hey Tina, how're you doing? Do you have a minute? I need your help with...." That interaction pattern works well in a synchronous setup. When you're distributed, you can't expect the other person to be looking at their chat app right at the moment that you are typing. Here's what happens when you apply a synchronous interaction pattern to asynchronous instant messaging:

> Co-worker, 10:20 a.m. Hey, Sumeet!

> Sumeet, 10:45 a.m. Hi!

> Co-worker, 11:01 a.m. Do you have a minute?

> Sumeet, 11:12 a.m. Sure, mate, what's up?

> Co-worker, 11:14 a.m. So, I was just looking at our backlog and...

See what happened right there? Between the two of us, we created five messages for what could have been one message. I know it may feel uncomfortable to just get to the point. And that's okay. Go ahead with the pleasantries, but just include it in a single message. Think of how you'd write the note if you were writing an email. Here's an example:

> Co-worker, 10:20 a.m. Hey, Sumeet. Whenever you have a minute, can you tag the Epics and Confluence pages that relate to the search feature? I'm putting together our road map, and the tag will automatically pull related artifacts into the document. Thanks a bunch, mate!

TARGET YOUR CONVERSATIONS

On some of my earlier teams we've used @mentions to gain the attention of colleagues, while keeping other people informed of the conversation. I've realized that while this seems transparent, it can easily generate a lot of noise and notifications for people who aren't involved in the discussion. Your IM platform may also give you features to manage these notifications, but it's best to be efficient with IM traffic in the first place.

Just like meetings benefit from the right audience, chat does too. If only three people care about the discussion, target the discussion to them alone. Not only will you have a more focused discussion, but you'll reduce noise for everyone else. When you're done with the discussion, summarize it on the team channel in one coherent message.

REACT, DON'T RESPOND

The cost of responding with an "LOL" or a "So true!" or just piling on a "Congratulations" on a personal chat group is incredibly low. It also has a negligible impact. In these groups, we sign up for the noise. It's not a bug; it's a feature.

In a work context, the noise is a good old bug. Every message generates a notification by default. A notification is an interruption. Interruptions are costly. So, in the spirit of limiting messages, use emoji reactions instead of responding to a message, as you see in Figure 11.3. On most chat platforms, reactions don't generate notifications. You can participate in the conversation without interrupting people at work.

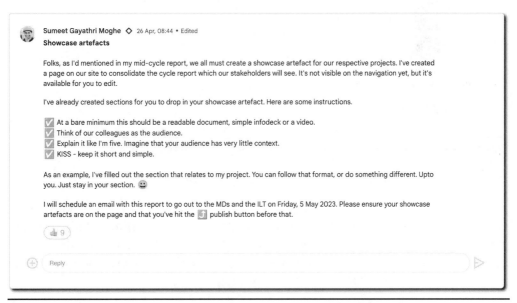

Sumeet Gayathri Moghe ◇ 26 Apr, 08:44 • Edited
Showcase artefacts

Folks, as I'd mentioned in my mid-cycle report, we all must create a showcase artefact for our respective projects. I've created a page on our site to consolidate the cycle report which our stakeholders will see. It's not visible on the navigation yet, but it's available for you to edit.

I've already created sections for you to drop in your showcase artefact. Here are some instructions.

☑ At a bare minimum this should be a readable document, simple infodeck or a video.
☑ Think of our colleagues as the audience.
☑ Explain it like I'm five. Imagine that your audience has very little context.
☑ KISS - keep it short and simple.

As an example, I've filled out the section that relates to my project. You can follow that format, or do something different. Upto you. Just stay in your section. 😊

I will schedule an email with this report to go out to the MDs and the ILT on Friday, 5 May 2023. Please ensure your showcase artefacts are on the page and that you've hit the 🔲 publish button before that.

👍 9

Reply

Figure 11.3 Reactions acknowledge the message and don't generate notifications.

USE THREADS: ONE PER TOPIC

Enough said, right? Threads make it easy to follow conversations on chat, like you see in Figure 11.4. We've all run into that situation where someone creates a new thread instead of replying to an existing conversation, and you know how it derails the discussion. If you're the person who makes this mistake, then fear not. Just delete your new thread and respond to the right conversation.

The converse also holds true. Don't hijack a thread with an unrelated topic. Follow a simple rule—one thread, one topic.

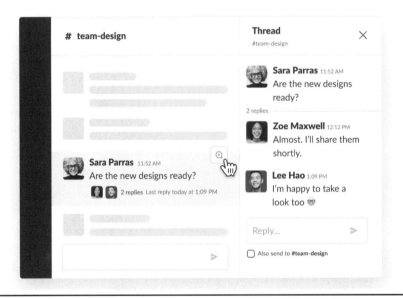

Figure 11.4 Use threads to make sense of conversations. Pictured here, Slack.

SLOW THINGS DOWN, AND DON'T ARGUE ON CHAT

Have you ever tried to argue with your significant other or your friends on chat? How many times has that ever gone well? You know the answer. Messaging and charged emotions don't mix well. IM is best for short, ephemeral discussions. Long discussions on chat add little clarity to the topic at hand, and they become an ineffective version of an all-day meeting.

The moment you see a chat conversation taking too long, slow things down. Write things up in a collaborative document and take it from there. If you see an argument developing, stop right there. Take some time away from the screen, collect your thoughts, and go synchronous when everyone has calmed down. It's easier to assume positive intent when you can see each other. Real-time video conversation can diffuse emotions much better than chat.

BEST PRACTICE

The API Mindset

Matt Mullenweg, CEO of Automattic, encourages people to "assume positive intent" (API). It's a simple concept. Read every message by assuming the best intent possible. And when you communicate, pay attention to how people may receive your message. Read, rephrase, refine. Use emojis to express yourself and to communicate emotion. The meaning of your message is the response it gets!

MAKE YOUR IM GUIDELINES VISIBLE

Following up from this chapter, write up your team's IM guidelines and make it a pinned post on the team's IM channel. That way, it'll never be out of sight. Every new member of your team will see it, and you must encourage them to read it as well. From that point on, everyone must be thoughtful about their communication, slow things down, and hold each other accountable.

RESOURCE

The EqualExperts Slack Guide

To create your IM guidelines, you needn't start from scratch. EqualExperts provides a handy usage guide that you can edit for your context. Their guidelines relate to Slack, but you can adapt them to any tools you use. Use their guide as a sensible default. Visit the book's companion site at https://www.asyncagile. org/book-resources for access to this resource.

MESSAGING: JUST NOT INSTANT

As you help your team tame the instant nature of messaging, you'll notice that the number of interruptions per person goes down. Not only will you create more space for deep work, but you'll also build a more empathetic team where all responses don't have to be ASAP.

CHAPTER SUMMARY

Messaging can be a useful tool on distributed teams, provided we use it effectively and reduce the interruptions and noise it can otherwise generate.

- Use chat as primarily an asynchronous tool and avoid thinking of it as "instant."
- For urgent matters, don't use chat. Use a channel suitable for urgent communication, such as a phone call.
- Name your chat channels intuitively so they're discoverable. If you can't get consensus on these conventions, start by naming the channels that are in your sphere of influence.
- Use your chat status to broadcast what you're doing right now and respect others' statuses as well.
- Reduce the number of notifications you generate for people by writing detailed messages, using emojis as reactions, and getting to the point in a single message.
- Target your conversations to the people who need to actively participate. Summarize these later for the group so you reduce noise.
- Use and respect threads so conversation is easy to follow.
- When things get complex, slow down and write things up.
- Don't resolve arguments on chat. Choose a synchronous medium instead to diffuse tensions.
- Write up your chat guidelines and make them a pinned post on your team channel. That way, they're easier to notice, follow, and reference.

By now we've addressed two major culprits that deny us the opportunity for deep work—meetings and instant messaging. Next, let's examine several meeting-heavy practices on software development teams and learn how to shift left on each of them. Coming up, the easiest shift left!

STANDUP MEETINGS: AN EASY SHIFT LEFT

Standup meetings have a rich legacy. The extreme programming movement popularized them in the early 2000s, but there've been variants of this practice in many other spheres. General Pagonis, for example, famously used standup meetings in the Gulf War.

My ex-colleague Jason Yip wrote the most famous article about standup meetings, aka *standups*. That was way back in 2006, 16 years before I had the idea for this book. It's a simple concept.

> The whole team meets every day for a quick status update. We stand up to keep the meeting short.

The most common, in-person version of this meeting format was for team members to stand in a circle beside the team's physical task board. They'd then share updates in round-robin fashion, all while referencing work on the task board. The standard format of the update would answer three questions:

- What did we do yesterday?
- What will we do today?
- What obstacles are we facing, if any?

I think you'll agree that a lot has happened since Jason's 2006 article. The biggest inflection point, however, was the pandemic triggered the remote-work revolution of 2020 and beyond. Those short, early-morning gatherings around a physical wall in the office aren't the same. For many of us, they are long, painful, teeth-pulling sessions over Zoom.

DISTRIBUTED STANDUPS CAN BE PAINFUL

In theory, distributed standups should be efficient and short because of all the tooling that's around. I'm sure there are teams out there that run these meetings well. However, I notice some common problems across most distributed standup meetings:

- Standups should be 15 minutes or less. I don't recall too many distributed standups that are any less than 30 minutes. Heck, I've been in standups that are longer!

- Physical standups move fast because you're either passing a speaking token or going around in a circle and speaking on your turn. In remote standups, people get confused about whose turn it is next. So, either a project lead is prompting people to speak, or, after an uncomfortable silence, people volunteer with "Okay, I'll go next."

- Often, these meetings are a mere formality. Since many people attend with their video off and on mute, it's hard to tell if anyone is paying attention. Even if people are listening, it's hard to build engagement when all you see is an avatar on Zoom.

- It's no longer a standup! Everyone attends these meetings sitting down, so there's no incentive to keep it short, unless of course there's a meeting right after!

All this pain would be worth it if there was an obvious benefit. It's tough to justify why, with all the collaboration tools we have, we need standup meetings to tell us answers to the three standup questions:

1. What did we do yesterday?
2. What will we do today?
3. What obstacles are we facing, if any?

If you're using your tools well, then you should have real-time answers to 1 and 2. And if 3 is important, then why are you waiting for a standup to get help? The killer with remote standups is when these happen across time zones. Imagine working till 10:30 p.m. in Bangalore just so you can do a standup with your colleagues in San Francisco to tell them the answers to 1, 2, and 3. Ugh!

In an async-first culture, meetings are the last resort. A standup meeting makes it mandatory for all team members to be present, regardless of what their personal commitments may be. Every. Single. Day. This is neither flexible nor inclusive.

By the way, spare a thought for the people who may miss a standup. No one documents these meetings. So, if someone misses the standup, that's it right there. Wait to hear a few days later, "Oh, didn't you know? We agreed _____ at standup on Thursday last week!"

There are a couple of ways around this problem. We can try our best to make distributed standups effective. With some discipline, this may be possible. However, in the interest of being async-first, I suggest the alternative of cutting the meeting from your rituals.

In this chapter, I outline a few simple ways for you to radiate the same information that you expect from a standup, minus all the pain of the meeting. As an individual, you'll get back a few minutes of your life every day. The bigger benefit? You can share updates continuously and at your own pace. From the team's perspective, you'll create an audit trail of communication and, of course, plow back the time savings into deep work. If that sounds worthwhile, let's begin.

USE THE PROJECT MANAGEMENT TOOL'S FEATURES

The first discipline is to use the features of your project management tool, like you see in Figure 12.1. Most of these tools allow people to sign up for work, or "task it out," and then use comments to have discussions about that piece of work, in context.

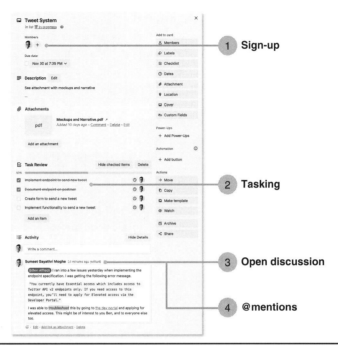

Figure 12.1 Using the task board for status updates.

Here's a straightforward way to radiate progress:

1. **Sign-up.** Whenever someone picks up a piece of work, they also sign up for it on the project management tool. That way, if anyone looks at work-in-progress on the tool, they know what everyone is up to.

2. **Tasking.** The first thing someone does when they sign up for something new is to task it out. When they complete a task, they just check the box. So, if anyone wants to know the status of that piece of work, they just need to look at the checklist.

3. **Open discussion.** All discussion about a piece of work happens on the ticket associated with it. Whenever you have an update to share, throw your notes into the comments. You'll have yourself a nifty audit trail in place. While you should add as many updates as you think are necessary, *I recommend doing at least one update when you wrap up work for the day,* just so everyone knows where you've left it before a long pause. An end-of-day update is fresher than

an update the next day when your memory about the previous day's work can be a bit foggy. This discipline doesn't just mirror the standup's cadence; it also triggers self-reflection.

4. **@mentions to get attention.** Need help? @mention the person who needs to help you. If you need urgent help (it better be urgent), call them on their phone. If you want to radiate information about the task to anyone else, add comments about that as well. Tools like Jira allow you to @mention the entire team, if necessary, though I'd use those notifications sparingly.

This level of atomic discipline helps answer the standup questions and allows people to be reflective about their own work.

┌─ **BEST PRACTICE** ───────────────────────────

Use the Eisenhower Matrix to Deal with Blockers or Problems

Since standup meetings were short by design, they didn't provide a way to address blockers, even if they became visible during the meeting. The standard practice was to "take it offline" so a specific group of people could address the issue by a specific time.

You can follow this pattern even with asynchronous status updates. If a problem needs a deep dive, a small group of people can address it separately. Be careful not to fall into the "always urgent" trap and default to meetings to solve problems. This is where the Eisenhower matrix can come in handy.

Dwight Eisenhower was a five-star general during World War II and an American president. His military and political accomplishments aside, we know him in the business world for his prioritization framework—the Eisenhower matrix.

Figure 12.2 shows what the matrix looks like. On the x-axis you have urgent and not urgent, and on the y-axis you have important and not important.

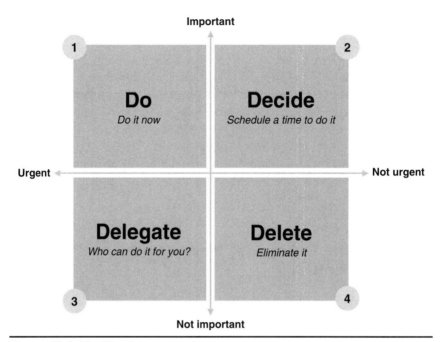

Figure 12.2 The Eisenhower matrix.

There's only one "do it yourself right now" quadrant. That's quadrant 1. It's the stuff that's urgent *and* important. For a software development team, this should be a tiny percentage of work. I have two qualifiers for quadrant 1 activities:

- They have a clear deadline, and there are dire consequences for not meeting the deadline.
- Only you or your team can perform this activity.

Beware of work from other quadrants that masquerade as quadrant 1:

- If the consequences of missing the deadline aren't too serious, this may be quadrant 2 work. Just schedule a time when you or the team can address it calmly. Agile software development is all about iterative improvements. So, how about you address this in a future sprint?
- If there are others who can perform this activity, then it may be quadrant 3 work. Yes, developers can address support tickets, but isn't that the support team's job? Yes, you can answer an urgent ad hoc question, but shouldn't people search the handbook first?

AUTOMATE THE RITUAL

In addition to, or as an alternative to, your task board, you may still like the safety of a ritual to get your standup digest. That's okay. There are ways to do this while being asynchronous. In this case, you'll need to implement a two-part solution:

1. **Use automation tools.** With IFTTT and Zapier, you can automate pretty much everything these days. However, I have two out-of-the-box solutions for you.

   a. If you use Jira and Slack or Microsoft Teams, then you can try Geekbot. It's a tool that prompts you with standup questions inside your instant messaging tool. These updates are visible to the entire team. Figure 12.3 illustrates how this works.

   b. If you're using Trello, then the Butler functionality on it can help you create a standup workflow. In fact, my last team did all its standup updates on Trello, courtesy Butler.

   Whatever tools you choose, be sure that all the updates go to one place, such as a #status channel on Slack or a specific list on Trello so people can control how frequently they get notifications.

2. **Agree on team commitments.** An async standup is pointless if people don't post their updates within a reasonable timeframe and if no one reads these updates. Depending on how distributed you are, your agreements will be different. That said, it's important to agree on a time by which everyone will post their updates and a time by which everyone will read them.

That's it, no biggie. There's the small matter of team discipline, though. Like all new practices, this may seem uncomfortable at first. As a team, take some time to agree on how you'll follow through with this commitment.

By the way, if you don't use Jira, Slack, or Trello and your company doesn't allow you to use IFTTT or Zapier, there are other ways to make your status updates async. A shared collaborative document, or a form connected to a spreadsheet, can do the trick as well. Tools like Basecamp and Fellow allow for automated standups, and you'll encounter specialized tools like Range as well. The world is your oyster—find your own adventure!

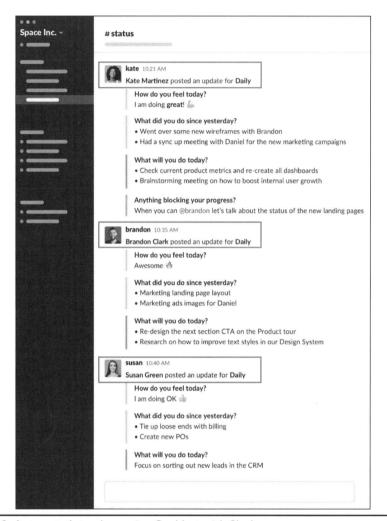

Figure 12.3 Automated standups using Geekbot with Slack.

Still Want a Standup?

Some teams like the ritual of meeting every day, if only to keep their connectedness alive. If that's how you feel as well, consider dropping status updates from the meeting. Instead, use this meeting to eyeball team, engineering, and delivery health indicators so you can trigger follow-up actions on them. Here are a few examples of such health indicators:

- Work-in-progress across workflow stages.
- Sprint goal vis-à-vis remaining number of sprint days.

- Blocked pull requests (PRs). Developers often use this feature to make contributions to a shared codebase that uses a distributed version control. GitLab refers to this same functionality as a merge request.
- High-risk code branches.
- People's availability, morale, and mental health.

Don't try to solve the problems on the standup. Focus only on the next action.

KEEP IT RELEVANT

I remember talking about asynchronous standups to a senior consultant some time back, and her response to me was, "Oh, I've tried that, and I find all those updates so overwhelming!" I left that conversation perplexed. Later, it occurred to me that she was a high-level manager and the low-level updates from various teams were not just overwhelming for her but also quite irrelevant.

My takeaway is that the standup is for the dev team. The moment you try to make it a one-size-fits-all exercise, either you'll dilute its purpose or you'll make it useless for some people. Jason's original article on standups has some wise words:

> Not all forms of reporting will be, nor should be, covered by the stand-up format. For example, overall project progress would be better communicated with a Big Visible Chart such as burn-down, burn-up, or a cumulative flow diagram.

Provide managers with an abstracted view of progress so it's easy for them to follow. That way, they don't feel overwhelmed, and your team can still sweat the details.

MAKE PEACE WITH LAG

When you take standups async, updates will initially feel slow and uncoordinated. You'll have all the information you need, but for some of you, the lag will feel disconcerting. Give yourself time to be comfortable with it. Asynchronous work is about making peace with lag.

If you're leading your team's shift left, then you might have to remind some team members to post their updates. That's okay—once they settle into the new habit and they see the benefits, you can get out of their hair. You may also hear of a gazillion "other benefits" you got from standup meetings. While those meetings perhaps weren't standups anymore, be empathetic to those concerns and keep an open mind. Find alternatives to achieve those benefits outside the notional standup. After all, if this is among the first practices you shift left on, you want your team to feel good about it.

STANDUPS = CONVEYANCE/STRONG RELATIONSHIPS

This chapter begins a sequence of practice-oriented plays that allow you to examine meeting-centric rituals in your development workflow so you can shift left where possible. Since standup meetings are about conveyance, for a group with a strong relationship, they are ideal candidates to shift left.

CHAPTER SUMMARY

Standup meetings for status updates can easily become an asynchronous activity. This frees up a few hours for the team each development cycle.

- Use the sign-up, tasking, and commenting features of your project management tool to make updates continuous.

- As an alternative to, or in addition to, using your tool's features, automate the standup using tools such as Geekbot or Butler.

- Avoid making it a one-size-fits-all interaction. For leaders and higher-level managers, create summarized reports of progress so they don't get overwhelmed.

- If you're leading your team, help everyone make peace with lag. You may need to remind them about their updates at the start so they get used to the new practice. And stay open to feedback.

While standups are the easiest meeting to eliminate from your development process, they're hardly the most time-consuming. If you're following scrum or a variation of it, you have several other time-sapping rituals that need a rethink. Let's examine those next.

TAKE CHARGE OF YOUR DEVELOPMENT CYCLES

In the previous chapter, we discussed how to make your daily standups more productive by moving them to a more asynchronous format. While standup meetings have been around for a long time, in the last two decades they've become ubiquitous because people follow them as part of scrum. And if you're following scrum, then you probably also follow a few other rituals to run your sprints.

If you're trying to work in an async-first fashion, these rituals represent heavy interruptions in your flow. So, how do you run an iterative development process while still being async-first?

SPRINT CEREMONIES CAN HINDER ASYNC WORK

If you've practiced scrum in your career, I expect you'll be familiar with the timeline in Figure 13.1. I've plotted the rough recommended duration of each meeting in this timeline, assuming a two-week sprint (per the official scrum guide). Your cycles could differ in length, but you probably follow similar rituals.

- 4 hours of sprint planning
- 15 minutes each day of the daily standup (aka the daily scrum)
- 2 hours for a sprint review
- 1.5 hours for a sprint retrospective

You may recollect the notion of "mass" from Chapter 9. In the case of the scrum process or its variants, you can accumulate mass by way of recurrent meetings.

Notice that just the four types of scrum ceremonies you see in Figure 13.1 sum up to 10 hours every two weeks…for every member of the team. This means if you follow scrum by the book, you lose almost a day and a half every two weeks to meetings.

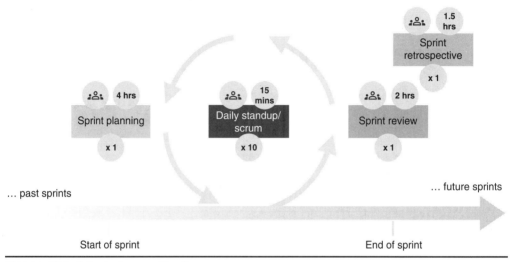

Figure 13.1 A typical scrum timeline.

A sprint-focused approach to running projects spends a lot of time nailing down sprint scope in a planning meeting. A review at the end of the cycle assesses how well the team has addressed that scope. While each of these rituals has its value, I've found the cost of coordination in a remote environment to be disproportionately high. So if you want to work async-first, I suggest you follow one of two approaches:

- Keep the two-week sprints, but embrace continuous flow instead of fixed sprint scope.
- Choose longer development cycles, and give small dev pods autonomy to solve a broad problem (aka the "shape up" approach).

Each of these approaches will work only in specific contexts, so let's explore them together, and then you can figure out which approach will work best for you.

APPROACH 1: EMBRACE CONTINUOUS FLOW

Those who already follow a variant of scrum will find that this approach represents the smallest change for your team and stakeholders. You'll retain the same cycle length as you've always had, while changing the way you size requirements, how you execute the cycles, and the way you report to your stakeholders. You may know this approach as "scrumban," i.e., a hybrid approach between scrum and kanban. I'll steer clear of jargon, though, and outline the key principles of such an approach.

Focus on Prioritization and Not Sprint Scope

Most businesses need to respond as quickly as possible to our customers. So, every stakeholder wants the flexibility to move requirements up the queue if necessary. Fixing sprint scope can be counterproductive to this. After all, once you fix the scope, nothing changes for the rest of the cycle.

Continuous flow is a simple concept that addresses this problem while minimizing the meeting overhead:

- Stakeholders ensure that the backlog always represents a descending order of business priority.
- The development team works through the backlog starting from the items at the top.
- Work-in-progress limits for each stage of your development process prevent bottlenecks and stop you from oversubscribing your team.

Figure 13.2 illustrates this process. Of course, this approach can descend into chaos if there are no rules. So, you must have three guardrails in place:

- Never context switch developers and testers. Work-in-progress should always be inviolate. All you can influence is the next item in the queue, be it a story or a bug fix.
- The product owner must collaborate with the business to ensure that items in the "ready for development" lane are always in descending order of priority.
- Nothing can enter "ready for development" until it meets the criteria that the team sets for these tasks. Teams often collectively refer to these criteria as "definition of ready" (DoR). Depending on the nature of the work, the criteria describe the level of detail a work item must have before the team considers it ready for developers to execute.

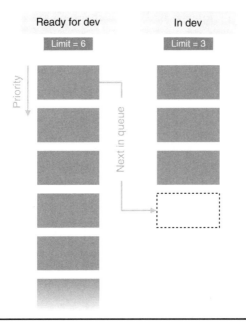

Figure 13.2 How a prioritized backlog works.

Use Throughput and Cycle Time to Optimize the System

In a standard scrum process, teams often compare the estimated scope they've delivered in the last cycle to an overall notion of scope they've delivered. Aside from giving them a sense of how much scope they can deliver in a sprint, it also helps them forecast when they can deliver the rest of the scope.

In a continuous flow–oriented process, we flip the script by delivering the most essential functionality first. Measurement is still important, though. Instead of spending time estimating each work item you execute, here are two other metrics to focus on:

- **Throughput**, i.e., the number of items delivered per sprint
- **Cycle time**, i.e., the time it took for an item to go from an "in-analysis" state to what your team considers a "done" state

I want to call out a few pitfalls and considerations here:

- Measuring throughput works well when you **scope items to have a similar size.** Between the teams' lead developers, testers, and product manager, you must eyeball stories to see that they're roughly the same size. This is an estimation exercise as well, albeit a rough one. You can't be 100 percent sure that all stories are the same size. Accuracy isn't the goal, though. The trick with this approach is to take minor errors in stride because they'll cancel each other out over time.

- It's still a good practice to **negotiate scope** at the level of a feature or capability. Often, when analyzing requirements, you'll notice that the scope may differ from your initial assumptions, when you first logged the requirement. In such cases, slice the requirement down to other similarly sized items and inform stakeholders about the impact on the backlog. Hammering scope this way also nudges you to focus on the simplest thing that works. You don't have to deliver all the tickets related to a feature for you to bring an initial version of the feature to your customers.

- Measure **throughput only for functional requirements.** This is a good thing. If you see throughput going down, it may mean that defects are slowing you down. This can then nudge the team to examine the regression test suite and to improve test coverage.

- The **cycle time metric nudges you to optimize your system.** Since the measurement applies to all functional items from "in analysis" to "done," it'll discourage you from maintaining a large inventory of requirements in analysis. Communicate rigorously with your stakeholders to focus on the things that are important. This will also help you ensure that nondevelopment tasks such as exploratory tests don't become a bottleneck. When you see these symptoms, a focus on cycle time can encourage developers to double up as testers.

Sprints as a Denominator for Measurement

When you adopt a continuous flow process like the one I've described, you won't really need the notion of timeboxes such as two-week sprints. However, I suggest keeping the idea of a fixed cycle, in the interest of measurement and reflection.

- Having a sense of your throughput per cycle can still allow you to forecast delivery timelines to your stakeholders.
- As a team. you can pause and reflect on your performance and collaboration and figure out ways to get better in the next cycle. Retrospectives are an effective way to trigger such reflection. We'll discuss this practice in detail in Chapter 14.

Demos Only When Necessary

Let's be honest. Teams don't always have something big to showcase every sprint. Without substantive demos, regular sprint reviews become a formality and a reporting exercise. Take a pragmatic approach to sprint reviews instead:

- Every cycle, create a report of what the team has achieved. This should include the stories from your project management system or task board, your delivery and tech metrics, and screenshots or video snippets where applicable. Add these reports to an area in your team handbook.

- Encourage your stakeholders to browse the reports asynchronously. They can respond with feedback in the form of comments, and if a meeting is indeed necessary, you can set it up on demand.

- When you have something big to showcase, for example, a new capability in the system, organize a full-blown demo. Pay special attention to these. Plan for them and get as much attendance as possible. They're an opportunity for the team to celebrate and to show off what you've accomplished. I suggest doing such demos every four to six weeks.

Can't Avoid Sprint Ceremonies? Make Them More Efficient

Contractual obligations may prevent some teams from moving to a system of continuous flow. For example, if a team has committed to delivering a fixed notion of scope by a certain date, sprint ceremonies may become unavoidable. In such situations, teams will estimate scope at the sprint level and use those estimates to track their progress toward delivery goals. Sprint planning and sprint reviews help keep such plans on track. They can also spark conversations about scope change and any risks to the plan.

If you're in such a situation and you can't eliminate sprint planning and sprint review meetings, find ways to make them more efficient. A tightly prioritized backlog can shorten sprint planning. Follow the ConveRel quadrants and split async information sharing from synchronous decision-making to make both meetings shorter. Aim to reduce the length of these meetings to an hour each per cycle.

APPROACH 2: USE "SHAPE UP" CYCLES

If you have an established product, then you're probably less concerned about contractual deadlines. Instead, your priority will be to enhance your product regularly. For such situations, I'm a fan of Ryan Singer's "Shape Up" approach. This approach has no estimates and no backlog. You don't need to track any scope metrics either.

Here's what you get in return. Your teams can work deeply on a problem for six weeks at a stretch, with little or no interruption. They create and manage their own tasks. They self-report using lightweight visuals. Most important, they enjoy full autonomy with execution. Sounds exciting, right?

To understand the approach in detail, read *Shape Up: Stop Running in Circles and Ship Work That Matters* by Ryan Singer. In the meantime, let me explain the process in brief.

The Shaping Process

Anyone can come up with ideas to improve the product. Before any of these ideas go into development, though, a group of people "shape up" the work.

- The product of the shaping process is a **pitch document**. This document summarizes the problem, the constraints, the solution, and the go/no-go areas. It doesn't have wireframes or mock-ups. No stories or architectural diagrams either. Designers and developers can figure out those details if they end up working on the problem. The document uses fat marker sketches and box-and-arrow diagrams to illustrate the potential solution.
- Not all pitches make it to development. Each cycle, all shaped pitches go to a **betting table**. This is where a team of people who are responsible for making decisions about a product decide which pitches to bet on. By betting on a pitch, they commit a team for six weeks to solve that problem. Why six weeks? Singer says that it's long enough for a team of two or three people to finish substantial work, and it's also a short enough time to plan for.

A Capped Downside

A key feature of the shaping process is the notion of a **capped downside**. The shaping team must be confident that a development team can execute the idea in six weeks.

- The six-week time box is also a circuit breaker. If the development team can't ship in six weeks, then it represents a shaping problem. Work stops, and the idea goes back into shaping.
- The corollary to the capped downside is that development teams get **uninterrupted time** to work on their problem. They also have the freedom and autonomy to "hammer scope," i.e., focus only on the absolute must-haves to solve the problem in their six-week cycle.

Asynchronous Status Reporting

Development teams divide their six-week project into broad scopes and constituent tasks. They **communicate status asynchronously and transparently** using hill charts, as you see in Figure 13.3.

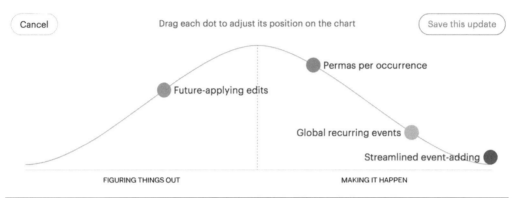

Figure 13.3 Using a hill chart to show scope and progress. (Source: Modified from Ryan Singer, *Shape Up: Stop Running in Circles and Ship Work That Matters*, Basecamp, 2022, p. 134)

On the left side of the chart are scopes where you're still figuring out what to do. On the right you're getting things done. One view with click-throughs to detail can show you where the team is at. When you compare different states of the chart, you get a sense of progress.

Two Tracks Drive the Process

The "shape up" method follows a **two-track approach**. Figure 13.4 illustrates the two tracks and their respective timelines. While development teams hammer away at their respective problems, the shaping team creates pitches to bring to the betting table. At the end of six weeks, the dev teams ship their software into the wild and get two weeks to cool down. During cooldown, teams don't just get a breather, but they can also tie up some loose ends, maybe making some minor bug fixes. This is also the time when the shaping team brings pitches to the betting table. Every eight weeks the cycle repeats itself.

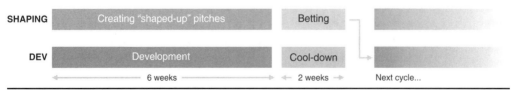

Figure 13.4 The "shape up" timeline. (Source: Modified from Ryan Singer, *Shape Up: Stop Running in Circles and Ship Work That Matters*, Basecamp, 2022, p. 134)

I encourage you to pick up Ryan's book and read it cover to cover. If you're responsible for an established product, you'll find that this approach allows you to facilitate autonomous teams. At the same time, you forecast only a few weeks at a time to keep your product and your ideas fresh.

Of course, this approach is very different from a standard scrum implementation and may not be something you can adopt immediately. At the time of authoring this book, I've tried it with only two teams, and it worked well because we didn't have strict contractual obligations. I leave it to you to figure out if this approach is suitable for you.

THE KEY TO ASYNCHRONY IS A STRONG PROCESS

Between the two approaches we discussed in this chapter, you probably noticed that a solid process helps eliminate frequent meetings in both cases. While each approach facilitates autonomy at the level of execution, they need more rigor than what you'd need to follow a standard scrum process. This may seem like a lot of work, but in essence these approaches take a lot of the value that we'd have achieved through sprint planning and sprint reviews and spread them across other activities.

CHAPTER SUMMARY

Sprint ceremonies can add several hours of meetings to each of your development cycles. These meetings can impede asynchronous ways of working. Two alternatives can significantly reduce the number of meetings you need to run your development process:

- Approach 1: Embrace continuous flow.
  - Work through a tightly prioritized backlog in descending order of priority.
  - Use throughput and cycle time as measures of productivity, instead of velocity.
  - Use the sprint only as a common denominator for measurement.
  - Release often, report regularly, but conduct demos only when you have something substantive to show.

- Approach 2: Use the "shape up" approach.
  - Operate in two tracks. A small group of people shapes pitches so teams can execute them in six-week cycles. They work in parallel with development teams that work on these pitches.
  - A dev team has full autonomy on how to execute the pitch. They hammer scope to achieve the outcome and report asynchronously using hill charts.
  - If a team can't ship in six weeks, work on that pitch stops. This represents a capped downside for the process.

We've addressed standup meetings, sprint planning, and sprint reviews. There's one more sprint ceremony we need to revisit: retrospectives. That deserves its own chapter, which is up next.

RUN MEANINGFUL RETROSPECTIVES

A retrospective is an event that allows teams to reflect on how they're working together, in a blame-free, safe environment. The goals of this event are to learn from their collective experience, to recognize the team's strengths, and to explore ways to improve the team's effectiveness in the future.

Agile software development is all about continuous improvement. The iterative process allows the team to learn from experience through feedback and reflection. Retrospectives are one of the most powerful reflective thinking practices in the agile toolbox.

Yet, teams conduct retrospectives or retros infrequently. In a distributed setup, they can be rather painful to orchestrate as well. Can an async-first approach help us run more meaningful retrospectives?

INFREQUENT RETROS LEAD TO POOR TEAM HEALTH

In their most classic form, retros are meetings. If coordinating these for distributed teams wasn't tough enough, the problem of infrequency exists as well. When teams don't retrospect frequently, it leads to a backlog of thoughts and ideas in people's heads. The day a retro happens, these ideas come in a deluge. We spend a major part of the meeting just collecting and synthesizing these inputs. You can use hard timeboxes to keep the meeting moving, but after a certain point, that becomes counterproductive. When retros don't yield meaningful outcomes, people lose faith in them, and they become tick-the-box activities.

Without a ritualistic forum to share their ideas, team members can feel unsure about whether constructive ideas are welcome. That lowers the sense of safety and openness for people—a prerequisite for effective retros. Even when people feel safe, they are likely to fall prey to recency bias. Only the most immediate problems come up for discussion. The team may overlook bigger, simmering issues only because they aren't top of mind.

Aim for a retrospective each month, if not more often. Most agile practitioners will agree with me when I say that a practice of effective retros is vital to the effectiveness of such teams. There's plenty at stake to make the ritual effective.

Let me explain how you can run regular and effective retros for your distributed team with an async-first approach. For simplicity's sake, I'll assume you'll run these retrospectives yourself. You can, of course, bring in a neutral facilitator if you have that option.

VIEW RETROSPECTIVES AS A PROCESS AND NOT AN EVENT

Let's revisit the ConveRel quadrants (see Figure 14.1).

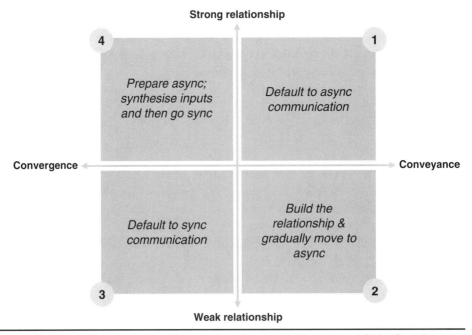

Figure 14.1 The ConveRel quadrants. (Source: Based on Luke Thomas and Aisha Samake, *The Anywhere Operating System*, Friday Feedback, Inc., 2021)

A retro is an activity that aims for convergence in a group that has a relatively strong relationship, i.e., quadrant 4. If you pare it down, you can view the retro as four smaller activities that I've illustrated in Figure 14.2.

1. **Collect inputs.** Depending on the format of the retrospective you want to run, your team will have to think about the time gone by and answer a few questions. The most common retrospective questions are these: What went well? What didn't go so well? What puzzles you? Other formats will have different questions.

2. **Synthesize inputs.** This is where a facilitator groups similar inputs together. When people have brainstormed independently, clustering their inputs allows you to see clear themes of what's on people's mind. Back in the day, we'd facilitate retros using sticky notes on a whiteboard or flipchart, and that approach lent itself well to clustering. In a remote setup, you can use collaborative whiteboards like Mural or Miro to achieve similar, or even better, results.

3. **Vote to prioritize.** You can't address all themes in a single sitting. So, you must prioritize what's important to the group. Typically, we do this by getting people to vote on the themes. That way, you can bubble up the top three or top five themes, depending on how many you have the appetite for.

4. **Commit to actions.** This is where the rubber hits the road. The team discusses the prioritized themes and commits to actions for each of them. It's good practice for specific people to sign up to complete each action. In fact, I recommend you track these actions on your team's task board.

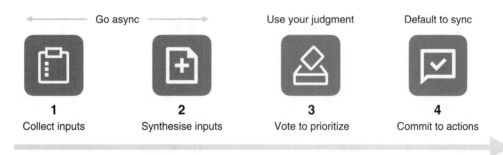

Figure 14.2 A retrospective timeline.

This timeline should tell you a few things.

- #1 and #2 can easily happen asynchronously. Get those out of the way. You'll give people the time to be thoughtful.

- #3 is possible to do asynchronously, but you need to phrase the themes in a way that people understand them well.
- #4 is also possible to do asynchronously, but be mindful of a few challenges.

  - If the team doesn't have a high level of safety, you won't get honest inputs in an asynchronous environment. Especially with newer teams, you'll find it easier to get inputs in a synchronous setup.
  - Agreeing on actions can benefit from a fast-paced exchange of thoughts. Speed is a feature asynchronous communication doesn't have. So even in a safe team environment, doing this asynchronously may feel like pulling teeth.

Of course, as you get more adept at working async, you may not need a meeting at all. Don't rush that transition, though. It's okay to shift left in baby steps.

COLLECT INPUTS IN SAFETY

While you can facilitate the retrospective on a collaborative whiteboard, it's tricky to collect inputs on the whiteboard itself. Not all whiteboards preserve anonymity, and if you're unsure of the team's safety level, this isn't ideal. So, I suggest using a survey form instead to collect these inputs.

┌─ RESOURCE ──────────────

Survey Form Example

You will find an example of an async, retrospective survey form on this book's companion site (https://www.asyncagile.org/book-resources). Use it to create your own version of such a survey.

Be sure to agree on a due-by date for survey responses; otherwise, you or your facilitator may have to wait indefinitely. If your team is new to asynchronous work and the accountability that comes with it, you may have to remind people individually as well. Once you have all the responses, you can convert them into sticky notes on your whiteboard and cluster them for everyone's benefit. Next, everyone votes on these themes.

Data-Driven Retrospectives

To ensure that retrospectives don't focus only on top-of-mind issues, you can bring data as discussion points for your retrospective. Here are a few examples of such data points:

- Is your cycle time and throughput getting better or worse?
- How well are you meeting your sprint goals and commitments?
- What percentage of your time goes to bugs and rework?
- How frequently are you able to deploy to production?
- How long are you waiting for code reviews, and how deep are they?

To make your retro data-driven, synthesize these insights during step 2 of the retrospective process so people can choose to act on them in the upcoming steps.

VOTING SYNCHRONOUSLY VS. ASYNCHRONOUSLY

As I mentioned earlier, it's possible to conduct voting asynchronously. If you do this, take extra care to name each theme in a manner that makes it easy to understand, even when stripped of context. You could choose to do this on the collaborative whiteboard as well, but then you'll need to set it up with an anonymous voting session that runs indefinitely. This can be a bit fiddly if you know what I mean. A cleaner approach, if you want to go asynchronous, is to send a survey form and to ask people to respond to it by a certain time.

However, let me tell you what I prefer. By this stage in the process, you've completed most of the conveyance work. Voting only takes a few minutes in a real-time environment. If you're going to meet anyway, then it makes sense to vote in that same meeting. You don't lose any context that way, and people have the chance to ask quick clarifying questions if something is ambiguous, which brings us to the retrospective board itself.

SETTING UP THE RETROSPECTIVE ENVIRONMENT

You can set up your retrospective board using any collaborative whiteboard such as Mural, Miro, or Google Jamboard. Tools like Parabol have purpose-built interfaces for retrospective meetings, so look at them, too. Whether you use a template or make your own, your board should have a few different sections to map to various parts of the retrospective meeting. Let me describe those to you.

RESOURCE

Retrospective Templates

If you've never facilitated retros before, you'll find a few different retrospective kits on the book's companion site.

These are Mural templates like you see in Figure 14.3. But even if you don't use Mural, you can create equivalent kits using another whiteboarding tool by copying the design of the templates.

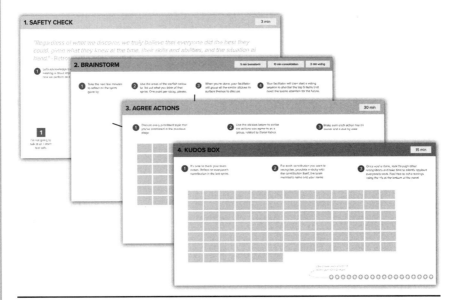

Figure 14.3 Representation of screenshot of the starfish retrospective kit.

Safety Check

This section calls out the retrospective prime directive, which goes like this:

> Regardless of what we discover, we believe that everyone did the best they could, given what they knew at the time, their skills and abilities and the situation at hand.

By stating the prime directive up front, you let everyone know that this is a blame-free environment. You can then ask people to anonymously indicate their level of safety, with 5 being the highest and 1 the lowest. *I prefer doing the safety check synchronously*, though you can do this asynchronously as well. You can choose to do this after collecting inputs or even earlier. It's a judgment call.

Experience Report: How to Respond to Low Safety in Retrospectives

I was once running a retrospective for a team of 18 people distributed across the world, from Australia to North America. The team hadn't done retrospective meetings for a year. When I ran the safety check, I saw an uncomfortable number of 1s and 2s.

Theoretically, if a team's safety isn't high, you shouldn't retrospect on that day and instead consider how you can address safety. This wasn't an option for the group. Wrangling a two-hour slot on their calendars was a feat in itself. Postponing the retrospective could have meant not doing it for weeks.

So, I had to improve the safety of the group during the retrospective itself. I asked the group this question and solicited anonymous responses to it:

How can we improve the sense of safety in this group so everyone feels comfortable to speak up?

The responses I got were well within my control as a facilitator. Your situation may vary, but you can still apply this method to understand what's behind people's low perception of safety. In my case, I had to reiterate the prime directive, so it was clear the retro was only about improvement and not blame.

I also assured the group that they could contribute their thoughts to the retrospective anonymously. If I needed them to write sticky notes, then I'd do this using Mural's Private mode. If there was a discussion they wanted to contribute to anonymously, they could just send me a one-to-one chat message. With those assurances in place, we reran the safety check. In this second run, the 1s and 2s had shifted to 3s and 4s. We acknowledged that some people felt less safe than the others, and the rest of the retro proceeded with that sense of empathy.

Brainstorm

This is where you bring in all the inputs and synthesize themes for everyone's benefit. When you conduct synchronous voting, people can cast their votes in this section as well. I recommend you give people 5 to 10 minutes after the safety check to review each theme and to ask clarifying questions. Once they're clear about what each theme stands for, you can run an anonymous or open voting session depending on the safety level of the group.

Actions

Once everyone has prioritized the themes they want to discuss, you can scribe all actions in this area along with the owners and the due dates.

Kudos

Retros can get overly focused on improvement and not enough on appreciation. Adding a kudos section allows the team to say thanks to anyone who enriched their experience at work.

If you use any of the templates I've created, you'll see facilitation instructions embedded. Follow them step-by-step and you should be on your way. When you're done with the meeting, be sure to find a central place to track the actions from the retro. As I mentioned earlier in the chapter, your team's task board is a sensible default.

RETROS AS A PROCESS, NOT AN EVENT

Figure 14.4 shows the timeline for an async-first retrospective process. In summary, when you're in a remote setup, think of your retro not as a meeting but as a process. You can extend that thinking to all communication.

Communication is a process, not an event.

The retrospective process has two parts: asynchronous and synchronous. How much you do asynchronously is totally up to you and how adept you feel with working this way. That said, it's best to give people async time to provide inputs and for you to synthesize those inputs meaningfully. So, I recommend a week for this part of the process. The rest of the process can easily happen within a 60-minute window. If you haven't had retros for a while, make it longer.

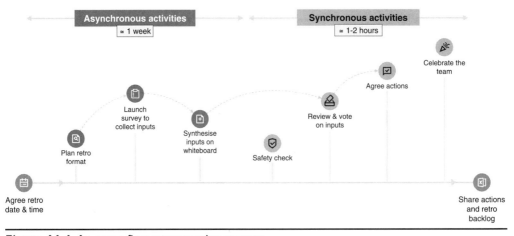

Figure 14.4 An async-first retrospective process.

— RESOURCE —

Run Fun Retrospectives

My colleague and author Paulo Caroli runs a terrific companion site for his book *Fun Retrospectives*. You can also use the companion app to make running retros easy for yourself.

SCRUM FOR THE 2020S

This chapter along with Chapters 13 and 14 address async-first variations to the standard scrum ceremonies. As you'll notice, the way I suggest running retros isn't "async only." It's "async-first and sync-next."

CHAPTER SUMMARY

Frequent retrospectives are an effective way to maintain a positive team environment and a culture of continuous improvement. However, we must approach retrospectives more as a process and not as an event.

- Going by the ConveRel quadrants, retros aim for convergence with a group that enjoys a strong relationship. So, you can gather input and synthesize them async.
- You can choose to asynchronously vote and prioritize issues for discussion, but since this is a short exercise, you may not get much benefit doing so.
- Be sure to set up the retrospective environment in advance with all the synthesis in place, so you can run the meeting effectively.
- You can use the Mural templates on this book's companion site to give yourself a head start with setting up the retro environment.

By applying an async-first mindset to your scrum ceremonies, you'll have made considerable progress already. But these aren't the only practices software development teams follow. We'll now change track to address several other meeting-centric practices on such teams that can benefit from an async-first approach. In the next chapter, let's first address story kickoffs and desk checks.

KICKOFFS AND DESK CHECKS: REDUCE RITUALIZED INTERRUPTIONS

When we were all still in the office, most communication was synchronous. In fact, in my company, each team would have a large table to themselves, and we'd all sit together. If you needed to collaborate with someone, you'd just walk up to them and get things done. When we work remotely, this communication pattern breaks down. This may be one of the biggest features of remote work and one of its most unrealized benefits.

James Stanier, in *Effective Remote Work*, says this:

> Engineers know that it's a pain to be interrupted mid-thought because the complex internal representation of a computer program in their brain immediately evaporates into thin air when somebody asks, "Have you got a minute?"

The "remote" feature of remote work makes it difficult for you to interrupt a colleague, so you reduce your chances of bringing down their productivity. This becomes an unrealized benefit when we try to slap on our old ways of working in the office when we work remotely.

In this chapter, we'll examine two synchronous collaboration practices: kickoffs and dev-box tests or desk checks. As with every other practice, I'll suggest ways to adapt these practices to a remote-native of working.

HOW TO MAINTAIN QUALITY WITH FEWER MEETINGS

Before you dive into the chapter, take a look at Table 15.1 for an adapted definition of each practice, as described in the book *Full Stack Testing*. The book refers to *user stories*, which are concise descriptions of functionality that customers want. For this chapter, we'll use the terms *requirement*, *story*, and *user story* interchangeably.

Table 15.1 Kickoffs and Desk Checks Defined

Kickoff	Desk Checks, or Dev-Box Tests
During the iteration, just before developers pick up a user story for development, a story kickoff happens. The story kickoff is a process where business, developers, and testers *discuss the user story's requirements and edge cases in depth.*	Dev-box testing is where the testers and the business representatives do a round of manual exploratory testing on a developer's machine to *verify the newly developed functionality.*

Agile teams use the kickoff and dev-box tests as ways to build quality into the process and to get fast feedback. They used to be impromptu yet ritualized meetings in a co-located team setup, and they work quite similarly online. For a team that works remotely, though, these meetings can disrupt flow and become an impediment to flexible hours and deep work.

To retain the value of these practices in an async-first environment, I suggest two approaches from my experience. These techniques work well in tandem with the continuous flow approach that we discussed in Chapter 13.

APPROACH 1: GO ASYNC WITH KICKOFFS AND DESK CHECKS

I prefer moving both these practices to a fully asynchronous mode. This allows you the highest amount of work schedule flexibility and minimizes interruptions unless they're absolutely necessary. To use such an asynchronous approach, you must have a few disciplines in place.

Step 1: Agree on the Definition of Ready and the Definition of Done

In Chapter 6, we discussed some basic team norms. From the perspective of delivering software requirements, you must agree on two criteria:

- **Definition of ready (DoR).** A requirement doesn't come into development before it fulfills the definition of ready criteria. Teams need to agree on the amount of detail they need in a requirement before developers pick it up. Sometimes, teams may want to estimate the fully detailed requirement and compare it with any initial estimates they'd attached to it. This allows them to quantify scope change, if any.
- **Definition of done (DoD).** These are a collection of criteria that the team must complete to term a requirement as "done." This doesn't just include business logic or acceptance tests. Depending on the team, the DoD can include logging, monitoring, and even documentation. Since getting a requirement to production can involve many steps, it's likely that different roles will play a part in meeting this criteria.

Why do we need these agreements? you ask. Well, the DoR allows the team to set a standard for user stories that developers pick up. In an asynchronous setup, you need more detail in the story itself. That's a good thing, because it leaves less room for ambiguity, and it helps everyone in the team understand the requirement. The DoD ensures developers aren't aiming for a moving target. It gives them a common standard to aim for with every user story.

I suggest making these criteria explicit using checklists. As Atul Gawande notes in *The Checklist Manifesto*, these checklists should be precise and "provide reminders of only the most critical and important steps." Figure 15.1 shows an example of such checklists. You can embed these checklists into the requirement templates on your task board.

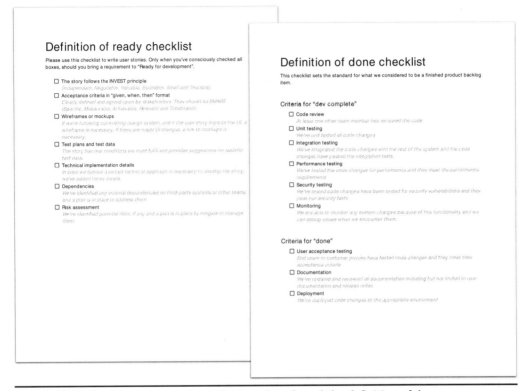

Figure 15.1 Checklists to state the definition of ready and the definition of done.

Step 2: Sweat the Details at the Story Level

Agile user stories provide a lightweight approach to communicate requirements. They also lower the stakes of development. Since the requirements are small, the blast radius of any mistakes is also significantly lower than with larger, traditional requirements.

A well-written user story can pre-empt the need for a kickoff meeting, especially if it follows the team's definition of ready. To reduce the need for meetings, your stories must have all the details developers need. This is where the three amigos—the product owner (PO), the test engineer (aka quality assurance analysts or QAs), and the tech lead (TL, aka lead developer)—must collaborate to produce these requirements:

- The product owner provides the business logic and the acceptance criteria.
- The tester specifies the testing approach, the test cases, and the test data.
- And the tech lead includes implementation notes, if any.
- If the story addresses a user screen, then it should link to a mockup or a clickable prototype. Your definition of ready should tell you what's the necessary level of detail in your stories.

Use collaborative documents to build out user stories so there's room for everyone to add comments inline. You can copy and paste these into Jira or whatever task board you use or attach them to the card if you want to leave the discussion history alive.

┌─ RESOURCE

Examples of Detailed User Stories

Since this isn't a book about user story writing, we won't address the details of how to write them effectively. However, I've created a few example user stories for a fictitious online grocery store. They'll help you learn how to craft effective user stories for your own team. You'll find them on the companion site.

Step 3: Queue Up "Ready" Stories in Advance

Asynchronous communication deliberately slows down communication to make it more thoughtful. If you slow down communication, though, you must give people time to respond. If you're a product owner, give your dev team a chance to see the stories before the sprint starts. Here's how I suggest you seek feedback:

- Queue up candidate stories well in advance. These should be in the "ready for development" queue on your task board. You can help your team filter them using a tag, such as "Waiting for feedback," as you see in Figure 15.2.
- Invite devs to read the stories they'd like to sign up for so they can ask questions using the comments feature that the PO, TL, or tester can respond to.
- This Q&A can enrich a story description and further reduce the need for a story kickoff.

Adopt the same approach as that of consent-based decision-making that we discussed in Chapter 6. If you don't hear any objections by the time the requirements hit the top of the queue, assume that everyone is fine with them. If any major objections emerge at the time of development, you can either add corresponding new backlog items or address them on a case-by-case basis.

Step 4: Replace Desk Checks with Recorded Video

A good practice with desk-check meetings is to time box them to 15 minutes. Otherwise, they can end up being full-blown exploratory tests on the dev's computer. The time limit ensures that you don't go into a manual testing rabbit hole. So, by nature, desk checks should be short and simple even when they're synchronous.

However, even when everyone's in the same physical space, sometimes no one is available for a desk check. Instead of waiting to synchronize, recorded video is an effective way to "default to action" until the PO and tester are available.

While a lot of obvious defects show up in these dev-box tests, you can preempt them with a checklist. Teams can develop their own checklist based on the definition of done. Developers can then enrich these checklists with the specific acceptance criteria for individual stories.

Once such a checklist is in place, developers can use it to create a simple recorded demo showing each of the test conditions and other completion criteria such as logging and monitoring. They can attach it to the backlog item and @*mention* the tester and the PO to do an asynchronous dev-box test. A team agreement on turnaround time can ensure that devs don't have to wait for too long. To create such videos, you'll find async video tool suggestions in Chapter 4.

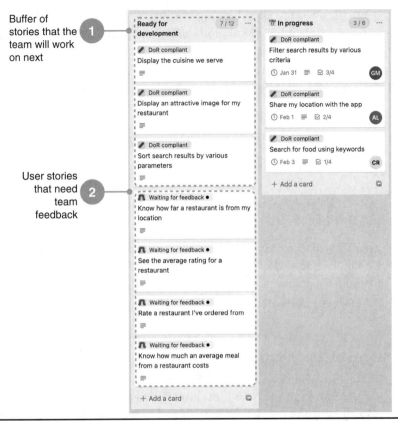

Figure 15.2 Queue up stories in advance so the rest of the team can share feedback.

BEST PRACTICE

Don't Make the Video Your Last Task!

It's a good practice to create the desk check video while there's still some minor work to complete for the story. That could include adding unit tests in parts of the code that you may have touched, refactoring some of the code you've encountered, making final changes to your own code, and writing up the eventual commit message. This ensures that even while you wait for a reasonable amount of time to get feedback, you don't have to sit idle.

Step 5: Meet If You Must

Whether it's to kick off the story or for a dev-box, there'll be times when you have to meet. For example, if the feedback's going back and forth, it'll be too slow and impractical to stay asynchronous. In such cases, set up a call and sort things out in real time. Just be sure to maintain two important bits of hygiene:

- Follow all the best practices for meetings.
- Learn from the experience and write up how you can make this async the next time around.

Remember, it's not about changing everything on day one. Small steps go a long way.

APPROACH 2: KEEP THE SYNC PRACTICES AND PLAN FOR THEM

There's a chance that your team wants to retain either or both the synchronous kickoff and desk check. While that's not what I'll recommend, it's possible that these aren't practices you want to tweak right away. In such a case, I encourage you to follow two key disciplines.

Step 1: Represent the Practices on Your Workflow

Your task board should be the primary signaling mechanism for your process. So if a requirement is waiting for a kickoff or a desk check, it should be evident when someone looks at the board. Making these gate checks visible on your task board also allows you to measure the amount of time that you spend on them. That data can be fodder for improvement. Figure 15.3 shows an example of how to represent these processes in your workflow.

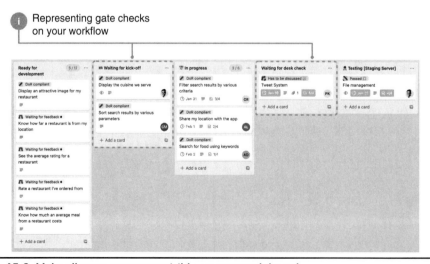

Figure 15.3 Make all team processes visible on your task board.

Step 2: Clarify Team Norms for Synchronous Activities

In Chapter 7, we discussed how members of a development team should have at least a four-hour overlap between them. Organizations that choose to separate their testing and development teams should keep this in mind, even when they want people to work asynchronously. When working asynchronously, a lower overlap can lead to a long waiting time and developers or testers might end up blocking each other.

In addition, you may have to agree to some team norms:

- Identify your hours for synchronous work. This goes together with the team play of agreeing on inviolate hours. POs and testers can make themselves available in those synchronous time slots and work flexibly during the rest of the time.
- On the first day of the sprint, testers and POs can set aside some extra time to respond to questions from developers.
- Create an instant messaging channel that testers and POs can monitor with greater urgency. Agree on a maximum turnaround time (TAT) for this channel.

MAKE YOUR FEEDBACK LOOPS "REMOTE NATIVE"

Within a development cycle, meetings can quickly add up with a kickoff and a desk check for each user story. Of course, these are feedback loops that exist for a reason, and we don't want to eliminate them without thought. Both the approaches we discussed in this chapter aim to adapt these feedback loops to a remote-native work setup. Your appetite for change and team environment will determine which of these approaches you choose.

CHAPTER SUMMARY

Story kickoffs and desk checks build quality into the development process. To adapt them to a remote work environment, you have two options:

1. Approach 1: Go fully asynchronous.
   a. Align on the DoR and DoD.
   b. Collaborate among the three amigos to detail the story well enough to pre-empt a kickoff.
   c. Queue "ready" stories in advance so developers can pose questions to the three amigos.

d. Use recorded video in lieu of desk checks and use standard checklists to guide these recordings.

e. If you still see a reason to meet, do so, and follow best practices.

2. Approach 2: Retain the synchronous practices, but plan for them.

a. Represent both kickoffs and desk checks on your task board and measure their impact on the workflow.

b. Ensure that you have enough overlap time to make both sync and async communication productive across roles. Agree to team norms such as turnaround times.

In their co-located, synchronous avatar, both these practices felt like a kind of a team huddle. These aren't the only huddle-like practices, though. In the next chapter we'll discuss another informal practice—the tech huddle.

QUESTIONS TO REIMAGINE YOUR TECH HUDDLES

Over the past few chapters, we've examined some common agile practices through the lens of async-first collaboration. You may have noticed that we're eschewing collaboration for collaboration's sake. Sometimes we give a free pass to any activity that seems collaborative. Before you know it, you've built half a dozen gate checks to deliver a single user story. Each of those "collaborative" gate checks doesn't just create interruptions and context switches. It also leaves an attention residue—your mind continues to think about the interruption even when you've switched to the task on hand. There is such a thing as a collaboration curse, as the *Economist* described some years back.

> Organizations need to do more to recognize that the amount of time workers have available is finite, that every request to attend a meeting or engage in an internet discussion leaves less time for focused work, and that seemingly small demands on people's time can quickly compound into big demands. Helping people to collaborate is a wonderful thing. Giving them the time to think is even better.

So, we must be smarter about collaboration, especially because remote work is a new medium for many of us. Even years after I've authored this book, it'll be a new medium in comparison to the synchronous, co-located model of the office. This new medium affords us new ways of working that may often be counterintuitive in comparison to the office model. A pattern that may have worked well in person becomes inefficient when you re-create it, as is, using videoconferencing and instant messaging. One such pattern among dev teams is the huddle.

THE WHAT AND THE WHY

Huddles, in their purest synchronous avatar, are short, standing meetings around a whiteboard. In their remote version, they're just like any other online meeting. Before I explain how I think about the "huddle" pattern, let me describe the two variations I've seen.

- **The ad hoc huddle.** Teams use these to solve day-to-day technical problems. The expectation is that you shouldn't need to look up calendars, and you can just pull a bunch of people into a conversation and thrash the problem out.
- **The scheduled huddle.** In this pattern, the dev team builds up a list of topics over a week and meets at a predictable frequency to discuss them.

While I think we have to reimagine both these patterns, the first one is often more problematic than the second. I'll explain that in a bit. On that note, let's discuss how you can get better value from async-first variations of these patterns on your teams. I want to explore this topic through a series of questions.

HOW MUCH AUTONOMY EXISTS IN YOUR TEAMS?

According to *Rob Cross, Reb Rebele, and Adam Grant in Harvard Business Review*, "Requests for time-sapping reviews and approvals can be reduced in many risk-averse *cultures* by encouraging *people* to take courageous action on decisions they should be making themselves, rather than constantly checking with leaders or stakeholders."

As we noted in Chapter 15, user stories are an effective way to specify requirements because they lower the stakes. Each requirement is so small that even if you go wrong, the risks are low. Teams tend to overcomplicate their development process for this simple unit and make it more heavyweight than it needs to be. Before you know it, there's a debate at the sprint planning meeting, a kickoff, a bunch of huddles, a tech check, a desk check, and whatnot to get just one user story out the door. Sure, you need feedback and collaboration, but does all this ceremony create the value that it promises? Or are you as a team being risk averse?

The teams I've seen being effective in a distributed setup devolve responsibility to smaller units where possible. If everyone is asking everyone before making every single decision, this creates noise in the system. This is model A in Figure 16.1.

 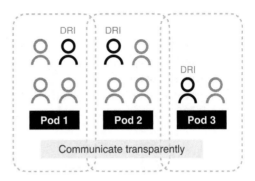

Model A: Chaotic communication   **Model B:** Decentralized, empowered pods

Figure 16.1 Distributed teams need calm, decentralized models to organize.

A better model, as shown in model B in Figure 16.1, is to create smaller decentralized pods inside the team. These pods can be as small as two people and no larger than four people. Here are some characteristics of effective pods:

- Align the pods to an outcome. It could be to deliver a feature or an epic.
- Nominate a directly responsible individual (DRI) for each outcome. This person is a "first among equals" (FaE) within the pod and can help make tough calls for the pod in case it comes to that.
- Resist the temptation to make DRIs part of multiple pods. It leads to too much context switching for the DRIs and avoidable coordination hassles. A dedicated DRI in each pod allows these individuals to address problems in depth as well.
- Pods operate autonomously, and the larger team encourages each pod to make its own decisions with help from its DRIs.
- To encourage knowledge sharing and to bust silos, keep the pods short-lived. When you achieve the outcome, disband the pod. Any longer than a month and you should question the existence of the pod.
- Except the DRI, you can rotate people across pods even before delivering the outcome, if that's something you want to do. Be aware of the trade-off, though. Although more people will be able to engage with the corresponding part of the codebase, you may lose the benefits from expertise and continuity.
- Radiate information across the team so everyone is up to speed with what's happening on each pod. That way, you also won't create walled gardens of information.

Now if you really need help, you have a smaller, more focused group of people to reach out to. The result—lesser noise and fewer interruptions in the system.

HOW NECESSARY IS THE "SYNC UP"?

In Chapter 9, we discussed how "quick syncs" may be in the flow for you but can disrupt the people you interrupt (see Figure 16.2). Your need to solve the issue at hand is important, but spare a thought for your colleagues who also need uninterrupted time to do their work. A little empathy goes a long way. Your proposed huddle may be a quick sync that could instead be async.

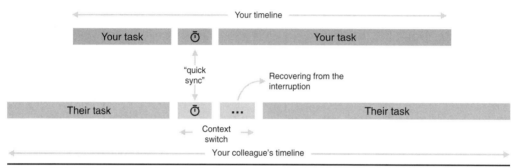

Figure 16.2 "Quick syncs" benefit the interrupter but disrupt the interrupted.

Instead of a quick sync, consider writing things up. If a sketch or a video describes things in more detail, add it. The artifact you produce can also speed up problem-solving. A precisely written problem description can aid someone who's trying to help to get straight to their inputs. Moreover, the chain of written communication can become a decision record for others to refer to at a later point in time. Often, writing and sketching things out can clarify your thinking and help you get to a solution without help!

As you've seen in Chapter 4, writing is your superpower to go deep and conquer those hard problems. Once you have a write-up, you can use it for async decisions, or even a meeting, if necessary.

WHAT IF YOU DEFAULTED TO ACTION?

Defaulting to action is a major goal and benefit of an async-first mindset. Every member of the team must cultivate the skill to work independently and make decisions. Managers must also look for this attribute when you hire people into your team. If you've built a team of high-ability individuals, then everyone needs the confidence to give the problem at hand the hardest crack they can. When some information or input is unavailable, the culture of the team should be to do the best they can and backtrack or refactor if necessary. Here are some ideas to encourage a bias for action:

- Help each other differentiate between irreversible decisions and reversible decisions. Most of your project decisions should be reversible. For these, use the consent-based decision approach we discussed in Chapter 6.

- Several agile teams practice pair programming. If you're one of those teams, then you already have two heads at the problem. You're mitigating some risks right there!

- If you're not pairing, you probably have a code review process to mitigate design and implementation risks.

- Create systemic approaches to highlight risks. Depending on the branching strategy you use, you may be able to identify high-risk branches using your code analytics and address these risks proactively.

Use "defaulting to action" as a way for team members to think deeply about their work and to build a culture of entrepreneurship and calculated risk taking.

IF YOU MUST HUDDLE, HOW DO YOU MAKE THE MEETING EFFECTIVE?

There will be times when you can't default to action. It's fine to meet up in such situations. But remember, meetings are the last resort, not the first option. Everything we know for a good meeting should still apply if we must meet. Here's what I suggest so we make these huddles productive:

- Don't start any such meeting without a written artifact that everyone has looked at. The least prepared person often derails the meeting, and it wastes everyone's time. You can use the six-page memo pattern that we discussed in Chapter 7 and ask everyone to consume the artifact in silence during the first few minutes of the meeting.

- Huddles should be tiny meetings with a tiny group of participants. Remember that these were supposed to be quick, standing meetings at a whiteboard. Over 30 minutes and a group larger than four participants, and you're probably doing this wrong.

- The decision to huddle and not go async or default to action means this was complex and high stakes. You must document the meeting and the decision for everyone's benefit. No excuses. We'll address decision records in some detail in Chapter 18.

The frequency of these last-resort huddles should give you a sign of how you're doing when building an async-first development culture. Too many huddles may mean you're not defining stories and implementation decisions clearly or that you haven't built a culture of autonomy in the team. Something needs fixing.

┌─ BEST PRACTICE ───

Free Calendars Enable Ad Hoc Conversations

The beauty of making meetings the last resort is that you end up with a relatively free calendar. This makes important, ad hoc conversations easier to organize. After all, you don't have to juggle a bunch of preexisting commitments to find 30 minutes to help your colleagues. A call for help can be as simple as the following:

> *Hey, Shree and I are figuring out ways to implement this new component, and we wouldn't mind bouncing some ideas off you. When do you have 30 minutes?*

In teams with cleaner calendars, you'll usually get help sooner than in teams where you pack your calendars with meetings that instead could be documents, text messages, or even email.

OH, AND ABOUT THE REGULAR, SCHEDULED HUDDLES...

So that was all about the great ad hoc huddle on agile teams. As I mentioned at the start of the chapter, the scheduled huddle is not as problematic. The way teams often do this is by first creating a backlog of topics they want to discuss. You then pick a day of the week to meet up, and you discuss items from the top of the backlog downward. Be aware that this pattern can't always address stuff that's vital to the project. It's a top-level triage of things to discuss. Examples could be a possible new library to try, a new static analysis tool to integrate into your pipeline, or how you plan to do an accessibility audit for your product. Whatever grabs the team's fancy! Once you decide on an action, it should go onto your backlog. From then on you track it, business as usual.

The value of doing these scheduled huddles isn't so much that the meeting itself is the most efficient. Think of it more as a social gathering for technologists to talk about things that fascinate us. In Chapter 7, we talked about being human. Having these fun sync-ups can help your team feel connected even when most of your work becomes asynchronous.

NOT A ZERO-SUM GAME

As you notice from both the previous chapter and this one, the async-first adaptation of certain practices may not be 100 percent async. How far you shift left on the spectrum of synchronousness depends on your context. In the case of tech huddles, I suggest unbundling some of these contextual parameters using questions.

CHAPTER SUMMARY

Tech huddles are usually ad hoc meetings to solve technical problems or make technical decisions for the project. They can also be scheduled conversations to address a wide array of tech topics that concern the team. To reimagine them for an async-first environment, lead with the following questions:

- How much autonomy exists on your teams? Consider a decentralized model of pods to devolve decision-making to smaller groups.

- How necessary is the "sync up"? If possible, slow down and write things up first and then take it from there.

- What's the worst that could happen if people default to action? Adopt a consent-based decision-making approach for reversible decisions.

- If you must meet as the last resort, then how can you make that interaction less disruptive, better prepared, and more productive? Follow the best practices we've learned so far.

- Lastly, scheduled huddles aren't as problematic as the ad hoc ones. Not only do they serve as a fast-paced triage of topics the team must discuss, but they also serve as a fun social gathering.

By now we've addressed several common practices on agile teams. There's one more practice to discuss before we switch to a different topic. So, in the next chapter, let's address an elephant in the async-first room: pair programming.

PAIR PROGRAMMING: THE ELEPHANT IN THE ROOM

When you have a hammer, everything looks like a nail. When that hammer is asynchronous work, we may think of making everything in our work lives asynchronous. We're going to take a break from that and address an elephant in the room. Pair programming is among the most frequent synchronous activities that agile teams practice, especially those that follow extreme programming (XP). To the uninitiated, here's a definition:

> *Pair programming is the practice where two developers work together on the same coding problem, sharing terminals on the same computer.*

Many teams pair all the time. So, it helps to spend some time examining this practice and how we approach it if we want to be async-first.

A POLARIZING TOPIC

I don't think that I'm overstating it when I say that pair programming or pairing is a controversial topic. Table 17.1 states the two viewpoints you'll hear about this practice.

Table 17.1 What You May Hear About Pairing

The Zealots	The Naysayers
"Pair programming is the only way to write high-quality code."	"Pairing is an unproductive waste of time where we make two people do the job of one."

Like almost everything else, there's nuance to the truth, and it'll often fall somewhere in the middle of those extreme views. In my view, pair programming can be a highly productive synchronous activity for teams that practice it regularly. The details of pair programming techniques are beyond the scope of this chapter and the book. My colleagues Birgitta Böckeler and Nina Siessegger have written a comprehensive article about pairing and its benefits, which I strongly recommend. For anyone who thinks pair programming halves the productivity of developers, though, Martin Fowler's flippant quip is a suitable response.

> That would be true if the hardest part of programming was typing.

LET'S START WITH WHY

The biggest benefits of pairing that I've seen on the teams I've worked on overlap with what Birgitta and Nina explain:

- **Constant code review.** Two people work together keep each other honest. You're on the constant lookout to refactor code as you go. Your pair provides you with a safety net to avoid cutting corners. The two of you can hold each other accountable to follow your team's coding standards.
- **Knowledge sharing and mentoring.** You can document a codebase to death, but a new developer will never have the confidence to navigate it until they've contributed code to it. As codebases get larger, the barrier to entry for new developers increases, and it gets more daunting to write code. Pairing reduces this barrier to entry by helping new, even inexperienced developers learn about the structure of the codebase. Constant rotations help seasoned programmers share their skills with less experienced developers. Even experienced developers can learn a thing or two from a fresh pair of eyes. Feedback in the flow of work improves resilience in the team.
- **Team bonding and camaraderie.** This is a benefit of pairing that we often overlook. Working in a paired setting helps you observe your co-workers at close quarters. Not only do you benefit from experiencing diverse styles of problem solving, you learn about each other's quirks and find common ground you may have never chanced upon otherwise. It's hard to place a dollar value on camaraderie, but anyone who has worked in a team knows it has as much value as any productivity measure.

There are challenges, of course, and Birgitta and Nina's article cover those too, but that's not the focus of this chapter. The benefits I mentioned are important for co-located and distributed teams alike. If pairing can be such a fruitful synchronous activity for a distributed team, how do we weave it into an async-first way of work? I have four things I want you to consider: designing for flexibility, using the right tools, encouraging personal discipline, and mixing pairing and solo work.

DESIGN FOR FLEXIBILITY

That people can work the hours that make the most sense for them is one of the biggest features of remote work. This is at odds with having to "sync up" with someone and to pair with them. To me, it's not an intractable problem, though. There are two ways to get around this problem—one that I prefer more than the other.

- You can institute "core hours" on your team when everyone is available to pair. While this makes things predictable, it can be heavy-handed. Every day isn't the same for every single person, so you'll end up making life difficult for some people on your team if you take this route.
- I prefer another option. Leave the timing to the individual pair. Let them figure out the hours that work well for them to sync up. This kind of decentralization makes your team's processes, in the words of Nassim Taleb, "antifragile." Regardless of the events of the day, two people can easily figure out how they'll work together. This works particularly well if you organize larger teams into small pods, as we saw in Chapter 16.

Figure 17.1 shows a pattern I've seen work remarkably well at an East European software development company. I call this the *baton-pass pairing routine*. The developer who started their day early would begin working solo. At some point, the second developer would join them, and they'd have a few hours of intense pairing. After the first developer logged off, the second developer would work solo. At the end of their day, the second developer would write up notes for the first dev. That way, the first developer could pick up the baton the next day. The practice of writing effective commit messages made this pattern even more productive.

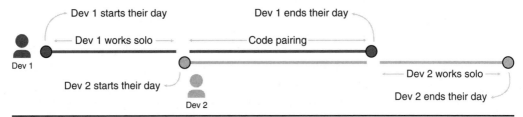

Figure 17.1 The baton-pass pairing routine.

USE THE RIGHT TOOLS

Pair programming is not screen sharing. Ask any developer who has tried to pair using Zoom or Teams, and they'll tell you that the experience is nothing like sitting side by side with someone. That's understandable, isn't it? Once you throw in features such as remote controls, videoconferencing tools become laggy and inefficient. It doesn't compare to the physical setup of two developers sharing a keyboard and a screen, sitting side by side.

If you don't have the right tools, remote pairing will be an uphill battle. You need specialized tools to do this. The two tools I've seen my colleagues enjoy are Tuple and Visual Studio Live Share. I've also heard wonderful things about CoScreen and Pop, but I haven't worked in a team that's used it extensively. There'll be more tools in the future, so I don't intend to be comprehensive with my tool recommendations. Just don't let us business types select pairing tools for developers. Listen to your developers and let them have the pairing tool that works for them.

Watch This Space: AI Pair Programmers!

At the time of writing this book, there are a slew of programming bots on the market. GitHub Copilot, Amazon CodeWhisperer, Tabnine, and Codeium are fast gaining popularity among developers. I suggest watching this space cautiously. Coding bots could become a promising innovation, where you may get some benefits of pair programming without the struggle of real-time collaboration. At the time of writing this book, though, there are concerns related to how supportable AI-generated code is. Since the AI models learn from publicly available source code, it's also likely that you could run into unintended licensing issues where you mix copyrighted code with public code that has no identified sources.

ENCOURAGE PERSONAL DISCIPLINE

Effective remote work is also about personal discipline, as we discussed in Chapter 5. When in a pairing session, you're responsible for your time and your pair's time. Distractions such as instant messages of meetings in the middle of a pairing session can disturb your partner's flow. Pairing works when two people immerse themselves completely in solving a coding problem. It's also as inefficient as the most distracted partner. A few years back, my colleagues at Thoughtworks created a hilarious video with several pair programming anti-patterns. While they shot the video in the office, all the lessons apply in the remote world as well. Let me summarize some of the anti-patterns you must avoid:

- **Hogging the keyboard.** Pair programming is a way to learn from each other on the job. If only one person writes code, it doesn't help the other person's confidence or morale. Share the keyboard periodically by using a driver-navigator pattern. One person guides, the other types. You can achieve this by trying one of two techniques:

  - *Ball and board* where one person handles the mouse or trackpad and the other handles the keyboard, and then roles swap.

  - *Ping pong*, where one person writes a failing test and the other person writes the code to pass that test. This can be a fun way to challenge each other while you also test-drive your code.

- **Pairing with the same person all the time.** When you pair with the same person all the time, you might build a strong bond with them. However, you lose the opportunity to learn from others on the team. You also risk creating skill and knowledge silos. Instead, find a cadence to reset pairs so you mix things up.

- **Being rigid about a problem-solving approach.** Pairing assumes that "two heads are better than one" when solving a problem. It doesn't help, then, if one person dominates the other in a pairing session. Listen carefully and ask questions to understand the other person's perspective. You may end up with a richer solution through the process.

- **Passive pairing.** The corollary to the previous anti-pattern is when one person just hangs back, leaving the other person to do all the work. This is worse than working solo, because one person is idle. Passive pairing may be a sign that at least one person doesn't find the pairing activity useful and is just going through the motions. I suggest having a frank conversation and being open to working solo if you can't convince each other to pair.

- **Leaving your pair hanging.** When busy senior developers pair with junior colleagues, they may often leave their partner hanging because they have to head out for meetings. You may as well work solo then. If you want to pair program, then make pairing hours inviolate. Clear your calendars and block all distractions.

- **Philosophizing.** Discussions during pair programming will often make the solution more robust. You must, however, avoid long philosophical debates that contribute nothing to the problem at hand. Learn to park such discussions for a more informal conversation. If you have disagreements, then pause to write your points of view on a virtual whiteboard or a shared document. That may help you weigh the pros and cons of each perspective and arrive at an agreement. In case you're still undecided, continue working on areas where you share common ground and let the directly responsible individual (DRI) for that project or feature asynchronously or synchronously break the tie for the debate.

MIX PAIRING AND SOLO WORK

When you see the value in pairing, it's tempting to pair all the time. Pair programming is intense and tiring; you'll find out when you try it. People will need a breather. The baton-pass routine helps with that. You may have simple coding activities that won't benefit from the intense code review of pair programming. These are great candidates for solo work that people can sign up for when they need a break from pairing.

Sometimes people must go solo, if only to build their confidence. Birgitta and Nina suggest a solution:

> Running into a problem ourselves is often a more effective learning experience than somebody telling us that we are going to walk into it. There are a few ways to counteract this. One is to let junior programmers work by themselves from time to time, with a mentor who regularly checks in and does some code review.

Andrew Montalenti advocates for a pair programming pattern where two developers act as each other's accountability partners. Figure 17.2 describes how this pattern plays out.

1. *Synchronously* lay out a plan or a rough design sketch.
2. *Asynchronously* develop some implementation prototypes and a few functions and classes.
3. *Synchronously* discuss the pros and cons of each implementation approach.
4. *Asynchronously* refine the prototypes based on each other's feedback, with the intention of arriving at a consensus solution.
5. *Synchronously* agree on a plan for how to implement the functionality and the tasks each person is responsible for.
6. *Asynchronously* work on individual coding tasks.
7. *Synchronously* integrate the individual pieces of code.
8. *Asynchronously* review the merged code and polish it further if you must.

A pattern such as this can balance the need to work at your own pace with the benefit of learning from a colleague's problem-solving approach. Whatever you do, resist dogma on your teams. Pairing has its benefits, but the agile manifesto also emphasizes "individuals and interactions over processes and tools." If you have great people on the team, your priority must be to find ways to collaborate in an effective and inclusive manner. Avoid practicing any technique without respecting the context.

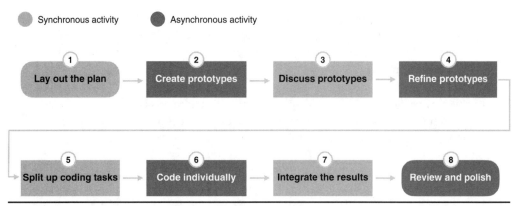

Figure 17.2 Pairing with an accountability partner.

IF IT'S FUN FOR YOU, PAIR BY ALL MEANS

As we've noted earlier, being async-first doesn't mean async-only. If your team enjoys pair programming and sees value in it, you must continue the practice.

CHAPTER SUMMARY

Pair programming is a highly productive synchronous activity, and if your team sees value in coordinating it, you should continue the practice. Here are some ideas to implement it in an async-first team:

- Design your work patterns for flexibility so pairing doesn't create a rigid work schedule. Try the baton-pass pairing routine as a way for developers to start and end their days at times convenient to them.
- Use the right pairing tools; otherwise, the dev team will struggle to pair efficiently. That in turn can be morale and productivity sapping.
- Everything we've discussed thus far about personal discipline becomes even more important. You're now responsible for two people's time.
- Be pragmatic. You don't always need to pair. Find ways for people to work solo and to learn from their own mistakes. Consider pairing as a way of having a design or accountability partner even if most of the work is asynchronous.

As a corollary to everything we've discussed in this chapter, if the team doesn't enjoy pair programming, it's not the end of the world. In such a circumstance you may need more diligence with code reviews and how you share knowledge in the team. Be pragmatic.

By now we've covered several agile techniques that teams commonly practice. Let's switch track to some documentation practices that'll help you in your async-first journey. We'll start with audit trails in the next chapter.

18

AUDIT TRAILS FROM THE FLOW OF YOUR WORK

You might remember a story from your childhood called *Hansel and Gretel*. I won't attempt to tell the entire story here. However, an interesting part of the story is the trail that Hansel leaves so the children can find their way back home. While the trail of white pebbles endures the day, they lose the breadcrumb trail to birds and animals. On projects as well, you'll need similar, enduring trails. Why? you may ask. Well, for the same reason: to find your way back. You need ways to resolve a bug, understand a decision, or identify the rationale for a code change.

THE "JUST ASK" PATTERN BREAKS DOWN

Back in the day, when we all sat around a table, you could "just ask" and get answers to questions. Couldn't resolve a bug? People would just huddle around and tell you what to do. Didn't understand an architectural decision? We'd "just ask." Someone would explain it to us. Frustrated with a code change? We'd say it out loud, and someone would give us a reason. While we'll agree that this was a distracting environment, we still got some answers.

The "just ask" pattern breaks down when you're working remotely. There's no one to huddle with and no one to holler at. We also don't want to interrupt each other with incessant chat messages. There must be an async way to backtrack, right? So, in this chapter, we'll learn how to be like Hansel. We'll discuss the five trails we create in the flow of asynchronous work.

An Audit Trail Doesn't Replace a Summary

All the audit trails we'll discuss in this chapter answer the question of "how we got here." While it's important to be able to backtrack from the current state of a project using an audit trail, it's also important to represent that current state clearly. Your team handbook should help your colleagues understand the current state of your project, well before they ever have to plow through an audit trail.

MEETING NOTES

Now that you don't sit with a team you can "just ask," think about the number of communication paths on a team. In a team of two, it's only one line of communication, but in a team of three, you have three lines. A team of four has six lines of communication, and a team of 10, a staggering 45 lines. This is why verbal communication may become a game of telephone as team size increases (Figure 18.1).

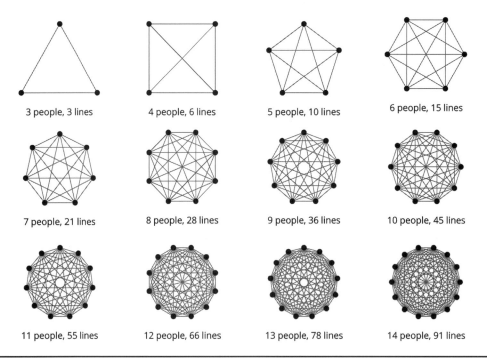

3 people, 3 lines   4 people, 6 lines   5 people, 10 lines   6 people, 15 lines

7 people, 21 lines   8 people, 28 lines   9 people, 36 lines   10 people, 45 lines

11 people, 55 lines   12 people, 66 lines   13 people, 78 lines   14 people, 91 lines

Figure 18.1 Team communication becomes more complex with team size.

If three people in a ten-person team have a meeting and they only rely on a verbal relay of information to share the output of that meeting, the best-case scenario is another meeting just to communicate the information. We've already discussed that conveying information in a team should be asynchronous by default. The worst-case scenario can be a number of additional meetings, again just to convey information. Before you know it, you can have a game of telephone going.

A better approach is to write a good, old-fashioned meeting summary. A succinct summary can help people consume the gist of a long meeting in a few minutes. Popular calendaring tools like Google Calendar and Outlook already build in nudges for you to make meeting notes. Confluence has a very practical template—any actions you decide from your meeting also become to-dos on your team's handbook. It helps you track due dates, and action-owners get notifications from the system. If your organization is willing to spend the extra bucks, there are tools to facilitate such documentation; Fellow, tl;dv, Hugo, and Otter come to mind. Tools and templates aren't the problem; discipline is.

It's not enough to just write meeting notes. You must make them easy to find and reference. Platforms like Confluence make this easy; all your meeting notes stay in one place. You can also tag people if you need their attention. If you use Office 365 or Google Workspace, you must decide where to host these notes. Don't expect everyone to keep up with the notes from every meeting. We don't want people drinking from a firehose, trying to consume every artifact the team produces. Instead, we want it to be easy for people to reference these artifacts, if they need to.

┌─ BEST PRACTICE

What Goes into Meeting Minutes?

Your meeting summaries needn't be verbose or complicated. Here are some basic components of such an artifact:

- Goals of the meeting and topics on the agenda—you'd have circulated these already, before the meeting.
- Attendees in the meeting—several tools allow you to @mention these colleagues, so you can fill this detail out fast.
- Key discussion points for each agenda topic—write these in bullet points so they're easy to scan through.
- Action items—who does what, by when. Some tools will allow you to track actions on your documentation system itself. If not, find a way to move these tasks to your task board.
- Decisions, if any—be sure to link these up to any supporting information, such as a decision record or a proposal.

BUSINESS DECISION RECORDS

Agile values "responding to change over following a plan." A part of that premise is that business needs and imperatives change over time, and software development should respond to these changes. This is probably something you experience day in and day out. The business makes decisions all the time—about prioritization, road maps, migrations, budgets, target groups, experiments, and whatnot.

The larger the team, the more the decisions, and the harder it is to keep track of them in our heads or through conversations. Distributed teams must adopt the discipline to document all business decisions in business decision records (BDRs). Joel Henderson has written an excellent guide for general decision records, which I'm sure you'll find useful. If you use Confluence, it has a built-in template that also allows you to populate all decisions at one place in your team handbook.

ARCHITECTURAL DECISION RECORDS

One of the central principles of extreme programming is simplicity and, by extension, simple design. In the recent decade, the idea of "evolutionary architecture" has gained popularity. Teams identify the fundamental technical requirements for a system up front but delay other decisions till the "last responsible moment." The benefit? You avoid up-front guesswork and allow yourself to decide when you have the necessary information.

This means your architecture will change with time, and in the future you may have to investigate why your architecture is a certain way. Architectural decision records (ADRs) help by providing an archaeological timeline of your project. Here are some benefits of using them:

- You can **align partner teams and stakeholders** at speed by using these artifacts to drive consensus, promote framework and code reuse, and even remove duplicative efforts.
- ADRs can help **onboard current and future team members** by helping them understand how the project's architecture has evolved and the rationale behind specific architectural decisions.
- **Project ownership transfer** becomes easier with ADRs. A new team taking over a project can use these decision records to understand how the system's architecture has developed until this point.

Joel Henderson's guide to ADRs is one I recommend; there are lots of templates that you can use to get started. Michael Nygard's original 2011 post on the topic follows the format of a standard ADR, so that's a great learning tool as well. I won't go into the details of ADR writing, but I do have a few pieces of advice:

- Like meeting notes, **ADRs should live in a central location** for the project. You can use collaborative file-sharing tools like Google Drive or wikis like Confluence. A sensible default, however, is to store them in source control, with your code.

- **No decision is too small** to document. In fact, the cost of your undocumented change is just as high as that of the first duplicated effort in your team or organization. ADRs are lightweight, so take a few minutes to write the change down.

- If you come across an undocumented decision, **be a good citizen**. Collaborate with your team to document it so you avoid confusion in the future.

- Last but not least, **write ADRs in a way that everyone on the team can understand**. You know your ADR is impactful when both techies and business folks can understand the rationale behind your decisions and the solutions you've arrived at.

RESOURCE

Simplify ADR Writing

ADR-manager is a tool that integrates with your GitHub repository (Figure 18.2). It allows you to browse and edit previous ADRs. If you want to create a new ADR, then it guides you through the process by providing a consistent format.

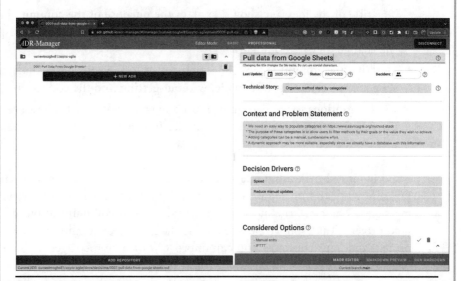

Figure 18.2 Use ADR-manager as a guide for writing ADRs.

A command-line alternative to manage your ADRs is adr-tools. You can configure it to use a text editor of your choice.

COMMIT MESSAGES

If you're a developer, you'll empathize with what I'm about to say. Do you remember a time when you had to fix a bug and you had to do the following?

- Check a vast number of logs with unhelpful commit messages such as "fix variable type."
- Understand the code corresponding to each commit, so you could find the root cause.

This is where effective commit messages come into play. Sure, at some point someone must dive into the code to fix a bug. Effective commit messages just make it easier to do a fast, first-level investigation to identify where the root cause may be. The anatomy of a commit message is beyond this post, but there are a few things I'd like to discuss here:

- There's no reason not to write a good commit message. You just need a **title of 50 characters or less** and a description, where **each line is less than 72 characters**. These character-length guidelines help you keep a balance between too much brevity or too much verbosity. If you're struggling to meet these constraints, it may mean your commits are too big. In that case, make your commits more atomic.
- The title of the message should **explain the purpose of the commit**. This helps someone examining multiple messages identify which commit corresponds to the change they're looking for.
- **Describe the commit** so anyone looking at it in the future can understand the scope of the change you've made, without getting into the code itself.
- **Use integrations** so your commits reflect on your task board. These are excellent proxies for status updates. For example, Jira integrates with GitHub, GitLab, and BitBucket.

I find Hoorvash Nikoo's guide and the Conventional Commits guide very useful. I'm sure you can find a dozen other useful guides to learn how to write commit messages. These are the most fundamental units of communication in a distributed project. Take some time to examine the quality of commit messages on your project and figure out how you can improve your own messages if you're writing code as well. If your tool allows it, you can apply the discipline you apply to code messages even to how you edit your team's handbook pages. A short message about what you changed on the page can save others the effort of comparing page revisions to nail down the changes.

┌─ RESOURCE ───

Train Yourself to Write Better Commit Messages

Simple command-line tools like Commitzen can teach you to write effective commit messages. All you do at the time of a commit is type git cz. The tool will then ask you a few questions and will then create a neat commit message for you.

PULL REQUESTS

Finally, let's talk about pull requests (PRs). I left this trail for the very end, because it's popular and controversial in equal parts. The feature, which most source-control systems provide (GitLab calls it a *merge request* [MR]), allows anyone who wants to contribute code to a project to package their changes so someone can review their code before merging it into the codebase. In theory, it's a systemic approach to facilitate code reviews.

No doubt, I know many teams use PRs or MRs as the means for code reviews. On the other hand, I know that many of my colleagues prefer a trunk-based development approach, combined with pair programming. My colleague and author, Kief Morris, considers this latter approach more aligned to continuous integration. Undoubtedly, PRs introduce a delay in the system. Consider this informal study by my colleague Ryan Boucher:

> Ninety-one percent of PRs had zero comments (about 7,000 in 2020), and the total time spent waiting (from creation to resolve) was about 130,000 hours in 2020.

Those figures highlight that code reviews driven by PRs may become a time-consuming check-the-box activity. The overhead of pull requests also has inadvertent consequences. For example, it's common practice for developers to refactor adjacent code when they're fixing a bug or writing a new feature. PRs seem to discourage this behavior. Here's what my colleague Dan Mutton says:

> On every project I've been on that uses PRs, the overhead has all but stopped people from doing small "just while I'm in the area" improvements (e.g., fixing a misnamed test, a readme change, a minor refactor). Refactoring in the feature branches still happens, but only really in places the feature is touching. Who really wants to go through the whole process of creating a branch, code, and PR

and then chase people for a minor change? Where they have done so, there are many examples of these PRs lying dormant, becoming quickly out of sync and then deleted in a half-yearly cleanup.

So that's the controversy. That said, PRs are popular, and you may not have a say on whether your team uses them. You may see more value in them than my colleagues do. If your team does not pair, then this may be an effective option to ensure code quality. If so, you must communicate clearly in your PR. Keavy McMinn's article is a simple guide to writing pull requests. Here are a few good practices I'd like to highlight:

- **Communicate purpose clearly.** Explain not just what has changed but why. For example, if you're adding new functionality, reference the user story you're implementing.
- **Use integrations** with your task board. As I've mentioned earlier, Jira's integrations with GitHub, GitLab, and BitBucket make it easy to reference the tickets in question.
- **Explain your implementation**, especially if some parts of it may not be clear by just examining the code. Use videos, sketches, or diagrams to clarify your explanation. Ideally, these should already be part of the task on your task board.
- If you're reviewing a PR, **be respectful when providing feedback.** Do your best to understand before you offer suggestions. Help the author understand the rationale behind your suggestions.
- If you're the author of the request, **be open to feedback.** This is your chance not only to improve your code but also to create a healthy engineering culture.
- PRs are notorious for the lag they introduce. Reviewers and authors need to collaborate with each other in a thoughtful and timely fashion, so **keep the waiting time minimal.** Track PR pickup time (the time a PR spends waiting for someone to start reviewing it) and review time (the time it takes to complete a code review and merge the code). Short pickup times and review times are indicators of a healthy collaboration and feedback culture.

— BEST PRACTICE ——————————————

Be Pragmatic About Pull Requests

Not every merge needs a full-blown code review. Tools like gitStream allow developers to merge small and safe code changes with an automatic approval. You can specify rules for higher-risk changes—such as to go through a specific reviewer or to go through more than one reviewer.

TRAILS AS THE MOST FREQUENT FORM OF DOCUMENTATION

We started discussing documentation in Chapter 10 when we addressed the need for a team handbook. This chapter covered the five pieces of documentation, aka the audit trails you'll create in the flow of everyday work (Figure 18.3). These'll help you make sense of where you are at any point in time.

─ RESOURCE ──────────────

Examples of Audit Trails

For your reference, the companion site (https://www.asyncagile.org/book-resources) has examples of all the five audit trails that we've discussed in this chapter. Use these examples to build your understanding of how you might create such artifacts on your team.

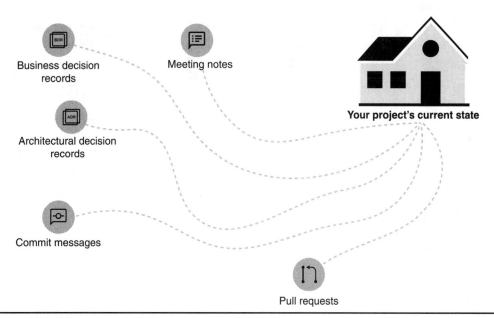

Business decision records

Meeting notes

Architectural decision records

Your project's current state

Commit messages

Pull requests

Figure 18.3 Five audit trails that your async-first team needs.

CHAPTER SUMMARY

Audit trails allow the team to backtrack from the current state of a project or codebase and understand why things are a certain way. These are the most frequent forms of documentation on a software development team:

- **Meeting notes.** These help you share outcomes of a meeting with the rest of the team, in an easy-to-consume format.
- **Business decision records.** These documents track the business-driven decisions you make as a team and for the software you're building.
- **Architectural decision records.** Each time you make a change to the architecture of the system, log the decision in an ADR document. These documents serve as a record of how the software's architecture has changed with time.
- **Commit messages.** Developers create these each time they make a change to the project. It helps the rest of the team understand how the code has changed and why.
- **Pull requests.** These represent a mechanism to contribute changes to a codebase and to receive feedback about these changes. If you manage these well, they can be a great tool for code reviews and a healthy collaboration culture.

You cannot build Rome in a day, so I suggest examining these audit trail practices one at a time. Commit as a team to improve at least one or two practices every two weeks or every sprint if you're following scrum. Find a champion for each of these practices so they can hold everyone accountable. As those audit trails become more apparent and frequent, you'll notice it's easier to find your way back home. Next up, let's look at some less frequent documentation to communicate ideas and about design.

COMMUNICATE TECH AND FUNCTIONAL DESIGN

Software development is a costly business. That's why we obsess over ways to reduce risk and cognitive load. Some examples are smaller requirements through user stories, pair programming, simple design, and unit testing. While it helps to break a problem into small, constituent parts, it's important to understand the big picture of where these small pieces fit.

A lack of shared understanding at the delivery stage can be chaotic, and the chaos increases exponentially with team size. In Chapter 10, we referred to the parable of blind people and the elephant. It's a metaphor for how different people with incomplete information can perceive the same thing differently.

The closer a piece of work is to development, the better you want the team to understand the design that leads to this work. You want to make the elephant visible. Purposeful artifacts can help you communicate design details within a team, at speed.

AN AGILE APPROACH TO DESIGN

Over the last decade and a half, the agile movement has found ways to bring design to the center of how we develop products. This has led to several little innovations in the way we design and deliver software, be it user story mapping, design sprints, dual track development, or any other design thinking–inspired approach you're familiar with.

In my experience, the agile design philosophy addresses two sentiments:

- **Build the right thing.** Converging on the ideas that have most value for customers of the product
- **Build the thing right.** Bringing those ideas to life through an iterative engineering approach that places a premium on quality

On many of my projects, my colleagues and I have addressed these two sentiments in parallel. Continuous delivery goes hand in hand with continuous tech and functional design.

The process of continuous design is beyond this book. I want to focus on how we communicate about design. So, in this chapter, I'll show you three techniques to share our design thinking asynchronously. All three techniques are relevant to in-flight projects, and they address technical, user experience (UX), and functional design.

┌─ RESOURCE ─────────────────────────────

Write the Docs

If you have an interest in documentation, consider joining the "Write the Docs" community. They organize regular conferences, have newsletters you can subscribe to, and also have a Slack network you can reach out to for help. Plus, their site map has tons of useful guides and templates to help you learn how to create effective documentation for your team.

IDEA PAPERS

Give credit where it's due. I didn't have a name for this before I read *Effective Remote Work* by James Stanier. In my teams, we'd just have a generic, unimaginative name for it. You know, something as boring as *shared document* or *wiki page*. I like the term *idea paper* much better. It's as straightforward as it sounds. It all starts with an idea. The trigger could be something internal, such as a clunky framework that's causing developers a world of pain. It could also be something external, such as usage data for your product or insight from competitor analysis. If you believe you have a way to solve a problem for your team or your stakeholders, write it down!

New ideas are fragile. They need care and nurturing. You must develop them without the pressure to explain them with charisma, in a room (or Zoom) full of people. When you take the time to write it down, you can make all your assumptions explicit:

- Enrich it with data and illustrate it if it helps.
- Do you expect questions? Add an FAQ.
- Are you clear about how to implement it? Throw in some implementation details.

It doesn't have to be long. In fact, I suggest you make your idea paper easy to scan and as crisp as possible. Once you write things up, everyone learns about your idea in a consistent fashion. None of that blind people and elephant stuff.

- If they have feedback; they add a comment. You respond and strengthen the idea.
- When they have questions, they ask inline. You can then enrich the FAQ.

By the end of a round of feedback, your colleagues have inspected your idea, and you've had the chance to enrich it. When everyone has the same information, it also facilitates decisions, especially if the team must agree to implement the idea.

As I say this, I must share what I think is the team's responsibility when reading an idea paper. The fine folks at 37signals say it much better than I ever will.

> We don't want reactions. We don't want first impressions. We don't want knee-jerks. We want considered feedback. Read it over. Read it twice, three times even. Sleep on it. Take your time to gather and present your thoughts—just like the person who pitched the original idea took their time to gather and present theirs. That's how you go deep on an idea.

You're better off slowing down this process than trying to rush through it. As we discussed in Chapter 11, speed and productivity aren't the same thing. If you take the time to let an idea develop, you'll see the payoff when you deliver it at speed.

FEATURE BREAKDOWN DOCUMENTS

Business analysts, product managers, and product owners usually work a few sprints or weeks ahead of the team to define the mechanics of certain features or system capabilities. Feature breakdown documents are a great tool to align the team on all aspects of implementation, from the business context to the details. Fear not—this isn't a long system requirement specification from the days of yore. Effective feature breakdown docs are brief and help connect various artifacts. They don't serve as product documentation. Instead, they're a reference for the development team. Here's what I include in my feature docs:

- Business context and success metrics, if any.
- A brief explanation of how it'll work.
- Links to any of the applicable artifacts:
  - Research about end users and feedback, if any.
  - Mockups, wireframes, or clickable prototypes.
  - User stories and epics that this feature relates to.
- A list of frequently asked questions. You can create this as you get reactions from people.

Confluence, Notion, and other tools have built-in templates to help you write your feature documents. The reason feature documents are powerful is that you can enrich them as you go. Often, we build the minimal version of a feature and wait for feedback to enhance it. When you get that feedback, guess where you link it up? The feature doc! What about new user stories? Where do you reference them? Of course, the feature doc. How about known issues? No brainer, eh? Use them well, and the document can be a powerful, single source of truth to describe the life cycle of a feature or system capability.

─ BEST PRACTICE ───────────────

Make Your Own Templates (MYOT)

After you've gained some experience writing these design artifacts, you'll settle on a format that works for you. Instead of starting from a generic template that your tools offer you, consider creating templates that the rest of the team can reuse. This'll also drive a consistent way to communicate about design within the team.

TECHNICAL DESIGN DOCUMENTS

The technical counterpart to functional, feature documents are *design docs*. If architectural decision records (ADRs) are the summary, design docs are often the detail that lead to that summary. Much like idea papers, design docs allow the team to slow things down and articulate various design aspects of architecture and software solutions. The team can use the design doc as the working artifact to refine their thinking, respond to each other's feedback, and build consensus. When the design process is complete, someone in the team can log the ADR as a summary of the process. A good practice is either to store the design docs with the codebase or to add them in a clearly signposted area of the team handbook.

Depending on the design decision you're taking, it can include several details. Here are some that are common. Figure 19.1 illustrates the structure of a standard design document.

- **Context and scope.** Describes the background, setting, and boundaries of the design problem being addressed.
- **Goals and nongoals.** Outlines the intended outcomes and what the design should achieve and what it should not do.
- **Actual design.** Explains the proposed solution in detail, including the system context diagram, APIs, data storage, code and pseudocode, and any constraints that must be considered.
- **Alternatives.** Discusses other possible approaches to solving the design problem and why the proposed design is the best option.
- **Cross-functional requirements.** Identifies and addresses any issues or factors that cut across the design and may impact its implementation or performance. These could include requirements such as security, privacy, usability, or monitoring.

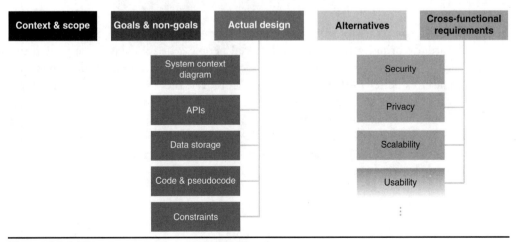

Figure 19.1 The structure of a technical design document.

A good design doc should be short enough to read in 15 to 20 minutes, though as the guide says, it's quite possible to write a one- to three-page "mini design doc." In fact, a shorter design doc is often a symptom of a smaller design problem—something all teams should strive for. The bigger the challenge, the hairier the solution and the longer it takes to build consensus around it.

This said, effective design documents also need detail. Even if you don't write them down, the details are out there. They're implicit. By not writing them, you play a game of telephone, where everyone has a different interpretation of the details. The broader the impact of the design you're proposing and the larger the team, the more misinterpretations will hurt you. So, get into the details and take the time to read the details.

RESOURCE

Learn from Examples

While the resources I've shared in this chapter will help you learn more about each kind of document I've described, I've also put together a few examples on the companion site (https://www.asyncagile.org/book-resources). In the interest of simplicity, I've chosen relatively domain-agnostic topics for each document. This'll help you learn from relatable examples.

SIMPLIFY COMMUNICATION COMPLEXITY

As team size increases, communication becomes more complex. Small teams will eventually bring in new people. Tenured people will someday leave your team. Such is life. Team size and churn aside, you'll find that complex decisions lend themselves better to the written word. Moreover, there are limits to what people can remember, so it makes sense to commit things to writing. In this chapter, we covered three kinds of documents that help you communicate about design in a software development team. So keep calm, slow down, and write the docs! Once you see how they help you drive shared understanding, there will be no looking back.

CHAPTER SUMMARY

When you avoid big up-front design, you will inevitably design your software in parallel with delivering it. To communicate ideas and functional or technical design, three kinds of documents come handy:

- **Idea papers** allow you to nurture fresh ideas by articulating them clearly. People can use an idea paper as a reference to share feedback and enrich the idea. Decision-making is also easier if everyone can understand the idea well.

- **Feature breakdown documents** serve as a single resource to catalog all information about a feature. As the team enhances the feature, this document becomes a single source of truth about it.

- **Technical design docs** are an efficient way to communicate about software architecture and technical solutions. These docs precede an architectural decision record. They benefit from detail, though brevity is an important consideration too.

In Chapter 18, we addressed the most frequent types of documentation you need: audit trails. In this chapter, we addressed slightly less frequent design documentation. To round off this exploration of documents, let's explore some even more stable artifacts. That's the next chapter.

TWO STABLE PIECES OF HANDBOOK DOCUMENTATION

Our discussion about documentation brings us back full circle to our handbook. The reason I've taken you on this journey is to explore the documents you'll create, from the most frequent to the most stable. While we've discussed the team handbook already in Chapter 10, there are two sections that deserve a detailed look. These relate to documentation that you'll create to help others join your team and hit the ground running without much fuss.

BEING AGILE ABOUT DOCUMENTATION

When you reflect on the previous two chapters, you'll notice that we're not aiming for comprehensive documentation. Instead, we're identifying patterns of documentation that help you communicate effectively in your team. Before we dive into this chapter, let me share five principles about documentation that I've followed on my projects:

- Documentation for the sake of documentation is problematic and wasteful. Documents must serve a purpose. As a corollary, when a document ceases to serve its purpose, we should archive it so it's clear to everyone that it may no longer be relevant.
- Prefer dynamic, automated documentation for things that change frequently, e.g., code. A team's writing efforts must prioritize documenting things that are stable.
- The lighter the documentation, the easier it is to consume and iteratively improve. Anyone writing documents must practice brevity as a skill.

- People consume documentation in specific contexts. This makes the location of the document just as important as its content. Writing a great document is not enough. You must also place it in the right spot so people can retrieve it efficiently.

- Outdated documents can shake a team's faith in documentation. This means that we should not budget only for the cost of creating documentation but also that of maintaining it.

In the spirit of focusing on stable, purposeful, and lightweight documentation, let's zoom into two areas of your team handbook. You'll remember that we visualized the structure of the handbook in two parts, as in Figure 20.1: project context and project content. Each of the two documents we'll discuss in this chapter sits in a different part:

- Ways of working, as part of the project context
- Codebase README files, as part of the project content

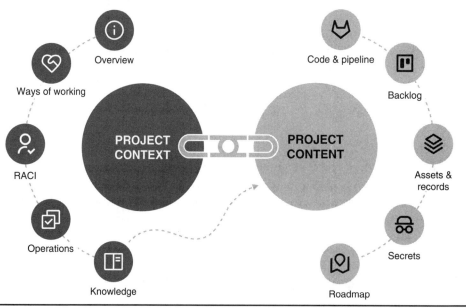

Figure 20.1 The structure of a project handbook.

Let's explore them in some detail.

YOUR WAYS OF WORKING

When a new team member joins your team, they're itching to start strongly. You want to minimize guesswork for them. We'll cover onboarding in detail in the next chapter. In terms of documentation, though, here are some questions you should answer up front, in writing:

- **How do you collaborate as a team?** Do you pair program by default, or do you work independently and do code reviews after? What's the process for code reviews? When teams pair program, they like to have some consistency in how everyone sets up their laptops. Do you have any guidelines for that?

  Add details about how you practice standups, story kickoffs, desk checks, and other collaboration techniques. Even within the same company, especially within consulting firms like mine, there are variations in how teams conduct the same practices, so it's best not to leave things to guesswork. Be sure to link up your team's communication protocols (Chapter 6) here.

- **What are the different environments you have on the project?** Different teams have different environments such as development, QA, UAT, staging, and production environments. Each of these environments will have different permissions and credentials, access control, and deployment protocols. If they need to set up access, then the instructions should be clear.

  Your developers will also need to know about what level of analysis, monitoring, and alerts you have set up so you can learn about the health of the system and fix issues when necessary.

- **How do you track project metrics?** It's tough to improve things we don't measure. Teams use tools such as LinearB, SonarQube, or Waydev to assess themselves on several parameters, including code quality, four key metrics, and nonfunctional requirements such as security, maintainability, reliability, performance, and a lot more. Even if your new developers don't have experience with all your tooling, it helps to give them a lay of the land right at the start.

While these are some fundamental aspects of your ways of working, you may be able to think of other aspects of collaboration that you must include on these handbook pages. The goal should be to provide anyone on the team with a reference of how you've agreed to engage with each other as a team.

┌─ BEST PRACTICE ─

Write a Team API

It's likely that your team doesn't work in isolation. Other teams may depend on you in some way, and vice versa. To help guide these interactions, a Team API comes in handy. Much like APIs describe how to programmatically interact with software, a team API describes to other teams how they can interact with you. Matthew Skelton and Manuel Pais provide a handy template for Team APIs as part of their work on Team Topologies. You can use that as a starting point.

CODEBASE README FILES

Depending on the size of your project, you'll have one or more repositories, and each of them needs some minimal documentation. We don't want to document things that will change frequently, for example, the code itself. Your code should self-document through the following:

- Using thoughtful naming
- Eliminating code smells
- Comprehensive unit tests

This by itself is a mindset shift. For code to be easy to read, the entire development team must acknowledge that code is documentation as well. Only then will you see the team adopt coding patterns and practices that support such clarity.

Aside from clean, readable code, you must document the stable stuff. These are things you don't want to say to each developer repeatedly. A suitable place to do this is right in the codebase, in a good, old README file, at the top level of your project folder. This is usually the first file people see on a project, so there's an incentive to make it useful. And there are tons of resources to guide you to do this well. I particularly like Kira's, aka hackergrrl's, "Art of README."

Here are a few sections you should include:

- **The project title and description.** Obvious, right? If you have a say in the project's name, please keep it intuitive. If you've inherited an unintuitive name, maybe explain where the name came from. You also want to explain what the software does.
- **Installation and usage.** A new developer will want to install and use the software to learn how it works. Simple step-by-step install instructions are helpful. Be sure to list dependencies, if any. You also want to show them how you run and use the software. If a video helps here, link it in. List terminal commands step-by-step. If developers need to specify some environment variables, list those as well. Be careful not to list privileged information here, though. Use other means to share project secrets.
- **Visuals and code overview.** If you have a high-level architecture diagram or a dependency graph or UML diagram, link it in here. Be as brief as you can when describing the code. Ideally, a picture should speak a thousand words, and you may get away with a few bullet points to supplement the images.

In addition, depending on the context, you may need to add contribution and support info, links to API specs, the ADR folder, and other details. Many sections of the README file will remain stable for a long time. By cross-linking to other artifacts, such as API specs, you can limit the number of updates you need to make to this file. A good practice is to set up a team reminder to review this file quarterly.

RESOURCE

Tools to Create README Files

If you haven't written a README before, fear not. Here are two tools that'll help you generate these files with the complete Markdown syntax. All you need to do is pick the sections you need in your file.

- Make a README
- Readme.so (Figure 20.2)

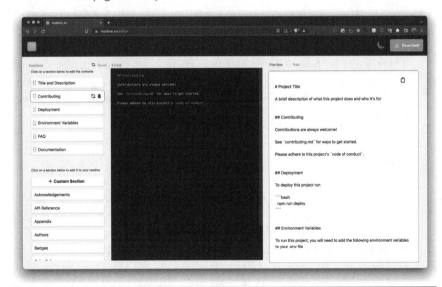

Figure 20.2 Representation of using readme.so to generate a README for your codebase.

DOCUMENTING CODE? THINK TWICE

Clean coding principles and a comprehensive test suite can preempt the need for traditional code documentation, such as code manuals, technical writing in separate files, or even detailed comments in the codebase, that separately describe the code. This is not to say that code documentation isn't necessary. It takes time for people to wrap their heads around even a very well-managed codebase. So, it helps to think about ways to simplify your developer experience. To avoid going around in circles with the never-ending task of documenting code, though, I recommend supporting your developers with automated solutions. Here are a few examples:

- CodeSee autogenerates interactive codebase diagrams on different tech stacks. This can help speed up people's understanding of the codebase and the impact of the changes they're making. The maps can also help simplify the code review process.
- StepSize allows developers to document tech debt in line with the code they're looking at right then. Your team has a clear incentive to ensure you're tracking tech debt, especially if it's easy to document it from within the IDE.
- Glean helps tie together multiple information sources on your project through a universal search. That way, if you have multiple tools like Jira, Confluence, or GitHub, you can minimize the number of clicks it takes to get to the right piece of information.

There'll always be new tools on the horizon, so the previous list doesn't seek to be comprehensive. It's merely a nudge so you think in the general direction of automating as much of the developer experience as you possibly can, especially tasks such as documentation.

GOOD DOCUMENTS REDUCE GUESSWORK

The best documentation is the one that scratches a real itch. You experience its power by writing once and running many times. By "responding with a link," you can cut down on several avoidable meetings. Of course, documentation works best when you focus on things that won't change often. This chapter rounds off our exploration of documents and artifacts for your team, starting from audit trails to design documentation and now ways of working and READMEs.

CHAPTER SUMMARY

To help new developers hit the ground running and to keep your entire dev team aligned, you need some stable, lightweight documentation.

- Clearly state your ways of working, especially how you collaborate in the team, your environments and access control, and your project metrics.

- Write a sharp README file for each code repository that helps developers start contributing to that codebase in a short time.

You'll find examples of both documents on the companion site (https://www. asyncagile.org/book-resources). Limit your documentation efforts to solve real problems. Where possible, automate documentation using modern tools so everything is always up-to-date.

Effective, lightweight documentation has one of its biggest payoffs in efficient onboarding. It makes sense then to discuss onboarding in the next chapter, before we close off this part of the book.

21

CRAFT AN EFFICIENT ONBOARDING PROCESS

Writing things up coherently takes effort. In fact, this makes asynchronous work feel daunting to beginners. If you look back at the principle of balance from Chapter 4, you'll notice that asynchronous communication optimizes for the future, even if it's tougher in the moment. This also helps your team become more productive and efficient.

Onboarding is an area where you'll see visible payoffs for the effort you spend in writing things up. James Stanier says, "Onboarding speed is a function of your technical, managerial and cultural efficiency." I agree.

So, in this chapter, let's explore a mindset shift and four ideas to help bring people aboard your team. Our handbook, developer documentation, and other artifacts will be among the key resources to power your onboarding experience.

WRITE ONCE, RUN MANY TIMES

Without written artifacts, onboarding can be a cumbersome process. You have to share all information in conversations and meetings. Not only is this redundant, it's hard to keep these conversations consistent. You could keep the information somewhat consistent by having just one person do all onboarding, but that makes the entire process fragile. Do you stop onboarding people onto the team if that person falls sick, goes on a vacation, or, worse, leaves the company?

Even if you have one person do all the onboarding, they'll eventually get bored. You'll then have to make your process inconsistent by bringing in more people to do this. The alternative is to let the same person have the conversation a little differently each time, just to keep themselves interested. None of these situations is ideal.

Well-written onboarding documentation is an upgrade to these fragile, redundant, and ephemeral conversations. Here are some advantages:

- When you share these assets so they're visible to everyone, the entire team can co-create and improve these assets.
- People can join your team any time—you don't have to batch and queue people for onboarding sessions.
- When people have questions, they can drop them in line with the materials. Anyone on the team can respond to these questions and either improve the materials or enhance the FAQ.
- Each time you onboard someone, they see the latest version of these materials. They're persistent, and they keep getting better.

To reduce communication overheads, we must shift our remote onboarding approach to being document-centric. Figure 21.1 illustrates this shift. And guess what! You've already created all of this content as part of your handbook and your developer documentation. You just need to curate it so you don't overwhelm your new colleagues. More on that in a bit as we get into the mindset shift and the four ideas.

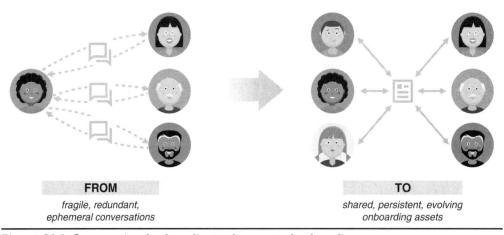

FROM	TO
fragile, redundant, ephemeral conversations	*shared, persistent, evolving onboarding assets*

Figure 21.1 Conversational onboarding to documented onboarding.

PRESERVE THE DUMB QUESTIONS BUDGET WITH AN FAQ

Joining a team in flight is hard. Even if everyone's friendly, new hires have many fears and trepidations running through their mind. In geeky organizational cultures, many new hires doubt their skills and experience, and they feel the fear of "being exposed." We know this as the impostor syndrome. There's also an implicit "dumb questions budget" in everyone's head. New hires want to seem competent. Given a chance, they'd like to ask only the questions that are necessary. Cate Huston, engineering director, DuckDuckGo, says this:

> Anything any new hire on my team wants to know is written down somewhere. They can find it out; they don't have to use their dumb questions budget. People often don't want to ask too many stupid questions that limit themselves. They can go and read whatever they want to read. And then they can come with better questions and have an interesting conversation.

No question is truly "dumb." It may be from your perspective, but not so much for someone new to your team. When structuring your handbook and your onboarding materials, be sure to expect these questions and answer them in an FAQ page. Enrich the FAQ as you encounter more questions. This is how your materials stay fresh and relevant. You also show empathy for your new teammates this way.

BUILD AN ONBOARDING CHECKLIST

When you think about onboarding at its most basic level, it's a series of steps that allow a new hire to contribute to a team. A precise checklist takes away the guesswork from this process. Document what the new hire must do, by when they need to do it, and how. Here are a few tips to design the checklist:

- **Focus on the essentials.** It can be tempting to throw the kitchen sink at your new hires. Instead, think of the shortest path to productivity. What's the least they must do before they make their first contribution to the project?
- **Start with verbs.** The checklist should have a list of actions for the new hire to perform. This could include reading some documentation, completing some paperwork, getting access, or studying a course. Phrase these checklist items such that they start with a verb. That way, the new hire knows exactly what they must do.
- **Make it the onboarding hub.** Link the checklist items to their associated resources. For example, if the new hire has to fill out a form, link the corresponding checklist item to the form. If they have to learn something new, link to the course they must complete. Be sure to provide a point of contact if you expect they may get blocked. These points of contact can be on a per-item basis or for the entire onboarding journey.
- **Provide due-by dates.** Just so the onboarding process doesn't drag on, provide a due-by date for each checklist item. That way, the new hires can keep themselves accountable. To make the checklist generic, you can keep the date ranges broad—e.g., what to do in the first week versus what to finish in the first 30 days.

- **End with reflections.** The last step in your onboarding checklist should be a reflection exercise. This is the ideal time for the new hire to look back at their onboarding experience and share what's gone well and what could be better. These inputs can help improve the onboarding experience for future team members.

The key here is to think like a designer. The design of your onboarding journey should be subtractive, not additive. That mindset will help you keep things lightweight so you don't overwhelm your new teammates. As Antoine de Saint-Exupery famously said,

> A designer knows he has achieved perfection not when there is nothing left to add, but when there is nothing left to take away.

— RESOURCE —

Example of an Onboarding Checklist

Figure 21.2 illustrates an example of a concise onboarding checklist, which you can download from the companion site (https://www.asyncagile.org/book-resources).

Welcome aboard!

To help you hit the ground running, we've put together a simple checklist for you to follow. Each item on this list links to related resources on our shared drive. By the time you get to the end of these steps, you should be able to achieve the following goals.
1. Connect to our project systems.
2. Learn how our application works.
3. Become familiar with how we've structured our tech stack.
4. Anchor a story card with another developer.

Task	How to complete	Who to contact
☑ Read the high-level developer notes	Read the document and use it as a reference to complete the remaining onboarding steps.	Buddy
☑ Connect to the VPN	Without this, you won't be able to access anything other than email without this. If you aren't able to access VPN, contact techops-support@thoughtworks.com	TechOps
☑ Gain access to BitBucket + JIRA + Confluence + CircleCI	Check your inbox for credentials. This is part of your systems onboarding package.	Project manager
☑ Explore how the app works and learn which release/features are in which environments	Play around with the application on the QA/ UAT environments. You can use the test data from _this spreadsheet_.	QA
☑ Understand the layers of our tech stack	Watch the embedded video. Feel free to ask questions on the document itself. One of us will respond and we'll also enrich the document if an additional explanation helps.	Tech lead
☑ Run full stack locally	_Refer to the list of commands and the process_ you must follow to run the full stack on your machine.	Buddy
☐ Develop a story card	Learn how to pull from master, create a branch for your card, and _our standard for commit messages_.	Buddy/ pair
☐ Create a pull request and push your code	Learn how to move your card from "pending merge" to "merged not deployed"!	Buddy/ pair
☐ Retrospect with your buddy and share feedback about the onboarding process	Pay it forward by helping the onboarding process get better the next time around.	Buddy

Figure 21.2 An example of an onboarding checklist.

FOCUS ON AUTOMATION AND REUSABILITY

If your team or department is onboarding developers regularly, then it helps to provide them with tools so they can set up their development environment quickly. Not only can they contribute to the project soon, it will also improve your team's overall efficiency.

For example, on one of my previous teams, we've used Vagrant to create a virtual machine on developer laptops, which contained all the software and components for the standard development environment. This kind of approach allows new hires to easily set up their development environment with a few documented steps, without help from anyone else.

Here are a couple of other options:

- Use a script-based solution to build and share your development environments. DevEnv is a great open-source tool that can help you do this using prebuilt packages for various tech stacks.
- You can use containers to run consistent development environments. For example, Visual Studio's dev containers allow you to use a container as a full-fledged development environment.

If you look around, the open-source community provides a variety of tools for you to define and share your team's development environment. At the time of writing this chapter, there are more than 1,000 different projects to solve this problem. Pick one that works for you.

On some larger, cross-functional teams I've been part of, we've built out a developer portal that makes everyday tasks easier. Through such portals, you can share a variety of assets and information:

- **Software templates.** Instead of starting from scratch, developers can build components from consistent starting points. These templates have some standard boilerplate code, which also helps drive coding best practices and patterns.
- **APIs and events.** Exploring APIs and events organized by domains allows developers to reuse existing system capabilities.
- **Developer tools.** Often you'll build starter kits and tools that can accelerate the developer experience. This includes proprietary internal frameworks.

As you may imagine, this kind of platform takes away guesswork for new hires by making it easy for them to reuse existing capabilities and patterns. But its utility isn't only for new hires. At Thoughtworks, such a platform has sped up ideas to outcomes by an average of 30 percent. Figure 21.3 contains a few screenshots of this platform that we call NEO. Backstage is a great tool to build out your development platform should you have the appetite for it.

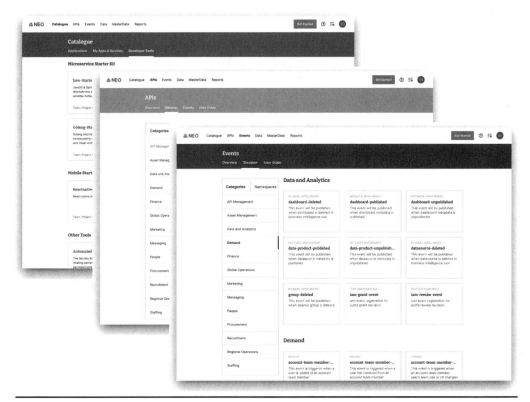

Figure 21.3 Representation of Thoughtworks' internal developer platform, *NEO*.

FIND THE NEW HIRE A BUDDY

Instituting a buddy system is an effective way for everyone in the team to participate in the onboarding process. Each time someone joins the team, pair them with someone else in a similar role. The buddy becomes the new hire's tour guide in the team. They can be a sounding board for questions, the person who makes introductions to others and also the first port of call for help.

Checklists can help set expectations for the buddy as well. Align the new-hire's checklist to the buddy's checklist to facilitate shared accountability. For example, if you expect the new hire to attend a team happy hours call, then expect the buddy to introduce the new hire to everyone else on that same call.

As more people become new-hire buddies, they'll learn about the onboarding experience. This'll create a feedback loop so the onboarding materials and the process stays fresh. Expect buddies to add ideas to improve the onboarding process in a shared space. This could be a separate backlog that the team reviews every few weeks.

FOSTER STRONG RELATIONSHIPS

What's a team without relationships? The sooner your new teammates experience the sense of togetherness and camaraderie, the easier they'll settle into your ways of working. An async-first culture needs trust. You trust people who you have great relationships with. So don't underestimate this part of onboarding. This is where meaningful synchronous interactions come into play. Real-time communication is great for building connectedness, so use them to integrate people into your team.

First, establish the reporting relationship for the new hire. Reporting managers must set up regular check-ins with their new hires. Use the first few meetings to set expectations with the new hire. These meetings should address not just their role and performance outcomes but also how the manager and direct report will work together. In Chapter 23, I'll address the topic of managerial relationships in more detail.

Second, include the new hire in team activities. We've already discussed why meeting in person is valuable and why you need shared team experiences. At the very least, organize a periodic team "happy hours" when you can catch up to chat without an agenda. This takes nothing to organize, except an hour off everyone's calendar, every few days.

Last but not least, encourage the new hire to meet people one on one. Some people may find it daunting to set up these conversations by themselves. Foster a welcoming atmosphere in the team where experienced teammates voluntarily set up one-on-one meetings to introduce themselves and to get to know their new colleagues. I've found that one-on-one meetings are among the quickest ways to get to know people deeply and to break the ice. Make it easy for newcomers so that regardless of their personality they experience a sense of warmth from their teammates.

ONBOARDING EFFICIENCY = TEAM EFFICIENCY

James Stanier adds that the onboarding equation isn't just about onboarding. Your onboarding efficiency is a proxy for how efficient your team or department is on the parameters of tech, management, and culture. When your new teammates report a high level of satisfaction and a low level of frustration with your onboarding process, you have a proxy for how efficient your team or your department is. When you extend this same efficiency to the entire organization, you'll notice that people can move across teams and departments seamlessly.

CHAPTER SUMMARY

Adopt a write once, run many times approach to creating onboarding assets. You can avoid redundant, ephemeral conversations this way.

- Enrich your FAQs to preserve new hires' "dumb questions budget."
  - Use checklists to take away the guesswork from onboarding.
  - Focus on automation and reuse.
- Use containers or scripts to automate the development environment setup for new hires.
- If you have the appetite for it, set up a development portal to share software templates and to help team members discover APIs, events, and shared developer tools.
  - Assign a buddy for every new hire so they have a friend to guide them in their initial days.
  - Use synchronous interactions to build connectedness and camaraderie with new hires.

Depending on your position in your company, you can improve things at a team, departmental, or organizational level. It's okay if you're not senior enough to change things for the entire company. As with every play in this playbook, first address the areas within your immediate control. Once you feel convinced about your blueprint, advocate it to others in the organization so they can learn from your experiences.

This chapter brings us to the end of Part III of the playbook—the practitioner's guide to being async-first. It's hard, however, to change ways of working without sufficient management and leadership support. In the next part of the book, we'll address practices to manage and lead with an async-first mindset. Even if you aren't in that position yet, you'll find Part IV useful to hold your leaders accountable.

Part IV

ASYNC-FIRST LEADERSHIP

It makes sense to adopt async-first practices at the individual and team levels first. Without effective management and leadership, though, teams may experience the pressure to regress to old, real-time ways of working. This part of the book describes how you can be a supportive leader and adopt an async mindset in your management style.

- **Chapter 22**, "The Async Leadership Mindset," explains the shift in thinking necessary to be an async-first leader. You'll also learn how you can be a champion for inclusion by applying such a mindset.

- In **Chapter 23**, "Manage Your People with Care," you'll learn how to be an effective people manager when you work async-first.

- **Chapter 24**, "Set Up Your Team for Success," helps you learn how to tweak and manage your team environment for efficiency and autonomy.

- Finally, **Chapter 25**, "Farm Tacit Knowledge in Your Company," dives deep into knowledge management at the company level. We'll explore the characteristics of systems you need to farm knowledge in a distributed company and how you can audit your current tools to find out what else you need. You'll also learn about the people you need in place to manage your company's knowledge ecosystem.

22

THE ASYNC LEADERSHIP MINDSET

It's time to shift focus from practitioners and individual contributors to leaders and managers. Asynchronous collaboration benefits from an async-first leadership mindset. Without such leadership, the team can succumb to organizational inertia and its own status quo.

What does it mean to build an async-first leadership mindset? Allow me to explain.

THE TYRANNY OF "THE WAY"

Over the last few years, when I've spoken to managers and leaders about asynchronous work, I've received a variety of responses. If they're remote-work naysayers, then there's an obvious skepticism. It's hard to convince tenured professionals with deeply held biases against remote work, so let's set that problem aside.

The interesting challenge comes from remote-work believers who listen carefully. There are some who can immediately think of ways this "asynchronous work thing" would work for them and their teams. Many leaders, however, see the value for their people, or maybe "other people," but claim it won't work for them. I hear statements such as the following:

> "Oh, but my job can't happen async!"

> "You know, my job involves talking to people. It's tough to do that async!"

> "I get it, but it won't work for me."

None of these concerns is unfounded. For example, many of us have learned that "the way" to lead is to manage by walking around and listening (MBWAL). You can't do that async, can you? Can you?

Let me make something clear. I don't disagree that there are parts of your work that need synchrony. We'll address those bits in upcoming chapters. But before that, let's examine the "Oh, but my job can't happen async!" mindset. I want to do that through a series of questions.

HOW CAN YOU GET THE MOST OUT OF YOURSELF?

Let's go back to first principles. Asynchronous work is not the goal. It's a means to an end. We've discussed the benefits of asynchronous work already. Which of these benefits would you like to experience in your own work life? I want to revisit a few ideas with you that may help you think about your work a bit differently.

Escape Recurring Meeting Hell

Take a good, hard look at your own calendar. How many meetings are recurring? Don't count your one-on-one meetings with your co-workers. Count the other ones. Chances are you're spending close to 15 hours each week on meetings that are begging for an agenda, not the other way around. Some managers I've observed have a recurring meeting to discuss the agenda for another recurring meeting. Let me restate this differently. These ongoing meetings can consume up to 38 percent of your time every week. That's two in every five hours lost to *meetings without agendas*.

Ask yourself some tough questions about these interactions.

- How many of these meetings have more than eight people? As we've discussed, such meetings can often be a waste of time. Most meetings like these are neither collaborative nor productive.

- How many of these meetings are about passive information transfer? Emails, documents, and even info decks share that information more efficiently. They are also more permanent than a conversation.

- How often do you actively engage in these meetings? If the answer is "occasionally," then must you lose time with them regularly?

I understand that in some work cultures, your bosses may want you to show up in meetings for you to seem "visible." That's a problem we can't solve at the individual level. However, if your organization gives you the autonomy to use your time effectively, then consider voting with your feet for an async-first culture. Decline those recurring meetings.

If you've set up some of these meetings, think about deleting them and freeing up your time. People can still meet up in smaller groups for *agendas that need meetings*. You'll give them back time to do exactly that!

Fewer Meetings, More Effective Meetings

The idea of "meetings as the last resort" exists not to demonize or ban meetings but to make them effective. The odd exception aside, we don't usually create new things in meetings. Either we facilitate the work that happens outside meetings, or we make decisions about that work. Olivier Sibony, Cass Sunstein, and Daniel Kahneman describe the concept of decision hygiene that leads to better decisions.

> Whenever you have different people making judgments, rather than assign the judgment to one person or gathering three people to talk about it around the table, get them to make their judgments independently and take the average of that. Or use some other variation on that theme. But essentially preserve the independence of people's judgments before you aggregate them. That's a big tool.

Think of meetings where you want to make some complex decisions. It's hard to accommodate all the data, surface all perspectives, avoid bias-cascades, and reach consensus inside that time box. You'll recognize many occasions when you've had to rush things just to finish in time.

When you make meetings the last resort, you can give yourself and everyone else time to work independently. Everyone can share their perspective related to the decision. The group gets time to synthesize the data and the information that's relevant. When you come to the meeting, you can now make the same decisions after considering all the data and viewpoints. In fact, your meeting can now be shorter and more efficient! Isn't that a good thing?

Reduce Repetitive Work

How many times do you have to say the same thing to different people? Leaders and managers do a lot of repetitive communication through presentations, walk-throughs, and sharing ideas. While there's value in using your charisma to present an idea live, only a few people get to consume the idea each time. Using asynchronous communication such as blog posts, documents, and recorded audio or video, you can reduce the number of times you say something. Your idea can go viral.

In Chapter 18, we discussed how communication becomes complex, even with relatively small team sizes. A synchronous communication strategy doesn't just force you to be repetitive. It also leaves a lot of room for interpretation and games of telephone.

When you commit something to writing, people can interact with it, ask questions, and leave feedback. This allows you to enrich that piece of communication by either simplifying it or adding an FAQ section. This way, your communication gets better with time and small, incremental efforts. As we've discussed already, write once, run many times.

Amplify Your Voice and That of Your Leadership Counterparts

Leadership and management groups should be diverse. Even if your leadership group doesn't have gender, racial, or caste diversity, you're all diverse in the ways you think and by way of your personalities. Synchronous collaboration often suits extroverts and native English speakers a lot more than it suits others. If you're the silent kind, this style of communication isn't giving you the best chance to express yourself. And if English isn't your first language, then I imagine it's hard to construct and express your thoughts effectively, in real time. Writing allows you to slow things down to your pace. A culture of asynchronous communication allows you to have a voice as well.

Even if you're an extrovert and you speak English fluently, going async helps you. You get thoughtful inputs from people who're unlike you. The diversity of your leadership group shines through. Being a champion of asynchronous communication is a terrific way to be an ally for your less articulate or introverted counterparts.

HOW CAN YOU BE AN EXAMPLE, NOT A BOTTLENECK?

When you're running from one meeting to another, you barely have time to think about work itself. Many conversations are superficial and off-the-cuff. This means people in your team can't collaborate with you the way they may collaborate with each other. You become the weakest link in the async-first culture that you want to create.

James Clear says this:

> Humans are imitation machines. We mostly learn what to do by copying those around us. In general, we imitate the habits of three groups.

1. **The close.** What are friends and family doing?

2. **The many.** What is the crowd doing?

3. **The powerful.** What are those with status doing?

As a leader, you're powerful. You're a role model everyone aspires to be like. If meetings are your first option, then you set the wrong example. First, you derail your team's ability to work asynchronously if they must collaborate with you. Second, anyone who wants to be like you will imitate your meeting-centric schedule and try that with their own colleagues. You don't want that, do you?

HOW CAN YOU AVOID BUSYWORK?

The Longman Dictionary of Contemporary English defines *busywork* as "work that gives someone something to do, but that is not really necessary." How much busywork do you end up doing? I must clarify, I don't want to demean your job. I just want you to make your work meaningful. Let's check out a few examples of busywork:

- Many project managers communicate on behalf of their teams. However, if the team has effective communication patterns already in place, the project manager can focus on something else.

- Managers often spend time on approvals and on ratifying decisions. Apart from high-stakes approvals and irreversible decisions, much of this managerial intervention is unnecessary. How can you remove pointless approvals and hand discretion back to your teams?

- A large volume of support and investigation calls often means something is wrong with the quality or user experience of your product. Should you be paying more attention there instead?

- Why be the internal journalist who consumes updates from the team and radiates it to others? How about championing an enterprise social network? That way, everyone is their own journalist!

The key to avoiding busywork is to take a systems focus over a transactions focus. Table 22.1 explains the difference.

Table 22.1 Transactions Focus vs. Systems Focus

Transactions Focus	Systems Focus
A transactions focus optimizes specific activities, without paying attention to processes, practices, or tools that may help simplify or eliminate the transaction altogether.	A systems focus evaluates the goal of several transactions and seeks to institute processes, practices, and tools that can achieve these goals with as little intervention as possible.

For example, the system of a team handbook eliminates or simplifies the transactions of explaining various aspects of your project to your team members. The system of audit trails creates a project archaeology. That way, anyone interested can make sense of project decisions after the fact. A system of written sprint reviews can eliminate the boring busywork of sprint review meetings, especially when you don't have a big enough demo.

Invest your time in creating systems. It'll not just simplify your team's job and give them time back for meaningful work, but it'll also help you drop busywork and pick interesting problems to solve.

HOW CAN YOU CHAMPION INCLUSION?

As a leader you must help people to bring their diverse perspectives and problem-solving techniques to the fore. Overdoing synchronous communication has its pitfalls. It makes it difficult for introverts, neurodiverse people, and non-native English speakers to be on even footing with extroverts and native English speakers. It can also be limiting for people in a faraway time zone or for people who find the time of the synchronous interaction inconvenient.

This isn't to say that you shouldn't synchronize. You just need to summon the "async-first" mindset and resist being trigger-happy with meetings. Here's how:

- **Unlink the notions of speed and productivity.** As we've discussed, these aren't the same things. "Slowing down" is a feature, not a bug. Thoughtful communication, idea development, and surfacing and interpreting data all benefit from slowing down. Encourage your teams to take their time with topics that deserve attention. The pause will help you include diverse perspectives. Help your team by shielding them from external pressures that could force them to rush the process. Start with enough time on hand so you can avoid cutting corners.
- **Encourage inclusive design.** Communication patterns such as writing level the playing field. Design your communication such that everyone has a voice, not just those who're the loudest, the most experienced, or the most fluent. This applies to your meetings as well. Embrace techniques such as silent meetings to surface independent judgments and inputs before you lean into discussions.
- **Treat communication as a process, not an event.** We can't solve complex problems with episodic, one-and-done communication. Each interaction, each artifact, builds on the other in a game of virtual tag, as you see in Figure 22.1. Encourage your team to empathize with those who may not yet be part of the conversation. Write things up. Use audit trails diligently. These are effective, lightweight methods to play the game of communication tag.

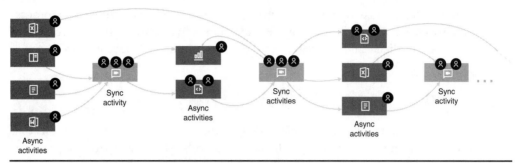

Figure 22.1 Async-first, sync next: communication as a process.

Most companies already provide a digital infrastructure for location-independent collaboration. Embracing asynchronous communication can help you take that infrastructure one step further. Not only will you avoid "Zoom fatigue," but you'll be a champion for inclusion.

HOW CAN YOU MAKE YOUR TEAM RESILIENT?

In the book *Antifragile*, Nassim Taleb describes the idea of "domain dependence."

> Humans somehow fail to recognize situations outside the contexts in which they learn about them… We're all in a way, similarly handicapped, unable to recognize the same idea when it is presented in a different context. It is as if we are doomed to be deceived by the most superficial part of things, the packaging, the gift wrapping.

Talking to leaders about asynchronous work also suffers from domain dependence. People can recognize how going async-first gives a developer or a designer more time and space for high-quality work. They also see how teams can be happier and more effective this way. What they struggle with is to see how asynchronous work can apply in their leadership domain. This makes their part of the organization fragile because many people depend on just one leader.

On agile teams, we have the concept of a "bus factor" to measure the resilience of a team. It refers to the minimum number of people that can suddenly disappear from a team before all work stalls. A synchrony-centric communication approach puts you at the center of information flow. If you disappear, the system can halt. Your bus factor is the lowest possible: 1.

Another world is possible. You make meetings the last resort. You foster thoughtful communication behaviors in the team. You encourage writing as a super-power.

Your systems and artifacts can improve your bus factor. Behavior change, process improvement, and skill building are leadership activities too. This way your team becomes resilient, and you don't need to be their human router anymore.

MAKE TIME FOR THE ESSENTIAL STUFF

At the start of this chapter, I acknowledged that there'll always be situations that need synchrony. As a leader, you'll make trade-offs—between speed and thoughtfulness, between gaining breadth or seeking depth, and between winning the moment or investing in the future. Connectedness will rank high on your priorities too. That's why those one-on-one meetings get a free pass. Spending quality time with people on your team can be among the most impactful things you do as a leader, as can solving difficult problems that'll make your teams' lives easier. To make time for these important pieces of work, an async-first mindset is essential, something we addressed in this chapter.

CHAPTER SUMMARY

If you're leading an async-first team, you must work async-first yourself. This requires a mindset shift.

- Start by thinking how you can get the most out of yourself. Here are a few ideas:
  - Scrutinize your recurring meetings and decline or delete the ones that are "meetings without agendas."
  - Meetings are the last resort. Use that rule to make the meetings you have more efficient.
  - Reduce repetitive communication and save time by committing them to a more permanent medium.
  - Use asynchronous communication to amplify your own voice and to be inclusive of your other leadership counterparts.
- Be the change you want to see in the world. By working asynchronously yourself, you set the right example, and you avoid being a bottleneck for others.
- Reduce the busywork you do by taking a systems focus over a transactions focus.

- Be a champion for inclusion. This involves rethinking collaboration.
  - Unlink the notions of speed and productivity. Many collaborative activities for software development benefit from slowing down.
  - Design inclusive communication. For example, use silent meetings to surface perspectives before diving into discussions.
  - Treat communications as a process and not an event. Use written communication and audit trails to connect various interactions.
- Improve your team's resilience by reducing their dependence on you. Use asynchronous communication, systems, and artifacts to improve your team's bus factor.

When you champion asynchronous work in your company, you won't give up all synchronous communication. You just need to be more thoughtful about it all. So lead by example. When we go async-first, leaders must demonstrate the behavior that they expect everyone else to follow. What you do will make your mindset visible to everyone else.

Next, let's shift the focus to people. Every leader may not be a manager, but every manager is a leader. So, how do you manage people with care? More on that in the following chapter.

MANAGE YOUR PEOPLE WITH CARE

In an async-first culture, the role of a manager is key. If the company is the mothership, the manager is the employee's bridge to it. As a manager, you're the individual who knows the most about your people, their skills, their abilities and strengths, their personalities, and their aspirations. Each of us needs a manager who leads with care.

As counterintuitive as it may seem, a human connection is essential to work effectively in an async-first culture. Managers own a critical part of nurturing these human connections.

CORRECTIONS IN THE RIGHT DIRECTION

In the tech industry the word *manager* is rather unpopular. Companies go to extreme lengths to say they're "flat" or that they have "no managers." They sometimes hide behind euphemisms by naming managerial roles "performance partners," "success catalysts," and whatnot. This doesn't lead to good leadership. The state of denial causes confusion. Since the company doesn't acknowledge that they have bosses, there's no obligation on anyone to be a good boss. At scale, the entire model breaks down, because employees don't see anyone who shows a personal interest in them, their work, and their careers.

I think our industry has overcorrected for the phenomenon of poor managers, aka "bosses." To be fair, it's likely that terrible bosses are just as common as incompetent technologists. It's just that bad bosses hurt more than, say, a designer who can't do their job properly. Instead of training people to be good bosses, we've propagated the myth of flatness. Anyone who's worked in a largish company knows that beyond a certain point there's always a hierarchy. I wish companies fessed up to it instead of tiptoeing around this obvious reality. It's okay. The world will not descend into a black hole if we accept that our "flat culture" has managers. We won't become a worse place to work overnight if we use that word. It'll only make responsibilities clearer.

Regardless of your formal job title, if you're leading people, you're a people manager. So, what can you do to be an *effective* people manager? Especially in an async-first setup? I have three suggestions.

MANAGE YOUR OWN WORKLOAD

First things first, revisit the people management relationships in your sphere of influence. It's hard to manage too many people with care. In many companies, the quest for flatness leaves the only official managers in the system with dozens of direct reports. You must mend this first.

Collaborate with your HR team to establish meaningful reporting relationships between people. This doesn't have to translate into a complex management structure. The idea is to find each individual, a people manager who's close to their work. For example, a tech lead can manage the developers on their team. An engineering manager can work with the tech leads. So on and so forth.

The rule of thumb is to get to a ratio of about 1:5 between managers and their direct reports. Why 1:5? Well, if you're managing people, then you need to spend one-on-one time with them. One hour a day will mean you can meet every direct report, each week. If you can't get to this kind of ratio, you'll always be behind the eight ball and find yourself in one of the following situations:

- You'll either compromise the time you spend each week with people and how well you understand their work.
- Or you'll stretch yourself and spend a lot of time in meetings with very little time for work.

And the second situation doesn't work. As Kim Scott says, you must keep the "dirt under your fingernails."

> In order to be a good partner to the people on your team, and in order to keep the GSD (getting stuff done) wheel spinning efficiently, you need to stay connected to the actual work that is being done—not just by observing others executing but by executing yourself.

The most effective managers don't just understand their people's work at a superficial level. They make time to get into the details. Knowing the details doesn't mean you micro-manage. It means you can help when necessary and that you have contextual, actionable feedback to offer. You can steer people and course-correct if you see the need. Lastly, your people can look to you for advice and coaching. Your presence adds value to their work.

MEET PEOPLE ONE-ON-ONE

That brings me to my favorite, ahem, synchronous, people management activity: one-on-one meetings. In my profession, I alternate between individual contributor and people management roles. My preference is to set aside an hour each week to talk to each of my direct reports. Over the years, I've developed a system for these meetings. Between my direct reports and I, we maintain a tracker, which has a running list of topics that need the other person's attention. The cool thing is that we resolve many of these topics well before the one-on-one by dropping notes in the tracker itself. That then leaves the meeting open for nontransactional conversations. You can use a variety of tools for such a tracker including a traditional task board, a specialized tool like Fellow, or a shared, collaborative document. Figure 23.1 shows a template to track your one-on-one interactions with Trello, a popular task board.

Figure 23.1 Representation of a Trello template to track your one-on-one interactions with a direct report.

Despite being an introvert, I surprise myself with how much I can talk at these meetings. In fact, that's an anti-pattern. This meeting is for the direct report;

give them the space to direct the meeting and take as much airtime as they need. There's always heaps to talk about. Here are some topics I cover in my meetings:

- **Personal well-being.** I like to know how people are doing, not just at work but also if they're comfortable sharing, in their personal lives. I try to be human as well and share what I'm up to. There's nothing special about me as a reporting manager. I just have a few more years or work experience or maybe a little more tenure in the organization. The more my colleagues see that, the more open they can be with me.

- **Sensitive conversations.** Some sensitive conversations can't happen on the tracker. For example, my colleagues may want to talk to me about interpersonal challenges at work. I prefer to address these conversations in a real-time conversation.

- **Progress on expectations.** The reporting relationship usually corresponds with a performance management process. One-on-ones provide a predictable time for both of us to agree on how much progress my direct report has made on their expectations. We don't have to do this each week, but having the space to do it is important. It also gives us room to course correct if we must. I often use this opportunity to evaluate their workload. People's time is a zero-sum game. If a new piece of work comes in, something else must go out. Understanding people's skills, their interests, and their capacity helps me shape their work so they always experience a healthy challenge.

- **Helping each other.** Reporting relationships aside, we're colleagues. I'm quite willing to ask my colleagues or manager for help, though I don't always wait for a one-on-one to do this. The value of the synchronous one-on-one is that both people can brainstorm ways to help in a fast-paced manner. If you're a manager, this is where it helps if you understand the work your people do. You can roll up your sleeves and offer meaningful help. Advice is cheap; execution is costly. By helping, you share some of that execution burden and build a strong relationship between you and your people.

- **Feedback.** In an ideal world, I wouldn't wait for a one-on-one meeting to share feedback. I enjoy sharing feedback in the work's context or the incident I'm giving feedback for. That way people have the chance to act on the feedback, and the specifics are fresh in their minds as well. If the trust level between me and my direct report is high, I'll often share feedback asynchronously as well, especially feedback to strengthen their confidence. However, if I'm trying to improve their effectiveness through feedback and we're still developing our relationship, I prefer waiting for a synchronous opportunity to talk. Sometimes the one-on-one is the earliest available synchronous opportunity.

PRACTICE RADICAL CANDOR

At the start of my Thoughtworks career, I was lucky to work with Patrick Kua. Among other things, Pat taught me that there's no such thing as "negative feedback." Feedback, Pat said, has only two purposes:

- **To strengthen confidence.** Tell the other person what they're doing well that they should continue doing.
- **To improve effectiveness.** Point out what the other person can change so they get better at what they're doing.

Each of these purposes comes from a place of empathy and positivity, so Pat argued that all feedback is positive. If in your mind the feedback is for some other reason, then think again. It's probably not feedback.

Over the years, I've read books like *Crucial Confrontations* that talk about addressing feedback conversations with safety. Between what Pat taught me and all my other reading, I've found the book *Radical Candor* by Kim Scott to be a memorable summary of an effective feedback approach. As Figure 23.2 shows, you display radical candor when you care personally about the people you manage and when you can challenge them directly about their work.

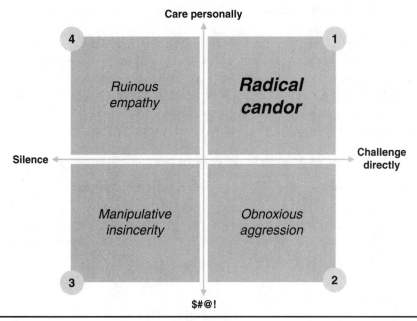

Figure 23.2 *Radical candor* exists at the intersection of caring personally and challenging directly.

While I suggest you read the book to understand the approach in its entirety, here's a summary:

- To **show care**, you must build trust. This takes time. When you share feedback about certain incidents, you can show care by acknowledging the other person's positive intent. You can create safety by asking them for their perspective.
- To **challenge directly**, you can follow the situation, behavior, impact (SBI) framework:
  - The situation you observed
  - The individual's behavior in that situation
  - The impact of that behavior

Here's an example: "Ravi, when we were in the sprint review meeting and I asked you to make a note of the client's feedback, you didn't acknowledge me or add the item to the meeting notes. This made me feel like you were ignoring me. We also haven't logged an important fix that the client wants...."

Kim also describes these anti-patterns to radical candor, which you must avoid:

- **Obnoxious aggression.** Challenging directly without showing personal care
- **Ruinous empathy.** Showing care without challenging directly
- **Manipulative insincerity.** Neither caring nor challenging directly

As a manager, learn this framework of building relationships and sharing feedback. It's best to share feedback in a timely and atomic fashion. When you let feedback pile on for too long, you'll construct stories about the other person in your head, and it'll ruin your working relationship with them. I mentioned earlier that you must build comfort with sharing feedback asynchronously. Table 23.1 summarizes how you can give and receive feedback async.

Table 23.1 How to Give and Receive Feedback Asynchronously

Giving Feedback	Receiving Feedback
Approach with the right intent. Feedback is to strengthen confidence or improve effectiveness or both. Apply only these lenses to your feedback and nothing else.	*It's not personal.* Avoid viewing feedback as a judgment on you as a person. It's a way to help you improve your work and how you operate as a teammate.

Giving Feedback	Receiving Feedback
Build safety: Apply the ConveRel quadrants to your feedback interactions as well. If the relationship is weak, async feedback may not be effective. Choose a sync medium instead. Outside the feedback interactions, make an effort to build a healthy work relationship with your colleagues.	*Assume positive intent.* Read feedback while assuming the best intent possible from the sender. If something offends you, reread it with a smile on your face. If that changes how you interpret the message, you may have misunderstood it the first time.
Include detail. Without being verbose, follow the SBI framework to make the feedback clear. Be sure to acknowledge the other person's positive intent, if that's apparent to you. When you're unsure of intent, don't assume it. Ask questions in your written feedback.	*Be grateful.* If someone took the time to write thoughtful feedback for you, that means they care about you. This is a good place to be. Thank them explicitly.
Make it timely. As we discussed earlier in the chapter, feedback makes the most sense in context. The more you delay it, the less one can act on it. Share your feedback about an incident as close to the incident as possible.	*Take time to understand.* We can all read relatively fast. But don't rush through the feedback. Focus on your takeaways. What can you continue doing? What can you do better?
Read it aloud to yourself. How does your feedback sound when you read it? Can adding an emoji clarify your tone? Would you find this feedback useful if you got it? Edit, sharpen, and clarify your message, before you share it.	*Ask for clarification.* Sometimes written feedback may seem vague or unclear. Don't be shy to ask questions so you understand the feedback better. People usually miss examples and suggestions when they give feedback. Be sure to seek these out explicitly.
Offer to clarify your feedback. It's likely that the recipient may have questions about your feedback. You can do this asynchronously, or if you believe it'll help the relationship, get on a call.	*Apply and validate.* Feedback is useful when you apply it. And if you do apply the feedback, be sure to let the person who gave you feedback know. This is a way to acknowledge that you appreciate the feedback. The corollary is also true. If you can't apply the feedback, respectfully make that clear to the sender. It's also okay if you need time to think things through. Just be transparent with the sender about this.
Try using new media. Sometimes a recorded audio or a video message can be more effective than written feedback. Feel free to experiment!	

And yes, the best way to build a culture of radical candor is to first solicit feedback. In Kim Scott's words, it "proves you can take it before you dish it out."

BE THE BRIDGE BETWEEN YOUR TEAM AND YOUR COMPANY'S CULTURE

If I could end this chapter with a piece of parting advice, I'll say this: *be there for your people.* Sometimes your direct reports just need an unscheduled chat or a phone call. There could be many reasons for this such as a stressful situation at work, an interpersonal blow-up, or just someone facing a tough time. There needs to be enough time on your schedule so you can address the unpredictable. That's all the more reason to make meetings the last resort.

CHAPTER SUMMARY

As a manager, you are the employee's bridge to the organization. To show that the company cares, you must show care as well. Here are the three ideas we explored:

- Aim for a 1:5 ratio or less between managers and direct reports. That way managers will have time to spend with their people without oversubscribing themselves.
- Run effective one-on-one meetings. Focus these meetings on building relationships, sharing guidance, and offering help. Avoid transactional discussions here.
- Share timely, atomic feedback. The radical candor framework is an effective way to do this.

Since we've spoken about being the bridge to a team and company culture, this chapter provides us with a segue to address the topic of culture itself. How do you shape a culture where asynchronous teams can thrive? Let's find out in the next chapter.

24

SET UP YOUR TEAM FOR SUCCESS

As technologists, it can sometimes help to imagine our teams as software systems. In this chapter, we'll address some environment variables that will affect your team's productivity and happiness. What are environment variables? I'm glad you asked. According to Wikipedia,

> An environment variable is a dynamic-named value that can affect the way running processes will behave on a computer. They're part of the environment in which a process runs. A running program can access the values of environment variables for configuration.

Like with software programs, you as a leader may need to define some environment variables dynamically, depending on the situations you find yourself in. Judgment, experience, and vision—you'll use all three to define these variables. Your choices will influence your team's productivity and behavior. Sound interesting? Let's dive in.

DESIGN FOR SUCCESS

In the book *Upstream*, Dan Heath repeats the sentence, "Every system is perfectly designed to get the results it gets." Your newly minted async-first team is a system. You can imagine it as a circle deep within a system of concentric circles: departments, divisions, the company itself. Each of these organizational constructs is a system that has its natural equilibrium. Systems can change when you apply force to them, but when you remove that force, they will tend to go back to their original state. The way you work is part of your team's equilibrium. To sustain your new way of working, you must design your team system for a new equilibrium.

As an individual leader, you may not be able to influence every part of your organization. It makes sense to begin with your sphere of influence. I have five variables for you to consider in the way you design your team and its surrounding ecosystem so you can make the change stick.

MANAGE TEAM COGNITIVE LOAD THROUGH TEAM TOPOLOGIES

We all have the desire to direct our work. This desire extends from the individual to the team as well. When a team can't work autonomously, you notice many symptoms:

- They're frequently blocked because of dependencies or a lack of ownership.
- The complexity of the system creates knowledge silos.
- It's unclear who you must interact with or who can help you move forward.

To address these issues, Matthew Skelton and Manuel Pais have written about the idea of team topologies. I encourage you to read their excellent book, which is all about organizing software development teams in a manner that reduces cognitive load and improves their ability to deliver—all while being clear about interaction patterns across teams.

Skelton and Pais recommend organizing across four kinds of teams—the fundamental topologies:

- **Stream-aligned teams.** These align to a flow of work from a segment of the business. An example is an iOS app.
- **Enabling teams.** These teams help stream-aligned teams to overcome obstacles. They may also help detect missing capabilities. An example is a team specializing in test automation.
- **Complicated subsystem teams.** These teams develop systems where specialized expertise is necessary. An example is biometrics-driven identity management.
- **Platform teams.** These teams provide a set of underlying services and APIs to accelerate delivery from stream-aligned teams. An example is a core banking platform.

The authors go on to describe the possible interaction patterns between such teams so the groups can communicate with each other in meaningful ways. They recommend only three interaction patterns across teams.

- **Collaboration.** This is when teams work together for a specific duration on a specific charter. For example, a platform team may collaborate with a stream-aligned team to agree on new API specs.

- **X as a service.** This pattern emerges when one team provides and one team consumes something "as a service." This kind of interaction shouldn't need much input from the providing team. And if it does need prolonged inputs, then it may mean that the teams involved should follow a collaboration pattern instead.

- **Facilitation.** In this pattern, one team with specialized knowledge helps and mentors another team. For example, the test automation team can help the iOS team build out its functional automation suite.

Figure 24.1 summarizes the four team topologies and the three interaction patterns. Work with other leaders and managers in your peer group to investigate if it is possible to reorganize your teams into these topologies so they have maximum autonomy to deliver their outcomes. This investigation may not be a trivial task, and it may need significant architectural changes. I understand if you discover that you don't have the appetite for it just yet. However, keep these structural improvements at the back of your mind. That way, when the time is right, you may be able to advocate for this way of organizing teams. The goal? Minimize each team's cognitive load and limit noisy interactions.

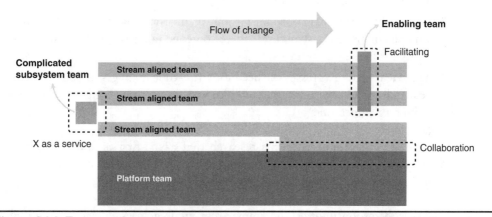

Figure 24.1 Team topologies and their interaction patterns (Source: Matthew Skelton and Manuel Pais)

REVISIT YOUR TEAM'S INTERNAL STRUCTURE

We've addressed the difference between makers and managers right at the start. Here's what that difference looks like on software development teams:

- **Makers** build stuff. This includes your designers, testers, developers, and writers.

- **Managers** oversee stuff. They coordinate projects, lead teams and people, and remove obstacles.

While managers perform yeoman service on many teams, asynchronous work is all about *optimizing for the makers*. Managers' schedules are incompatible with those of makers, as we've discussed. So, you must keep that management layer as thin as possible. If you don't, you'll frustrate all your makers, because the managers will want them to be in meetings just to get the hang of what's happening.

I understand if you find what I'm saying obvious. I say it because in some organizations a maker-first thought process isn't natural when structuring teams. Leaders often think about the management layer before they staff the makers. Before they know it, they construct a thick layer of overheads. The thicker your management layer, the more bottlenecks and the more box-ticking your makers will have to do.

I suggest going about it another way:

1. Staff your teams with the best makers you can find to solve the problem at hand.
2. Once you feel good about that team, staff the thinnest management layer you think you can get away with.
3. If you think the team can do without a full-time manager, institute a first among equals (FaE) structure, where someone takes the additional responsibility for management tasks.
4. If the team later expresses the need for a full-time manager or you see a gap in leadership and coordination, you'll know that you're solving a real problem, not an imagined one.

Liam Martin has found from his research that async-first organizations have a "50 percent smaller managerial level than their synchronous counterparts." Let me paraphrase his findings:

- Clear job responsibilities and transparent goals help employees operate more autonomously than otherwise.
- Since async-first teams create artifacts in the flow of work, it makes communication and documentation atomic. This reduces a lot of communication overhead that a full-time manager has to bear.
- With the right automation in place, many reports become real-time. All they need are minor, atomic disciplines such as keeping task boards up-to-date.

Even when you need people in managerial roles, this async-first discipline takes away a lot of otherwise boring work from a leader's life. Be ready to embrace that efficiency.

REDUCE PRESSURE, CREATE CALM

While researching materials for this book, I read a post by a senior leader at a major tech firm advocating for asynchronous communication. It sounded poetic until he wrote about how he has free time after dinner to read anything that anyone sends him, despite how crazy his day gets.

Think about that for a moment. We're not advocating for crazy days at work. We're aiming for calm, happy, productive teams. Being async-first is not about **a second shift** just to consume written communication. And no, dear leader, you shouldn't do that either. It's a poor example, and it sends the message that communication is not part of your day job.

The other mistake is to **expect results too early**. We've discussed earlier that change is rarely a straight line. Figure 24.2 illustrates the Satir change curve, which plots the usual trajectory of change initiatives. When you introduce a new way of working on a team, results will flag for a while, as the team copes with the change. Teams and their leaders get impatient at this stage and ditch the change, saying "it doesn't work." Be courageous and stay the course. Attempt to shorten that period of chaos and resistance, but remember—that dip in the graph is natural.

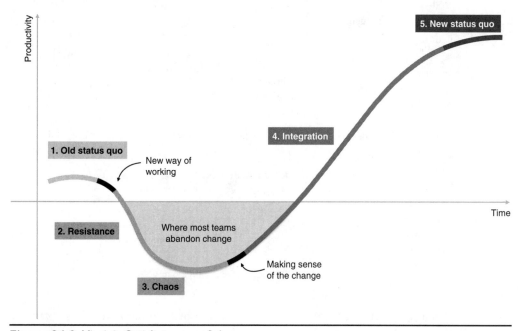

Figure 24.2 Virginia Satir's *process of change.*

Like with any change, it helps to guide your team using metrics and indicators.

- Leading indicators help you sense that you're making a change in the right direction.
- Lagging indicators help you look back at a period or major events such as big releases and understand how you're delivering value.

Table 24.1 lists potential indicators aligned to the SPACE framework. Use these to build your team's feedback loops and to help everyone own the shift.

Table 24.1 Indicators to Help You Sense and Guide the Shift to Asynchronous Work

Satisfaction	Performance	Activity	Collaboration	Efficiency
How fulfilled, happy, and healthy individuals are.	*The outcome of your processes.*	*The count of actions or outputs.*	*How people communicate and work together.*	*Working with minimal delays or interruptions.*
Lagging	**Lagging**	**Leading**	**Lagging**	**Leading**
ESAT scores	Cycle time	Volume of:	Onboarding time	(lack of) Interruptions
NPS scores	Deployment frequency	• Commits	% of successful knowledge searches	Hours of deep work
Intent to stay		• PRs		Number of handoffs
Diversity and inclusion		• Design docs	Expertise discoverability	Review time
		DAU/ MAU = Daily active users/ monthly active users		Meeting hours per individual contributor ($\leq$5) and manager ($\leq$10)
Leading	**Leading**	Compliance on:	**Leading**	
Reduced stretch hours	Throughput	• Decision documentation.	Review pickup time	
	Velocity		Review depth	
Flexible work hours	Rework rate	• Meeting documentation	Review waiting time	
Forty-hour work week			Decision velocity	
			Documentation hygiene	

Last but not least, there's the chaos of being **too busy to improve**. This is true of both teams and leaders. There's always something important to do such as an upcoming release, an upset client, people rolling on and off the team, production issues, and whatnot. There's never an ideal time to introduce change. If the team is under the gun for a dozen other deliverables, improving their collaboration practices will be the last priority. You might as well not try. Your job as a leader is to make space for the team to think through this change so they can own it and absorb new practices into their ways of working. Good things take time!

CONSCIOUSLY BUILD A TEAM CULTURE

One of the common concerns with any kind of location-independent work is that it may be difficult to maintain a "strong culture." I've always found culture to be a rather tricky word to deal with, because everyone can have a different definition of it. It becomes even trickier when people use loaded terms to describe culture. You may have heard some of these:

- The X-factor
- Our secret sauce
- Magic!
- The special something
- Our DNA
- Who we are as a company

I prefer a slightly more observable approach to maintaining a healthy culture on my remote teams. The inspiration comes from the world of hiring, where I've noticed a shift toward assessing "values alignment" over "culture fit." The most important reason for this shift is that it's easier to observe behaviors that are congruent with your values than to judge a fuzzy notion of culture. It also stops cults from emerging in the workplace that define culture in a manner convenient to them.

This thinking extends to team culture as well. Instead of thinking about a broad notion of culture, think about its constituent parts. Agreeing on your team's values helps you identify congruent behavior and discourage counterproductive actions.

Your company probably already lists its values. Defining team values doesn't undermine your company's beliefs.

- First, team values can help to align the goals and behavior of team members with the overall goals and values of the company. This can create a sense of purpose and direction for the team and help team members understand how their work fits into the larger mission of the company.
- Second, team values can help to create a positive and cohesive team culture. By explicitly stating the values that the team holds dear, team members can be more mindful of how they interact with one another and work together, which can improve communication and collaboration.

- Finally, team values can serve as a guide for decision-making and problem-solving. When faced with a difficult decision or challenge, team members can refer to the team values to help them determine the right course of action. This can help to ensure that the team remains aligned and focused on its goals.

BEST PRACTICE

How to Identify Team Values

There are several exercises you can use to identify team values. These can range from short sessions to full-day workshops. My preference is to err on the side of starting with a short session and then refining our understanding of team values over time. Here's an exercise I've tried several times with success:

1. Begin by using sticky notes to list a set of core values on a collaborative whiteboard. James Clear lists 57 core values as a starting point. You can add your company values to this list if you want to attempt overlapping with them. This is also where you can add values that have emerged from your own introspection, i.e., reflecting on the values that drive this shift to asynchronous work.

2. Ask your teammates to read the values in silence and identify the ones that they hold most dear, by "dot-voting" on them. Limit them to a maximum of five votes each.

3. Once the team has identified the initial set of values, move these to a new canvas. Now ask team members to describe the values they voted for. Encourage them to add sticky notes around each value to describe why they find it important and how one may behave in line with that value.

4. Now that you have descriptions and associated behaviors for each value, run a second voting session. This time, encourage team members to read the descriptions and associated behaviors and identify the top three values that resonate with them.

5. After the voting session completes, you should have a list of your team's top three (or top five values). Time to celebrate!

6. As a follow-up, codify the values on your team handbook and add the descriptions and behaviors you came up with during the workshop. Encourage your team to revisit this page in your handbook and to enhance it by adding examples of behavior that are in line with the values. You must also question every few months how well these values are serving your team. This is an especially useful good practice to follow when you have new people on the team who may challenge the status quo.

RESOURCE

Mural Template to Discover Team Values

To help you discover team values, I've created a Mural template called Team Values Discovery, shown in Figure 24.3. You'll find it on the companion site (https://www.asyncagile.org/book-resources).

Use this template to run the values discovery exercise in your team. Feel free to reuse the design of this template even if your team uses another whiteboarding tool.

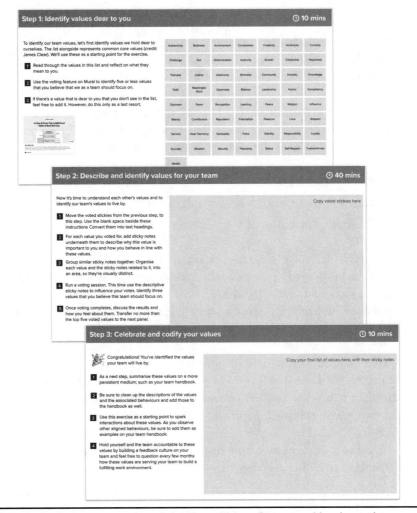

Figure 24.3 Representation of the Team Values Discovery Mural template.

ALIGN ON A COMMON PURPOSE

Your people don't buy what you do; they buy why you do it, and what you do simply serves as the proof of what you believe.
                    —My variation on a quote from Simon Sinek's TED Talk

Everyone wants to be part of something bigger than themselves. The one other thing that binds people together is a sense of purpose. I suggest that it's not enough to stop at an organization's purpose. Individual employees may find themselves too small to contribute to a grand organizational cause. Teams can benefit from defining their own purpose.

This is particularly useful for remote and async-first teams. Without the visual feeling of being together, you can feel like just another freelancer on a disjointed team. A clear purpose helps the team build a deeper sense of connection than otherwise.

In the book *Essentialism: The Disciplined Pursuit of Less*, Greg McKeown advises that you make your purpose, what he calls *essential intent*, both concrete and inspirational. This is different from the following:

• Mission statements that are inspirational but not concrete
• Values that can tend to be general and bland
• Quarterly objectives that are concrete but not inspirational

I've used McKeown's framework (as in Figure 24.4) to brainstorm a purpose with every team I've led in recent years. Nothing fancy. Just a simple line that everyone can understand and rally around. For example, when I was on a team building a data visualization platform, we all agreed that our purpose was to "help our clients use data to drive better decisions."

That simple phrase led to a sense of ownership. For every feature, every enhancement, we'd ask if it would indeed "drive better decisions." There was a healthy tension to do the right thing. The team would come up with ideas for the product with this purpose in mind. It was at the center of our existence.

Could your team benefit from having its individual purpose? How can you encourage them to define and own it?

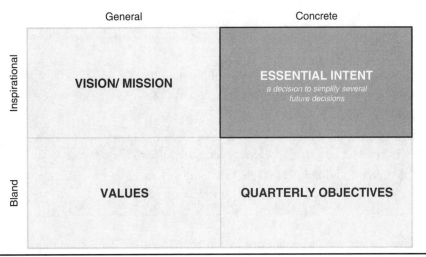

Figure 24.4 Think "concrete and inspirational" when defining your purpose.

YOUR VIRTUAL WORKPLACE NEEDS CONFIGURING

The five environment variables we discussed in this chapter influence the configuration of your virtual workplace. Keep a close eye on them, because they'll influence how your team works together. They will also give your team more space to experiment and a greater sense of autonomy and purpose. What do you gain? Well, better team cohesion and, ideally, better results.

CHAPTER SUMMARY

Leaders of teams that go async-first must use their judgment to decide a few factors that influence the team's success and the environment they'll work in. I'm calling these five factors *environment variables*.

1. Organize team boundaries and interactions to maximize autonomy and flow. Matthew Skelton and Manuel Pais's team topologies provide you with a framework to think about organizing your teams.

2. Create a lean, maker-centric team. Add pure management roles only when necessary.

3. Keep a calm work environment when going async. Avoid these common mistakes:

   a. Creating second shifts for communication

   b. Expecting results too early

   c. Being too busy to improve

4. Be conscious about building a team culture. Spend time identifying team values and encourage behaviors congruent with them.

5. Align on a common team purpose. In the long run, this will help you retain team cohesion and a sense of collective ownership.

This chapter concludes our discussion about team- or department-level leadership. In the last chapter of this part of the book, we'll shift to a broader, organizational topic: knowledge sharing across the company.

FARM TACIT KNOWLEDGE IN YOUR COMPANY

Remote work has renewed many companies' interests in knowledge management. Considering one can't walk up to co-workers for a quick clarification, could we instead ask a system for an answer? In an async-first, remote culture, a solid knowledge strategy can be a productivity power-up. The converse is also true. Without a proper knowledge strategy, your people will frustrate themselves searching for answers to the problems they face at work.

Depending on where you sit in the organization, you may or may not have an influence on the way you surface and share knowledge in the company. Understanding the levers for knowledge sharing may, however, help you make an effective case to influential leaders. And while the company takes its time to make change, you can use these levers to build a locally optimized knowledge strategy for the people you lead.

BEYOND HANDBOOKS: INTO COMMUNITIES

We've discussed the value of creating a team handbook. GitLab and other organizations have public handbooks to run their company! These are the kinds of knowledge that I refer to as *stocks*. With complex knowledge work, though, the approach of creating stocks of well-structured knowledge has its limitations.

We often solve problems where there is no established practice to follow. I argue that much of software development is just that. Tech stacks, markets, domains, customer preferences, and methodologies change faster than we can catalog them. This is the reason you may need to supplement your knowledge stocks with peer-to-peer networks. These networks enable flows and streams of knowledge.

In the 2020s, knowledge can take many forms.

- **Traditional forms of knowledge.** Process docs, templates, toolkits, and learning materials are ideal for stable practices and information.
- **Modern forms of knowledge.** Questions and answers, videos, and podcasts work best for ground-breaking, emerging practices. A lot of know-how about such practices is tacit.

Lew Platt, former CEO of HP, says this:

> If only HP knew what HP knows, we would be three times more productive.

How should your organization farm all this tacit knowledge? In this chapter, you'll learn how to create a knowledge ecosystem that keeps pace with your people's know-how. I argue that we have much to learn from the consumer internet. Allow me to explain using a two-part structure.

CREATE POROUS WALLS

Many of the tools we use at the team level make collaboration free-form and frictionless. However, they can be point-to-point, "walled-garden" solutions. Let's take the example of Workspace by Google, which is Google's collaboration platform. It's all about team collaboration.

- Send someone a message.
- Chat with the team.
- Start a video call.
- Share a document with your team.
- Create a site to catalog your work.
- Store all your team documents in a shared folder.
- Communicate with people using a Google group.

It's beautiful, but it focuses *only* on making you and your team more productive. It does little to generate signals for other people who may be peripherally interested in the work you do so they can learn from your experience. If you're not explicitly part of a team or a group, you know nothing about what's happening in its walled garden.

By the way, this isn't about Workspace by Google's limitations. To be fair, many platforms behave the same way. They focus on making teams effective when collaborating with each other. They don't really help all these teams come together as one organization where we learn from each other's tacit knowledge. Instead of walled gardens, we need porous walls.

So, What Capabilities Do Knowledge Systems Need?

Well, we need all the collaborative features that team productivity suites offer us. To farm tacit knowledge, though, these features must align with a few other, key capabilities, which Figure 25.1 illustrates. The more of these capabilities your toolset provides, the more robust your knowledge strategy will be.

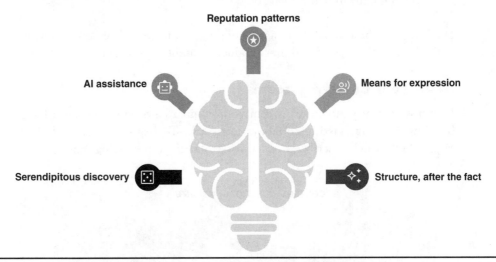

Figure 25.1 The key capabilities your knowledge ecosystem needs.

- **Serendipitous discovery.** The way to find information in your company should mirror how you find information outside of work. This is much like how you find things using Google or on news apps and social media, even if it's from people you don't know well.

- **AI assistance.** Think of how Google Assistant and Siri understand your interests and help you find information you'll appreciate. Modern AI models like GPT provide you with conversational interfaces to navigate information. In a comparable way, effective knowledge management systems help you discover relevant content. Of course, such approaches must also respect privacy.

- **Reputation patterns.** The internet makes it easy for you to find people who share your interests. You can also find reputable people in those fields of interest. Media manipulation aside, a lot of this happens due to the body of work people share on the internet, aka their *digital exhaust.* Your knowledge management system should also help you surface expertise and common interests.

- **Means for expression.** On the internet, you can post content on your blog, Instagram, YouTube, or other platforms without spamming anyone. People can follow you if they want and engage with that content. Or not. It's their choice. How can enterprise knowledge systems provide similar means for expression?

- **Structure, after the fact.** Finally, effective knowledge systems make it easy to organize information after the fact, not unlike Wikipedia. They also allow people to create their own ways to structure and navigate content, like they do using Pinterest, Diigo, or Evernote. Everyone can contribute without restrictions, and the system helps you reorganize these contributions in a way that makes sense for the company and at the personal level.

Don't look at these capabilities as a shopping list. Instead, keep these capabilities at the back of your mind and first conduct an audit of your existing systems.

Audit Your Current Systems

It's unlikely that you can transform your company systems overnight. I suggest building on your existing collaboration stack. To begin this process, refer to Figure 25.2, which describes a framework to audit your existing tool stack.

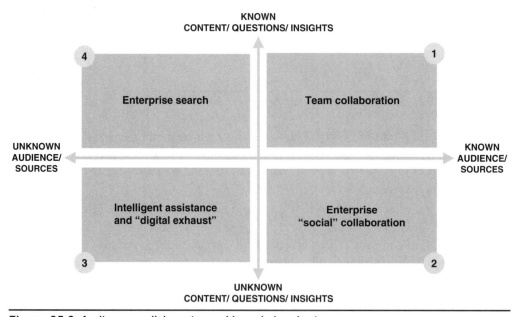

Figure 25.2 Audit your collaboration and knowledge sharing systems.

Start by evaluating your existing toolset across two dimensions:

- **Audience and sources.** How easy is it to identify your knowledge source and intended audience? On the left of the x-axis, your audience and sources are unknown; on the right, they're known.
- **Content, questions, and insights.** How easy is it to define your content's insights and/or questions you seek to answer? At the bottom of the y-axis, you have the unknowns and, at the top, the knowns.

Table 25.1 describes each quadrant of this 2 × 2 matrix.

Table 25.1 Tools and Solutions for Each Quadrant of the Knowledge Systems Audit

Quadrant	Audiences and Sources	Content, Questions, and Insights	Possible Tools
1	Known	Known	This is the most addressed quadrant for modern enterprise software. You know what information you have or are seeking. You also know who you're sharing it with or who you're getting it from. Team collaboration tools such as mailing lists, team sites, chat groups, and collaborative documents are ideal for this combination of people and knowledge. Examples include Workspace by Google, Microsoft 365, Notion, and Basecamp.
2	Known	Unknown	On the internet, we follow people, blogs, social handles, or websites without being able to predict exactly what value we'll get. We find content creators who represent our interests, and we bet that they'll produce useful content for us. This is a two-way street, and just as we follow people, some of them follow us back, and the interactions are richer for it. Examples include Workplace from Meta, Yammer, P2, and LumApps.

Table 25.1 *continued*

Quadrant	Audiences and Sources	Content, Questions, and Insights	Possible Tools
3	Unknown	Unknown	Your social networks, digital assistants, news, and entertainment apps give you "intelligent" content recommendations. I'll grudgingly admit that this does enrich our digital experience. There's the concern about privacy, no doubt, and enterprise software must be doubly careful about this concern.
			Let's not discount the role of "digital exhaust" here. When you come across interesting content, you follow the author and discover their other, as-interesting content. One discovery leads to another, much like a trail of breadcrumbs.
			Examples are Workgrid; recommendation engines within your quadrant 1, 2, and 3 tools; custom recommendation engines; and employee profiles on your enterprise social network.
4	Unknown	Known	Often you know what knowledge you're looking for but don't know where to look or who could give you that information. Google comes to the rescue on the internet and at work; enterprise search can help.
			Examples are Elastic and Glean.

Once you've completed this exercise, you'll learn how you can improve your knowledge-sharing infrastructure. The toolset should ideally have coverage across all four quadrants. If a quadrant is empty or if the experience across quadrants isn't tight enough, you'll know what investments you need. Use this analysis to make a business case to leaders who can sign off on such investments.

FACILITATE FLOWS WHILE YOU MANAGE STOCKS

In a fast-changing business environment, explicit knowledge as an asset has diminishing returns. It gradually becomes outdated or irrelevant with time. A century ago, it would take 35 years for half of an engineer's university syllabus to become defunct. Today, that half-life is down to somewhere between 5 to 10 years.

People and companies must adapt to the fast pace of knowledge change by creating a culture of continuous learning. This may involve mentorship, observation, and hands-on experience in addition to formal training.

To adapt skills to a new domain, individuals may also rely on the tacit knowledge of others and build relationships with those who can help them learn. This form of learning relies on knowledge flows rather than access to information stored in a repository or training program.

Optimize for the Strength of Weak Ties

It's natural for us to share knowledge with groups that we have strong ties with. But Mark Granovetter's 1973 paper "The Strength of Weak Ties" argues that weak ties, or acquaintances, can help individuals access knowledge they may not reach through strong ties alone. This concept is relevant today as we have many weak ties in our professional networks, which require less effort to maintain and can be sources of valuable information.

The Dunbar number suggests that humans can maintain stable relationships with only around 150 people. Weak ties can, however, help us expand our networks beyond that limit. Ask yourself: how many people do you have strong ties with? Compare that with the number of people in your company that you know in passing. Which number is bigger? My guess is that *you already have more weak ties than strong ties*. The key is to leverage those acquaintances.

Granovetter's work provides inspiration for knowledge management use cases. While wikis and productivity suites help people with strong ties work together, enterprise social networks (ESNs) can create and multiply weak ties. They also give people the ability to express themselves through blogs, videos, and other media. Your people can then access "potential" new connections based on common interests. Figure 25.3 summarizes the different kinds of systems you may want to implement to enable different kinds of ties between people.

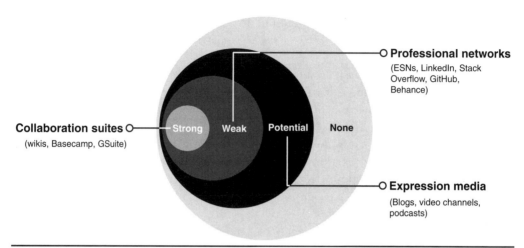

Figure 25.3 Types of ties and the systems that support them.

Your Community Platform Is Your Knowledge Platform

To enable flows and leverage weak and potential ties, I suggest a flipped knowledge strategy. Create those stocks, but go about things in this order:

1. **Implement a community platform** where people can self-organize and share content. Make all content accessible to everyone by default. Confidential information should be the exception, not the norm.

2. **Allow free-form content creation.** Videos, blog posts, discussions, files—everything should be kosher.

3. **Give people a way to build their own profiles** through contributions to the system. This will build their identity or brand for others to connect with them. Job titles become irrelevant this way, and content becomes king.

4. Provide means for people to **add metadata through tags, descriptions, comments, and reactions.** Let the most popular and the most relevant content bubble to the top.

5. Add structure to the most popular, well-reviewed content. **Update that structure constantly** so it represents the "state-of-the-art" for your part of the company. Some of this curated information can make its way into company or departmental handbooks.

This brings me to the distinction between community-based knowledge systems and team or company handbooks. A handbook contains stable knowledge. The more stable the knowledge, the more it lends itself to structure. Community platforms are ideal for volatile, emergent knowledge. Balance how you structure stable knowledge with how you nurture emerging practice.

All Systems Need People

A truly democratic and free-form system allows everyone to contribute to the collective—free-form, without friction. To enable this, I recommend two levels of "sense making," which you'll notice in Figure 25.4.

- **Community managers.** This group should exist at every community, practice, center of excellence, or department level in your organization. While the best content will bubble up, these people help add metadata and organization, so it's easy to access the "state of the art" at a later point in time.
- **Curators/knowledge managers.** These individuals help create an information architecture that mirrors the structure of your organization. They ensure that your knowledge ecosystem is "browsable and navigable."

The sense-making structure in Figure 25.4 is similar to the one on Wikipedia. While we all can enrich the system with our contributions, dedicated editors help interlink pages and organize them in the right hierarchy. Editors also watch pages, so they can review changes when necessary.

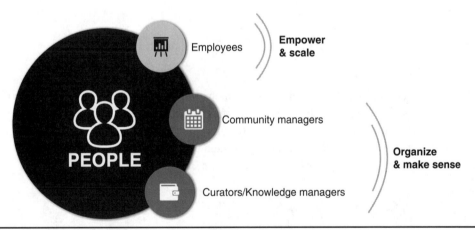

Figure 25.4 People who run your knowledge ecosystem.

Today, AI can manage many of the mundane tasks that a community manager or a curator would do: adding tags, updating metadata, and creating newsletters and digests. If you can get to this level of sophistication, your community managers and curators can take charge of more human activities. Here are some indicative activities that your community managers and curators can take part in:

- Being cheerleaders and creating opportunities for people to connect outside the system

- Building personal connections with and between valuable contributors across organizational boundaries
- Breaking silos where they may exist
- Fine-tuning recommendations and search results
- Blurring the boundaries between work, knowledge sharing, and learning by embedding the content creation process into work itself
- Enabling peer review and feedback mechanisms for content
- Helping people get answers to unanswered questions

These sense-making roles are the building blocks for nurturing communities and knowledge sharing in a distributed workplace. Successful distributed organizations are "intentional" about everything they do. Companies that care about communities, knowledge sharing, and serendipity can't leave this to chance alone.

With the right systems and the right people in community management and curation roles, you can brew the perfect storm of "organized serendipity." I daresay that this can work better than the proverbial watercooler encounter.

FROM TEAM KNOWLEDGE TO COMPANY KNOWLEDGE

I understand that knowledge management may not be your primary focus. That said, without effective knowledge management, it can be difficult to collaborate asynchronously, especially at the company level. So, use what you've learned in this chapter to assess knowledge management at your own company and to suggest better alternatives where you see a gap.

CHAPTER SUMMARY

Handbooks and documentation are only part of your company's knowledge management solution. Holistic knowledge management solutions also help you farm tacit knowledge and build connections between people.

- Point-to-point collaboration tools make teams efficient, but they also lead to knowledge silos.
- Over and above team collaboration tools, invest in systems that offer most of the following capabilities:
  - Serendipitous discovery

- AI assistance
- Reputation patterns
- Means for expression
- Structure, after the fact
- To decide which tools you may need, start with a systems audit. Map your systems across two axes.
  - Audiences and sources (known or unknown)
  - Content/questions/insights (known or unknown)

  Aim to cover all four quadrants of the previous matrix and use that to drive decisions about investments in an improved toolset.
- Stocks are important for stable knowledge. For emergent practice, though, you must also enable flows between people.
- Focus not just on the strong ties that exist in the team but also on weak ties across the organization and outside. This is where serendipity happens.
- Build your handbook, but also implement an internal community platform. This will help keep knowledge up-to-date in your company.
- In addition, staff community managers at the level of each community and curators at the organizational level. They add a layer of "sense-making" to your stocks and flows.

With that, we come to the end of Part IV of this book. Until now, we've seen only the benefits of async-first work and how to enable it. But every way of working has its pitfalls. In Part V of the book, I discuss a few obvious ones so you can guard against them. Let's go there next.

Part V

NAVIGATE THE PITFALLS

Async-first and remote work isn't without its pitfalls. This part of the book will describe a few common pitfalls in detail so you can prepare to avoid them.

- **Chapter 26**, "The Great Hybrid Kerfuffle," describes the trap of going "hybrid" without knowing what it truly means. You'll learn why a remote-first, async-first mindset makes more sense than forced-hybrid models.
- In **Chapter 27**, "The Async Island," you'll learn about the risks of being the only team that works async. I'll also share four strategies you can employ to mitigate these risks.
- In **Chapter 28**, "Toxicity in the Virtual Workplace," you'll learn about the ways a virtual workplace can breed toxic behaviors and how you can guard against them.

26

THE GREAT HYBRID
KERFUFFLE

When you have a diverse workforce, diverse preferences and workstyles are natural. At the time of writing this chapter, there's a visible divide between remote-work absolutists and those who prefer office-centric work. And there are those in the middle of that spectrum.

When we find ourselves divided across extreme positions, we reach for the middle ground. In the brave new world of remote work, *hybrid work* sounds like that middle ground. Some commentators even call it the "best of both worlds." I see it more as a pitfall, especially if you want to adopt an async-first workstyle. First, asynchronous work lends itself more naturally to remote work. It's not impossible to work asynchronously when you're working in the same physical location with others. It just feels unnatural to most people. Second, and most important, "hybrid" may not be the best of both worlds. Let me tell you why.

PEOPLE'S PREFERENCES ARE HEADING REMOTE

The term *hybrid* gained popularity somewhere in the first half of 2021. The world was fighting back against the pandemic, and it felt like "forced remote" would soon be history. My research told me that work preferences varied across people. Table 26.1 summarizes data from two consecutive years of surveys at a major Indian tech firm.

Table 26.1 Shifting Preferences for Remote Work

How Many Days per Week Do People Want to Work Remotely?	2021	2022
5 days	15.47 percent	44.57 percent
4 days	12.15 percent	16.17 percent
3 days	34.25 percent	22.2 percent
2 days	24.45 percent	11.13 percent
1 day	6.08 percent	2.25 percent
Never	7.6 percent	3.67 percent

I want you to examine this data. You'll notice that in the space of one year, work preferences shifted a lot. The percentage of people who wanted to be all-remote had almost tripled. Of course, please read this with a grain of salt. When I conducted the 2021 survey, India was in the throes of a debilitating second wave of COVID-19. People were more isolated than ever, and we still don't know what the mental health impacts of those times were. Between then and 2022, COVID-19 had almost become endemic, and people had gotten better at working remotely. That explains why almost half of the people wanted to be remote all the time.

This has some interesting implications for the future of work. One, it indicates where people's preferences are heading. It also shows us that one-size-still-doesn't-fit-all, at least not right away. So, in the sections of this chapter that follow, I want to explain a perspective to "hybrid work," which many think of as an effective compromise. First, let's address misunderstandings about this term.

HYBRID ORGANIZATION, NOT HYBRID EMPLOYEES

Even when I used the word *hybrid* in 2021, I was conscious of this spread of preferences. As a remote- and asynchronous-work evangelist, I must also admit that working from home works for only certain people. Those who have a home office setup are likely to thrive over those who are adjusting with temporary hacks. Working from home is toxic for anyone who doesn't have a great emotional environment at home. A victim of abuse, for example, doesn't want to be stuck at home with their abuser. If you have a disproportionate share of household responsibilities, you need the contrivance of "going to work" to take a break from daily chores.

My idea about "hybrid" has always been to respect people's choices. When you hire capable people, they want to do meaningful work. Trust them to choose where they'll be happiest and most productive. Given the spread of work preferences, you will have a "hybrid organization." This is the nuance that many organizations have missed. *Instead of thinking of a hybrid organization, they're thinking about "hybrid employees."*

This misunderstanding of nuance leads to abominations like the 3:2 model: "three days in, two days out," or vice versa. Let's look back at Table 26.1. Now let's check who may be happy with a 3:2 model at that company:

- If you take people on each extreme of the spectrum (people who want to work remotely for zero, one, four, or five days), then right off the bat you'll annoy two out of three, i.e., 67 percent of your people. The middle ground doesn't work for them.
- Even the people in the middle won't be happy. Depending on the version of 3:2 that you employ, you'll upset 11–22 percent of your people because the arrangement won't match their preferences.
- That leaves you with 11–22 percent of your people who may be happy with the arrangement. News flash: even they want flexibility. They don't want you to tell them which days to come to the office.

As an organization, your systems must elevate everyone to their highest level of productivity and happiness. The 3:2 model and its equivalents bring them down to the lowest common denominator of unhappiness.

AVOID A MOVE BACKWARD

Between 2020 and 2022, the operations teams of most tech organizations have had to innovate. Two years of remote work meant companies learned to hire from anywhere and staff projects from anywhere. Teams are distributed by design these days. In large organizations, teams find themselves spread across multiple locations.

In-person training, which was not just costly but cumbersome to organize, made way for virtual classrooms and online learning. I can tell from my experience that I've designed virtual workshops that are far more effective than their in-office versions. There's also industry evidence of this phenomenon. Simple media creation tools have lowered the cost of production for content. No wonder this resulted in a boom in online learning.

In addition, teams have woken up to the inadequacies of the all-office environment. They understand they're more productive when they choose where they work from. It's clear as daylight that copying and pasting the office working model onto a distributed workforce is stressful and doesn't work. Indeed, that's the premise of this book!

Misunderstanding "hybrid" can erode all these gains. Here are some questions you may struggle with:

- If you've spread team members across a country, how does a 3:2 model or something similar bring them together?
- What will you say to people who you hired from a place where you don't have an office?
- Are you willing to let go of the flexibility to hire from anywhere and staff from anywhere?
- How will you match the scale and efficiency you got from adopting virtual classrooms and online learning?

AVOID NEW COSTS FOR ALL STAKEHOLDERS

A poor understanding of hybrid work is also costly for all stakeholders. Let's start with employers. I suggest a thought experiment. For the firm in Table 26.1, calculate necessary office capacity on the back of a napkin. You'll notice that all they need is office seating capacity for 25 percent of their workforce. You may discover something similar for your company. Don't forget, you reduce your electricity, maintenance, water, and sometimes food bills as well, depending on what your offices provide, of course. A "three days in, two days out" setup needs you to have seating capacity for 40–60 percent of your workforce. That right there is 60–140 percent additional cost. And these costs grow as your company grows. When you allow your employees a true *work-from-anywhere* setup, people will become more proficient with remote work, with time. You don't need to grow your offices each year.

Let's not forget the owned-office versus leased-office nuance either. Many companies that have taken a hard stance about a forced-hybrid schedule own large campuses and office spaces. They can't get rid of these spaces in a hurry. They may as well call employees back to the office for a few days each week to use these facilities. In contrast, most companies lease their office space. They can foreclose their leases or give up space when the leases expire. If you work for such a firm, then don't blindly follow the lead of companies who own their offices. Think about the operating expenses you can save each quarter by just respecting your people's preferences.

Infrastructure is another cost we don't think hard about. Hybrid work needs you to provide your employees with three things.

- A world-class office infrastructure
- A world-class remote-working environment
- A way to straddle both worlds

The companies that are betting on this way of working are also making massive investments in purpose-built technology. Take Google's experiments with Campfire, for example. Many companies gloss over this part of the hybrid solution and focus only on the marketing spiel instead.

Next, let's talk about employees. Each of us knows colleagues who've moved to a smaller town or closer to family. These colleagues enjoy a better quality of life and save more of their salaries. A forced-hybrid model takes that way of life away from them. If they must be in an office two or three times a week, they can't stay in another town anymore. They have to move away from their families and accept a higher cost of living.

Lastly, let's discuss society. This part of the puzzle is so big that I should break it down into smaller subsections.

Facilitating Brain Drain

The Tulsa Remote project seeks to reverse the "brain drain" from Oklahoma. It attracts people who can work from anywhere to come live in Tulsa, Oklahoma. The reward? A $10,000 bounty! While that's cool, it underscores a lesson for every small town around the world.

Take India, for example. Most of our knowledge work happens from eight tier-one cities. These cities are expensive and get most of the attention from the government and private service providers. The congestion in these cities makes them increasingly unlivable. Household savings and the quality of life aren't great, though people take home decent sums of money.

There is another India, which lives in its 97 tier-two cities. These include some very livable places such as Coimbatore, Kochi, Visakhapatnam, Mysore, Jaipur, and Pondicherry. People have gone back to these smaller towns and are contributing to the secondary and tertiary economies of these places. For once, corporations can reverse the brain drain they're historically responsible for. In return, they benefit from having an expanded talent pool to hire from. Reverse brain drain can lead to many positive consequences, such as the following:

- Reinvigorating the local community
- Creating opportunities for mentorship
- Fostering an environment for innovation

Here's what Prithwiraj (Raj) Choudhury said on *Freakonomics Radio*:

> It's potentially great for emerging markets to get talent back. That's what I'm most excited about. I think India could get a lot of talent back from the West, but it's not only India. I think the smaller Indian towns could be the winners. Because there are tier-two, tier-three cities which have enough of an infrastructure that you could work remotely and there's all the benefits of lower cost of living. And I think they could be the real winners instead of Bangalore, Hyderabad, or Delhi.

Through forced hybridism, tech firms may facilitate another great migration and a repeat brain drain, away from the smaller towns and villages and into the big cities. And for what benefit?

A Blow for Inclusion

It's no secret that women share a disproportionate burden of household responsibilities. We also know that women make more sacrifices for their careers than men ever do. Even before the pandemic, we knew that if we were to be inclusive of women in the workforce, we had to mitigate the reasons for which they would otherwise exit the workplace. The industry made a rather half-hearted attempt to embrace "flex work" back in the day. Flex work has its minor benefits, but imagine yourself as a woman working from home. When most of your team hangs out in the office, the environment can turn exclusionary despite people's best efforts. Remote work during the pandemic somehow leveled the playing field for everyone. I imagine that this is a far more inclusive situation for anyone who's hard-pressed to come to the office every day.

Consider a different demographic: people with disabilities. If you have a motor disability, India is one of the worst countries to get around in. This has had a nontrivial impact on career options for people with disabilities. If people with disabilities can work out of their home offices, it's an epic win for inclusion. Raj Choudhury says this:

> ...work from anywhere allows companies to hire from anywhere and create a more inclusive workforce based on gender, based on disabilities. So, my prediction—and of course, this is testable—is that companies that do not offer this option are going to lose the right tail of the talent distribution.

Companies that force people back into the office, if only for a few days, will find themselves on the wrong side of history as they'll exclude such people from the workforce. Companies that care about a diverse workforce are also more innovative and productive. Is that something we should let go of easily?

The Nontrivial Impact on Environment

While this topic needs nuance, we must acknowledge that the daily commute has an environmental impact. In his *Harvard Business Review* cover story, Raj Choudhury put out some interesting data.

> In 2018 Americans' commute time averaged 27.1 minutes each way, or about 4.5 hours a week. Eliminating that commute—particularly in places where most people commute by car—generates a significant reduction in emissions. The USPTO estimates that in 2015 its remote workers drove 84 million fewer miles than if they had been traveling to headquarters, reducing carbon emissions by more than 44,000 tons.

I don't know of any tech firm that doesn't recognize the climate crisis we're in. Are we willing to give up even small wins for benefits that we can't justify?

EMBRACE SCIENCE, NOT SUPERSTITION

I know what you may be thinking. You probably see execs who've instituted a hybrid-work policy for their companies. There may even be some data to support their decision. They've surely thought through the benefits of their approach, haven't they? Maybe. Maybe not. Let's examine some reasons we've heard in favor of forced hybridism. And then, you decide.

Productivity or the Lack of It

There's enough research to suggest that people are more productive when they work remotely. Productivity was probably never an issue. Tech companies wouldn't have made a killing in 2020 and 2021 if that was the case. All-remote companies such as GitLab and Automattic have been around and growing for years. Shouldn't they have folded by now if remote work was unproductive?

In 2022 and 2023 we're headed into a global recession, but market performance is barely an indicator of employee productivity. Your people may have been very productive in the office environment; let's concede that for a second. If they were just as productive, if not more, in an unfamiliar, all-remote setup, does it say much for the magic of the office anymore? Or is that just superstition we're hanging on to?

Serendipity Through Only "Bumping into Each Other"

You can't build a distributed, multi-office, multi-continent culture by hoping that people collide at the water cooler. As Raj Choudhury says,

> The truth about hallway conversation is we only had it with people close to us in the physical office. You meet and talk to the same 10 people every day. And people talk to people just like them—sales talks to sales, R&D talks to R&D, and interns talk to interns.

Depending on the size and design of your office, sheer presence on the same campus cannot guarantee serendipity, as Tom Allen discovered many decades back. And what about the people they need to interact with in other locations? Let's not forget, introverts aren't at ease with these gregarious interactions. The watercooler pattern is not just unscalable, but noninclusive. In distributed organizations, employers must be intentional about serendipity. You must use technology better, including enterprise social networks, chat rooms, and company intranets. We addressed this in Chapter 25.

The Notion of a "Secret Sauce"

Culture is more than just people sitting near each other. Clay Christensen talked about it as a combination of your resources (in tech that's often your people), your processes, and your values (spoken and unspoken). This culture should be visible in and out of the office. As a consultant, I've often worked for clients at their office. That didn't stop me from living what I thought was the culture of my employers.

Forced hybridism for the sake of culture creates the illusion that it's all about in-person activities. In their book *Remote: Office Not Required*, David Heinemeier Hansson and Jason Fried state,

Having people work remotely forces you to forgo the illusion that building a company culture is just about in-person social activities. Now you can get on with the actual work of defining and practicing it instead.

DON'T CREATE A PERCEPTION OF ASYMMETRY

Even if one were to concede the arguments about culture, productivity, and serendipity, there's a problem of asymmetry in forced hybridism. As I write this chapter, most executives who've driven a mandate for hybrid work or for a "return to office" (RTO) have also retained optionality in their work lives. They can work remotely when they please. Such a perception can drive a wedge between people and their leaders.

Even when leaders say they'll return to the office in solidarity with their workforce, they can become victims to this perception. After all, it'll still be a decision *by a few, for the many*. A forced-hybrid arrangement reduces people's feeling of autonomy at work.

Such a perception poses a risk to how you retain talent in your firm. I write this chapter during a global recession. That said, the tech industry will continue to grow in the long run. What then? Raj Choudhury says top talent drives workplace trends. If top-talent values flexibility, then inflexible organizations will see an inevitable exodus. Organizations that put people first will have a competitive advantage.

TREAT EVERYONE AS "REMOTE"

While I've questioned organizations and execs who may employ forced hybridism, I admit they may also have good intentions. The path to hell, however—you know how the cliché goes! The aim of this chapter is to outline the dangers of misunderstanding what a truly hybrid organization should look like.

Here's a piece of advice: avoid the term *hybrid* altogether. It's a loaded word, too many people misunderstand it, and it's fraught with risks. Instead, adopt a remote-first, async-first mindset.

GitLab, Invision, Buffer, Basecamp, Doist, Automattic, and others were the early innovators of async-first remote work. More recently, companies like Shopify, Dropbox, EPAM, and Slalom have joined the party. As early adopters, they're already reaping benefits. There's still a window of opportunity for firms to be the early majority, as you see in Figure 26.1. Companies that miss this window will lag the innovation curve in designing the workplace of the future.

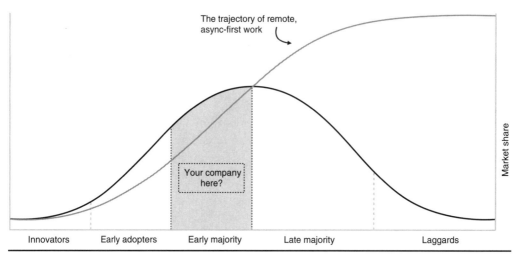

Figure 26.1 Organizations can still stay ahead of the curve (adapted from *James Stanier*).

Working asynchronously helps you participate in this future, while giving people the work–life balance they want. I also see this to be inclusive of people who would otherwise be invisible in our industry. A forced-hybrid model is the antithesis of such a work philosophy. It sacrifices flexibility and inclusion and limits scale. The arguments in its favor, be it productivity, serendipity, or preserving the cultural secret sauce, don't bear themselves out in empirical evidence. Well-intentioned leaders must think deeper about these problems. Another world is possible.

- If you care about connection, give people time, space, and the budget to create social connections. This can be through purposeful face-to-face interactions, through sponsored travel, and through company organized team events and retreats.
- If you care about learning, give people discretionary spend, the right systems, and on-the-job learning opportunities.
- If you care about serendipity, invest in the right tools and systems.
- If you care about productivity, move to an asynchronous way of working.

Oh, and if you retain your office space, your workforce will still be "hybrid." Just don't impose "hybrid" on every individual. Make location irrelevant in your way of working.

People can still have in-person interactions in your offices if they choose. Instead of telling people where to work, let them make that decision. If you don't feel comfortable devolving these decisions to the individual, then let teams decide how much in-person time they need. That may be the best way to balance the needs of the collective with the needs of the individual.

Create a culture of collaboration, where you *treat everyone as remote*, regardless of their physical proximity to each other. Always be inclusive of those who aren't in the same physical premises. This is a conscious shift that you must precipitate as a leader.

CHOICE AND AUTONOMY ARE THE KEY WORDS

Hybrid is a popular term and a seductive idea. I believe that poorly orchestrated hybrid work can be the biggest obstacle for an async-first way of working.

CHAPTER SUMMARY

It's natural to believe that a "hybrid" work policy where every employee spends a few days remote and a few days in the office is a "best of both worlds" approach. In fact, this is the hardest work mode to orchestrate.

- If organizations respect people's work preferences, they'll automatically be hybrid. There's no need to make every individual hybrid. This lowers everyone's productivity to the lowest common denominator.
- "Forced hybridism" threatens to erode gains in operational efficiency over the last two years, in areas such as hiring, staffing, and training.
- Forced-hybridism is also a costly move. Employers pay for infrastructure and office space; employees pay with a poorer quality of life; and society pays with poorer inclusion, brain drain, and environmental impacts.
- Many arguments in favor of forced hybridism are weak. They stem from a status-quo bias and a lack of deep thought, rather than from data or research.
- When leaders force their view of hybrid work on employees, the decision may seem asymmetric. There's negligible impact on leaders' work lives, but employees pay a disproportionate cost in comparison.
- The perception of asymmetry could eventually leave companies vulnerable. Top talent will migrate to employers that offer a flexible workplace.
- Instead of forced hybridism, employers should consider making the right investments in systems, people's learning, retreats and social events, and new ways of working. This will help them stay ahead of the future-of-work curve.

Even when your company adopts a remote-first mindset, everyone may not be async-first. If your team is alone in being async-first, you may find it hard to maintain your new ways of working. So, in the next chapter, let's understand the risks of being an "async island" and how you can mitigate them.

27

THE ASYNC ISLAND

If you look back at all the advice in this book, you'll notice that I recommend a "part-guerrilla, part-advocate" approach to change. With your team, you can be opportunistic and introduce async-first processes and ways of working wherever they make sense. As an advocate, you can use your successes from these experiments to justify a shift for the rest of the organization.

It makes sense to start small. That's the essence of agility, isn't it? But in large organizations, it's difficult for a small team to cling to its subculture for indefinitely. It's not impossible to have an "async island of excellence"! It's simply hard.

UNPACKING ORGANIZATIONAL INERTIA

When you introduce change in any part of a company, there's always a tension between the push and pull for change versus the inertia and anxieties against it. To understand this, let's build a model to think about teams within large companies.

The forces in this model aren't unique to async-first ways of working. The same forces apply to any other change you introduce in a team. I think of the forces across three categories:

- The change agent
- Internal forces
- External forces

To understand how these forces collide, let's spend some time understanding them.

FORCES FOR AND AGAINST CHANGE

In Figure 27.1 you'll see the three kinds of forces at play. We'll explore these from left to right.

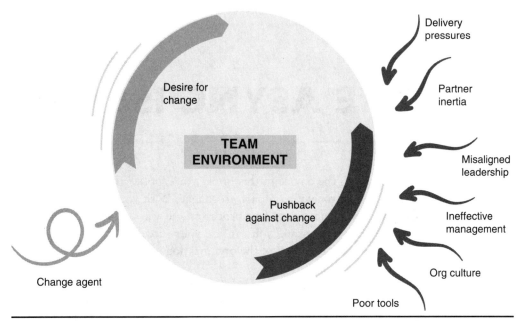

Figure 27.1 The colliding forces of change.

The Change Agent

The change agent refers to any external influence that precipitates a shift in the team. This could be a combination of various things. Here are a few examples that may come to your mind:

- An external consultant
- Technology or collaboration trends
- Performance objectives
- Market or compliance needs
- Current ideas from books, conferences, or other learning experiences

Internal Forces

These are the forces that either catalyze or stall change within a team. The team could **desire** the change because either or both of these reasons:

- They see that their current approaches don't work.
- They see better alternatives to the status quo.

On the other hand, the team could **push back** against the change for multiple reasons. We discussed some of these reasons earlier.

- Theory-induced blindness stops people from seeing flaws in their favorite approaches to work and thinking.
- Loss aversion stops people from adopting fresh approaches for fear of losing something they already have.
- Temporary, unaccounted-for productivity dips may cause teams to lose faith in the change.
- Since we can't foresee the future, we discount the problems we may face several months later. We avoid change and focus on the most immediate issues at hand.

Teams gain internal momentum for change when their desire for it overpowers their pushback against it.

External Forces

In my experience, these are the forces that have a disproportionate impact on a team's ability to sustain change. Here are some examples of such organizational factors:

- **Delivery pressures.** When you have tight deadlines and unrealistic go-live plans, it'll drive a chaotic work environment for the team. An async-first work culture aims to calm the team atmosphere through protocols and thoughtful communication. It's almost impossible to manage chaos asynchronously. In such situations, teams will sink back into a sync-first way of work.
- **Partner inertia.** Many companies collaborate with partners. It may not be possible to insulate your own work processes from those of the partners, especially if the power dynamic is in their favor. For example, if your partner is a client and they skew toward being synchronous, then your team will struggle to maintain an async-first approach.
- **Misaligned leadership.** We've addressed the role of leaders in an async-first culture. When leaders at any level don't model async-first behaviors, they influence people who look up to them. Depending on how powerful the leaders in question are, it can make the async-first teams seem like rogue subcultures in the company.

- **Ineffective management.** Remote and asynchronous work needs a fresh approach to management. We discussed several of the shifts earlier. For example, you need an outcomes focus over an inputs focus. Managers must relinquish their positional authority. An effective way to do this is by making processes and documentation clear. You should be able to respond with a link. Counterintuitively, you must care personally for your team and know enough about their work to challenge them directly. If managers don't adapt, the async-first shift doesn't stick.

- **Org culture.** Any team exists within an organizational culture. It's impossible to preserve a subculture that's different from the rest of the organization. Such teams stick out like sore thumbs. It's tough to rotate people in and out of these groups. Hiring into these teams can be a challenge as well. Interdepartmental collaboration can become a nightmare. All systems have a state of equilibrium. Organizations are systems as well. They will always gravitate back to that equilibrium. An oddball team can resist for only so long.

- **Poor tools.** I mention this last only because it seems like a trivial topic, but it isn't. Thankfully, most companies in knowledge work have decent collaboration tools. Sometimes, however, there are gaps in tool capabilities that can slow teams down. For example, if a team decides to pair-program and there's no specialized software for it, the practice can be cumbersome. A handbook-first culture is central to asynchronous work, but what if you have no tools to create one? Introducing new tools to just one team in a large company is an arduous task. You need to watch out for approvals, compliance, integration with systems, and whatnot. While all these processes are important, they also represent corporate red tape, especially in larger companies. It can be months or years before a team gets the tools they're happy with. Many teams will lose all motivation for change by then.

I've enumerated all these forces because I want to illustrate how async-first teams will find the odds against them if the rest of the company doesn't also appreciate and adopt this new way of working. If the forces against change are stronger than the forces for it, the change will be difficult to maintain.

ASYNC WORK IS A NEW SPORT

If you follow sports, you'll note that we play many of them with similar equipment. For example, golf and disc golf, hockey and ice hockey, ping-pong and tennis, and T20 cricket and test cricket are different sports with somewhat similar equipment. Regardless of the country and culture you're from, you'll find some of these examples. But even when sports look similar, their rules, nuances, and context are different. It also takes something special for a player who trains in one sport to succeed in another. It's not impossible, but it needs a growth mindset.

In an analogous way, sync and async-first ways of working are different sports with the same goal, same equipment but different techniques, different skills, and a different mindset. The defaults for both ways of working are different too.

Just like you don't expect a ping-pong player to play tennis (or vice versa), you can't expect people to switch between different modes of working. I mention this because organizations will inevitably want some people to work across teams. You may rotate people. You'll also hire new people.

What happens when an async-first player must now work with a mostly synchronous team? What about the reverse?

- How do you hire people so their work habits are complementary to those of the team?
- If you share the hiring pool with the rest of your company, how will you interview for the characteristics your team needs to maintain an async-first culture?

The bigger the organization, the tougher these questions get. Organizations eventually need to be decisive about what their default way of working is. They need to decide which sport they're playing. Multiple defaults lead to unlimited confusion.

HELP YOUR SYSTEM GET BETTER

To explain my point about multiple defaults, let me explain the conscious competence model or the four stages of competence that you see in Figure 27.2:

- **Unconscious incompetence.** *You don't know what you don't know.* Neither the deficit in skill nor the utility of the skill in question is obvious to you. You need a stimulus that'll kick-start your learning.
- **Conscious incompetence.** *You know what you don't know.* You understand the need for a specific skill, and you know you don't have it. But you still don't know how to execute.
- **Conscious competence.** *You know what you know.* You've learned the skill and can perform it when you concentrate and follow the steps consciously.

- **Unconscious competence.** *You don't know what you know.* You've had so much practice with the skill that it's now second nature. In fact, you don't even stop to think about it when you execute.

Figure 27.2 Four stages of competence.

Adapting to a new way of working also goes through roughly the same process. You achieve a state of nirvana when everyone on the team follows the team's practices without having to think too much about them.

But what if someone has to switch between two separate ways of working frequently? They'll always have to recalibrate themselves to the norms of the team they're working with, like you see in Figure 27.3. Most of the time they'll switch between unconscious and conscious incompetence. With some difficulty they may get to conscious competence, but it's almost impossible for them to make a way of working second nature.

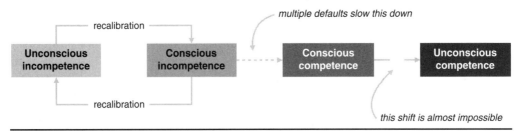

Figure 27.3 Lack of a sensible default stalls the learning process.

If you want to rotate people across teams, you must extend your sensible defaults across the organization.

PROTECT AND EXTEND THE ISLAND

So, this is where the rub is, and this is where I come full circle. *Part-guerilla, part-advocate*, of course! Teams are the smallest unit to drive change with, so start there by all means. However, as you play the guerilla, don't forget to play the advocate. A single team can be a nursery to develop an async-first way of working. However, if that shift must last, you must spread the seeds wide. At some point, the entire company must join the party.

Having said that, I suggest a few strategies to protect or extend your async ways of working. Depending on the stage of your shift, use the ones that work for you.

Recruit a Vertical Slice of Your Company

When you start on your async-first shift, in a company that works mostly in a synchronous fashion, it'll be tough to convince everyone to change. Therefore, we've focused on shrinking the change to your immediate team. To sustain this change for any duration of time, though, you must also garner support from other layers of the organization that you interact with. For example, as we saw in Part IV, managers must embody async behaviors in the way they work. Even executives, stakeholders, and partners who interact with the team occasionally shouldn't pull the team back into a synchronous way of working. So, you need the support of the entire vertical slice of the company that the team interacts with. Figure 27.4 illustrates the concept of this vertical slice.

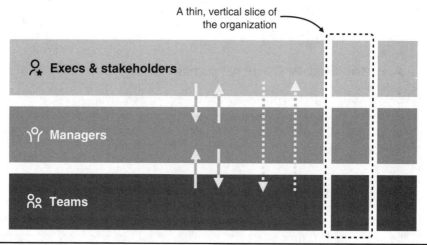

Figure 27.4 Support from all layers of the company, with a limited radius.

As a change agent, you're responsible for enlisting such support across company layers. Explain the rationale for the change to each layer of people in the company who the team collaborates with. It helps to take an interaction focus here. In Chapter 20, we learned about Team APIs; this helps teams define who they interact with and how. Use this artifact to drive alignment with those outside the team but who are part of that thin organizational slice.

Get Your Department or Division to Go Async

If you've gone async-first for a while and you're seeing benefits, you should have some evidence to say that this has worked well for you. You still may not be able to influence the entire company, but you may be able to influence other teams that you work with. For want of a universal term that describes different organizational structures, let's call this a "department."

I suggest using data to influence your departmental colleagues. In Chapter 24, we discussed how you can use indicators aligned to the SPACE framework to track your own progress. You can also use these indicators to show your colleagues the before-and-after story of your async-first shift.

You'll find it helpful to also reiterate that this isn't an all-or-nothing shift. Just as you'd have shifted left in small steps, on the spectrum of synchronousness, so will every other team. Remind your departmental colleagues that they can choose their own plays to drive this change in their context.

┌─ BEST PRACTICE ─────────────────────

Aim for Stable Counterparts

Even if your department is slow to change, you can help your team maintain their ways of working by identifying stable counterparts in other teams. These are people in other teams and functions with whom you'll maintain a long-term work relationship.

Not only does a stable counterpart allow for trust to develop between individuals, but it also helps you limit what you're asking from colleagues in other teams, when it comes to ways of working. The one-on-one relationship between stable counterparts also provides an avenue to influence departmental colleagues, over a period. You can use team topologies (Chapter 24) and the Team API (Chapter 20) to define the purpose and nature of these inter-team interactions.

Create a Community of Practice

Ultimately, the goal of going async is to work more effectively in distributed teams. We can say with some certainty that the time of five days in the office is behind us. Every team will be remote and distributed to some degree, and I suspect that degree of distribution will become more extreme each year. This is where a community of practice that focuses on effective remote and distributed work comes in handy.

In Chapter 25, we discussed the value of communities to knowledge sharing in the company. How you implement them will depend on the tool stack you use. It can be as simple as a Slack channel or as sophisticated as a group on Workplace by Meta. The advantage of creating this distributed and remote work–focused community is that you'll have a place to share your learning and to also learn from everyone else who cares about effective remote work. It'll bring like-minded people from the company together. You'll also find other evangelists who can influence their part of the business to adopt async-first practices. When there's enough critical mass, you can also lean on this community to develop hiring attributes that'll help you assess if a candidate can work asynchronously. The possibilities are endless!

Share Tools, Templates, and Sensible Defaults

Most change seems daunting because people don't know where to start. Even books such as this one have their limitations. People are busy, and there's little time to pause and consider how the techniques in this book may apply to their context.

If you've had the time to pause and think about this for your team, you can make the shift easier for everyone else.

- Share contextual advice for going async first by detailing what you've specifically done on your team.
- From your experience of change, describe what the sensible defaults may be. These would be the simplest, initial steps that you believe any team in your department or company can take when they go async first.
- Share tools and templates with other teams. For example, if there's a template you use to write DoR stories, make it available for everyone. If you've written an automation rule for standup updates using Trello Butler, share it with others as a starting point.

RESOURCE

The Async-First Method Stack

If you need a way to share the methods and techniques we've discussed in this book, use the async-first method stack (https://methods.asyncagile.org) as a starting point (Figure 27.5).

I've organized all the plays by category, and you can search through them to find the specific play you're looking for. You can also use the instructions for each play as a template that you can modify and adapt to your own context.

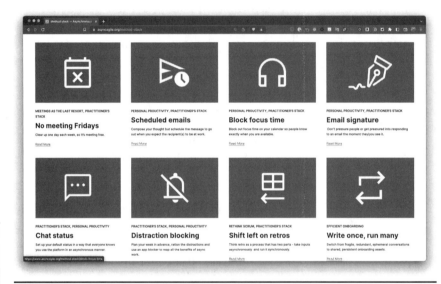

Figure 27.5 A representation of the async-first method stack.

All these steps will help you ensure that your team doesn't stick out like a sore thumb for too long. If you can proliferate these ways of working to other teams in the company, it'll also help you rotate people into your team more easily. People from your team will also find it easier to move to other teams when it's time. In Chapter 29, we'll extend the concept of sensible defaults, when I introduce you to the async-first starter kit.

WHILE BEING A GUERILLA, DON'T FORGET ADVOCACY

The most logical place to start an async-first shift is your immediate team. But if the organization doesn't eventually follow along, it'll be tough to sustain the change.

CHAPTER SUMMARY

A team that's an "async island" is an anti-pattern that any async-first advocate must avoid in the long run.

- External organizational forces can overwhelm a team that has a vastly unique way of working from the rest of the company.
- Async-first and sync-first ways of working need different skills and different mindsets. Few people can switch between them. This makes rotations and inter-departmental collaboration hard.
- If you don't have an organizational default way of working, people will always have to recalibrate themselves based on the team they work in. This makes it difficult to gain fluency, where the way of working becomes second nature.
- To protect your team's way of working and to precipitate change in the rest of the company, we discussed a few strategies.
  - When you start your journey, enlist support from the entire vertical slice of the company that your team interacts with. This includes managers, execs, stakeholders, and partners.
  - As you build evidence for the success of the async-first approach, share these stories with departmental colleagues so they can learn from your experience. Use data to tell these stories.
  - Create a community of practice focused on effective remote work. This will help spread your ideas further than your sphere of influence.
  - Share tools, templates, and sensible defaults so you can make it easy for others to adopt this new way of working.

The first two chapters of this part of the book focused on organizational traps your async-first team may face. In the final chapter of this part, we'll shift focus to some internal pitfalls. I'll describe four harmful anti-patterns that remote teams are particularly vulnerable to. You'll also learn how to avoid such toxicity.

TOXICITY IN THE VIRTUAL WORKPLACE

Every work model has its traps. While the office, particularly the open office, had its interruptions, monocultures, and cliques, it's not as if a remote workplace can't go south. An async-first remote culture looks to foster a calm, respectful, flexible, fun, and inclusive workplace that values deep work. Those are great intentions. Both leaders and team members must preserve those characteristics of the workplace.

In this chapter, I explore some anti-patterns I've seen in remote-first and "hybrid" organizations that can make your workplace toxic.

TOXICITY BUILDS: ONE BENIGN STEP AT A TIME

No one plans to make their workplace toxic. Often, it's a series of well-intentioned missteps. Some of these are by-products of old habits that die hard. Others are unintended but not uncommon consequences of a remote workplace.

When you know of these possibilities ahead of time, you'll be able to pre-empt them and put the right guardrails in place for your team. Let's explore some of these anti-patterns.

CELEBRATING THE HARD WORKER

A few days before I wrote this chapter, I saw a team at a company I admire celebrate a few of their superstars. I enjoy celebrating my colleagues as well, but there was something about that celebration that bothered me. One of the leaders at that event celebrated an individual for "going above and beyond their regular workday and for straddling opposing time zones to deliver results."

The problem with a celebration of this nature is that it sets the wrong precedent. When a leader celebrates long work hours or an unsustainable work pattern, it lays down unwritten norms. Before you know it, everyone believes they must work long hours so their company values them. It may be tempting in the short term to even encourage your employees to give it a good, hard crack, or, as some of us like to say, "hustle." The truth is that an unsustainable work environment hurts you eventually. Research from Clockwise confirms many of our fears, but there are two I want to point out:

- **The impact on diversity.** Women are twice as likely as men to feel that their work culture is unsustainable.
- **The likelihood of attrition.** Workers at companies with unsustainable cultures are more than nine times as likely to say they don't see themselves at their company in the next 12 months.

This doesn't mean you shouldn't recognize people's efforts. Do that, but instead of focusing on how long someone worked, celebrate the results they drove. Coach and encourage your colleagues to maintain a work–life balance and celebrate the people who help others have a sustainable pace at work. This preserves the culture of appreciation, while avoiding the toxicity of long work hours.

DIGITAL PRESENTEEISM

The twin phenomena of proximity bias and visibility bias have a deep impact on work relationships.

- Those who are physically closer to company leaders enjoy a greater influence on them and have a better chance at advancing their careers.
- Only when people can "see you" working do they believe that you're being useful.

Of course, that isn't fair. The whole premise of asynchronous work is that hours and locations don't matter. Then again, we're human. All our actions aren't rational, and our biases come with their corresponding blind spots. Despite our best intentions, we may end up recognizing our "visible" colleagues more than the ones who are just silently hammering away at their work.

Abby Peel, co-lead of the mental health network at the UK government's digital service, says this:

Digital presenteeism happens when you feel under pressure to always be available online, via video calls, phone, email, chat, or Slack. It's when you've done a full day's work but feel pressure to log on or reply later than your normal or preferred working patterns, even if you feel exhausted or unwell.

In the remote workplace, this can lead to a bunch of toxic behaviors and responses.

Some colleagues appreciate other colleagues who're always active on Slack or other communication platforms. Soon, everyone feels the need to be present and responsive on Slack.

- The boss appreciates people who respond to emails after hours. Before you know it, everyone is monitoring email if they're awake.
- People who attend meetings are the only people who get access to certain information. This breeds a culture where everyone wants to be in every meeting for the fear of missing out (FOMO).

Even our tools don't make it easy on us. Read receipts and presence indicators on digital collaboration tools add to the phenomenon of digital presenteeism.

Like in the case of celebration, keeping a focus on results and de-emphasizing the notion of presence are helpful. By instituting communication protocols, moving most task-based communication to your task board, and making meetings the last resort and not the first option, you'd have already taken systemic steps to avoid this toxicity.

If you're a leader at any level, then you also have a key role to play here. Don't send messages or emails after hours. The more you do it, the more others will follow. In fact, at the time of writing this chapter, some countries, such as Belgium, France, Portugal, and Italy, have gone so far as to ban employers from contacting staff out of hours.

Let me risk sounding like a broken record here. Be sure to rate people fairly on their work and not based on how visible they seem. When people have the confidence that their results matter more than digital schmoozing, you have a greater chance of avoiding the digital presenteeism trap.

TALKING TO THE DOCUMENT

When you work asynchronously, the design of the team's workflow prioritizes written communication and time for deep work. Writing has its benefits, of course, but there's always too much of a good thing. When things go off balance, we risk veering into toxic territory.

We must avoid a false sense of urgency for obvious reasons. Not everything needs an immediate response, and everyone wants uninterrupted time to work. Urgency is overrated. An ASAP culture is toxic. Keeping someone blocked, though, is insensitive. When someone can't move forward with their work even though they have a bias for action; or if they need some time-sensitive input, we can't ask them to "talk to the document." In such cases, a short conversation is much better than an endless asynchronous back and forth in a document or, worse, over email or IM. The toxic aftertaste of such inefficient communication can erode people's faith in an async way of working. It does more harm than good to the culture you're trying to create.

The ConveRel quadrants from Chapter 7 give you a simple rubric to decide whether you should go sync or async. As you'll remember, most communication about "convergence" is best suited for a synchronous medium. This also exploits what synchronous communication is good for: speed and connectedness. It doesn't matter how experienced the team is at working remotely. Revisit these fundamentals and course correct if you notice the team pushing too far in either direction.

NOT INVESTING IN MEANINGFUL SYNCHRONY

Asynchronous work is not "anti-meeting." It's about meetings as the last resort and not the first option. But there will always be situations where we must "sync up." The trouble is that the world of work has a poor track record with meetings.

A few years back, the *Harvard Business Review* published an article called "Stop the Meeting Madness." The article shared some sobering statistics about how ineffective meetings can be. These figures came from a survey of 82 senior managers in a range of industries:

- 65 percent said meetings keep them from completing their own work.
- 71 percent said meetings are unproductive and inefficient.
- 64 percent said meetings come at the expense of deep thinking.
- 62 percent said meetings miss opportunities to bring the team closer together.

When a team gets used to working asynchronously, there's a tendency to avoid even the useful meetings because of our biases against them. Before you know it, you'll introduce more lags into your system than you'd have bargained for. The key is to make these sync-ups productive and not feel like a drain on our time. That means your team needs to follow meeting best practices, day in and day out. Some of this is harder than it sounds. It needs discipline. There's also the matter of skill.

When you are intentional about the meetings you have, the stakes for each meeting will be quite high. This may sound like a terrible thing, but it isn't. Meetings are costly activities, so the stakes better be high. Skilled facilitators can manage these high-stakes situations and help you make the most of your synchronous interactions.

I'm not suggesting that you must hire a facilitator for every meeting you have. You can do that for a workshop or two, but otherwise, it's impractical. You can, however, staff each team in a way that it has at least one or two people who are passionate about facilitation. They don't need to be experts. Even keen learners will do. Support their interest by helping them learn these skills. Sponsor their training if possible. Find them a mentor if you can. Give them the chance to practice their skills by asking them to plan and lead the few team meetings you have. Encourage them to try new patterns and formats for meetings and workshops so they expand their facilitation toolkit.

When people take care to design and run meetings effectively, it has a few effects:

- You'll get the value you expect from these interactions: a sense of connectedness, speed, a broad range of ideas.
- Your facilitators will keep raising the bar for what makes for an effective meeting.
- People will learn from the facilitators and take away inspiration to build their own facilitation skills.

If you're lucky, the facilitators you find at the start may not be the only facilitators on the team. As people learn from each other and as you set the standard for effective meetings, other people on the team will step up and lead. Wouldn't that be a great side effect?

AS A LEADER, STAY VIGILANT

In his book *A World Without Email*, Cal Newport mentions a term called *collaborative pacing*. Douglas Rushkoff defined this term first in his book *Present Shock: When Everything Happens Now*. The idea is that "groups of humans may converge toward strict patterns of behavior without ever actually explicitly deciding that the new behaviors make sense." One person behaves a certain way, another follows, and before you know it, a pattern appears.

Toxic anti-patterns at work appear in a similar fashion. For organizations and teams in transition, you already need to battle the status quo bias of naysayers. Since remote work is newer in comparison to office-bound ways of working, every anti-pattern in a remote workplace will face a disproportionate amount of scrutiny as compared to the office. So, teams and leaders that want to protect their new ways of working must be vigilant and pre-empt the toxic anti-patterns we've discussed in this article. This is as important to the success of your transition as employing the right practices.

CHAPTER SUMMARY

When working apart for long, remote, async-first teams can become victims to some toxic anti-patterns. Here are four major anti-patterns that you must guard against as you transition to a remote native, async-first way of working:

- Celebrating long hours and unsustainable pace sets the wrong example among people. It'll eventually burn people out. This benefits no one.
- Proximity and visibility bias can force an always-on culture. People may feel obliged to be in every meeting, every chat, and every email exchange. This leaves little time for work and erodes the efficiency of our communication systems.
- Going async doesn't mean being insensitive and not talking to people when there's a good reason to do so. If anything, when we neglect time-sensitive work with a slow, asynchronous back-and-forth, it can shake people's faith in this way of working.
- Async-first isn't async-only, or anti-meeting. We must invest effort in better meetings as well. Effective facilitators can help in a big way. Promote effective facilitation by helping people on your team build these skills.

That brings us to the end of this penultimate section of the playbook. In the last, albeit short, part, we'll wrap things up. I'll introduce you to a toolkit that'll help you lead your team into an async-first shift before we look ahead to what the future of work may hold for all of us.

Part VI

BRING IT ALL TOGETHER

We've reached the last part of this book. It's now time to bring together everything we've learned to shift left with your team and adopt an async-first mindset.

- **Chapter 29**, "The Async-First Starter Kit," describes a set of tools that will help guide your team to kick off their async-first shift.
- To conclude this book, **Chapter 30**, "A Brave New World of Work," looks ahead to the future and the trends that may shape how we work with each other.

THE ASYNC-FIRST STARTER KIT

Here we are, almost at the end of our journey together. We've discussed several ideas and plays in this playbook. I'm certain that a subset of them will be relevant to your team's context and work.

In Chapter 2, we discussed how you can build a mindset for change in your team. In Part II of the book, we addressed how to create a scaffold for this change. And in Part III, which was the longest part in this book, you learned about several ways practitioners can collaborate asynchronously with each other.

However, I understand that too many ideas can be overwhelming. Where do you start? How can you get a few quick wins? How can you encourage your team to take ownership of this async-first shift? In this chapter, I introduce you to a set of tools and templates that'll bring some of your learning together and help you facilitate your team to own this shift. Sound good? Okay, then.

FIVE STAGES OF SENSIBLE DEFAULTS

Before I explain how to use the starter kit, let me clarify that this isn't the only way to go async-first. Think of this kit as a set of sensible defaults that should help a broad range of teams. In most cases, you may have to make minor tweaks to suit your context, just like you may not stay with the factory defaults of the gadgets you purchase. So, don't take this as a prescription. It's more a starting point that'll save you some design effort.

I've organized the starter kit (see Figure 29.1) into five stages. You can be flexible in how you go through these stages with your team. Many activities can be asynchronous if your team is already up for it. However, if you want to run these activities as synchronous workshops, in the interest of building connection and commitment, that's okay too. Each stage should take an hour or less. Your mileage will vary, of course, so use your judgment, and stretch or compress as you see fit.

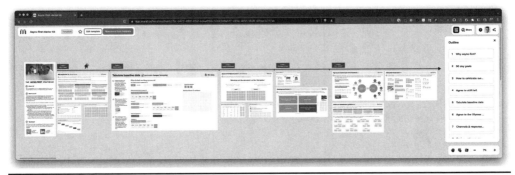

Figure 29.1 Representation of the async-first starter kit on Mural.

In the interest of brevity, I'll describe each stage without going into granular details. You'll find those details and step-by-step instructions when you access the materials on the companion site (https://www.asyncagile.org/book-resources).

While I've created the tools using Google Workspace and Mural, you can re-create them using a similar design on tools of your choice. All these materials are available under a Creative Commons license. Enough said. Let's get into each stage.

STAGE 1: ALIGN ON GOALS

Figure 29.2 highlights the exercise panels from stage 1. As we saw in Chapter 2, we first want to align on the benefits we're trying to achieve by going async. In this stage, you'll begin the conversation about going async-first by introducing your team to the six key benefits of going async:

- Work–life balance
- Diversity and inclusion
- Knowledge sharing
- Optimizing for scale
- Deep work
- Defaulting to action

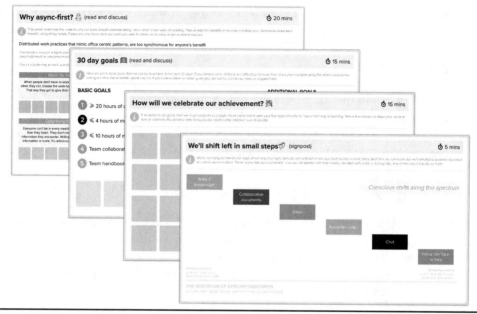

Figure 29.2 Representation of the activity panels for stage 1.

Allow your team the time to absorb what each of these benefits mean and encourage them to add their comments to each benefit using sticky notes. Address any objections or concerns and emphasize agreement before you move ahead in this stage.

Next, agree on some basic goals for the first 30 days of your shift. To make things easy for you, I've listed five simple but impactful goals that you and your team can aim to achieve without much effort:

- 20 or more hours of deep work, per person, per week
- 4 or more hours of meetings per week, per individual contributor
- 10 or more hours of meetings per week, per manager or lead
- Team collaboration charter in place
- Team handbook in place

As with anything else in the kit, you can modify these goals to something more ambitious or less daunting. You can also add goals if you think you have the appetite for them.

Once you've agreed on the goals you want to achieve, you must also agree how you'll celebrate your achievement. This will be a full team effort, so it pays to recognize that effort. It could be a team outing, a dinner, or conference attendance budgets for everyone—leave it to the team to decide. As the facilitator, feel free to let the team know if there are any constraints they should keep in mind—for example budgets.

As a last step in this stage, use the spectrum of synchronousness from Chapter 2 as a signpost. Reassure everyone that this will be a team-owned, gradual shift. Encourage everyone to think how they can move every interaction further left on the spectrum. After this, take a pause before you move to stage 2.

STAGE 2: TABULATE BASELINE DATA

Data is often an objective way to track how any change is impacting your team. You'll notice that we've set some quantitative goals for ourselves in stage 1. Some of these relate to how people spend their time. I find it intrusive to measure such parameters using tracking software. Instead, I prefer that people self-report how they're spending their time.

This is also a suitable time to assess how the team perceives its discipline on the following aspects:

- Use of distributed work artifacts
- Effective meeting practices
- Onboarding practices

To help facilitate this data gathering, you'll find a survey form in the starter kit. You'll also find the survey questions in a document so you can re-create the form using tools of your choice. Once you've collected people's responses to the survey, you'll have to convert some of their responses into a quantitative measure. While it's much easier to do this using business intelligence (BI) tools like Google's Looker Studio, I've created a rudimentary spreadsheet, which has a "score spitter." All you need to do is to input data from the survey results, and the formulae on the sheet will give you scores on various parameters. I suggest running this survey every fortnight to see how people's perception changes with time. Figure 29.3 shows the survey and the score calculator.

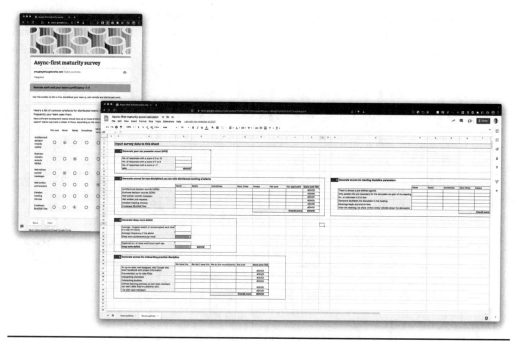

Figure 29.3 A representation of an async-first maturity survey and score calculator.

Once you have done your first round of data gathering, tabulate it on the dashboard you see in Figure 29.4. You'll notice that beside each data entry field, there's an indicative goal for that specific metric. This helps you and your team assess how you may compare to elite, async-first teams.

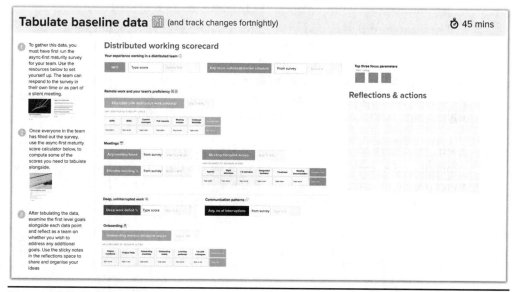

Figure 29.4 Representation of the tabulate baseline data from the async-first maturity survey.

That comparison may encourage your team to consider other goals for this shift. Set aside some time for reflection. Ask your team to add their comments using sticky notes. Group similar comments and agree on any actions that you all must take.

> ## Find More Elegant Ways to Track Data
>
> While the starter kit provides you with a space to tabulate some data for the first time, this is not a flexible way to track such indicators over time. The survey also doesn't track other indicators of team health, such as the ones we discussed in Chapter 24. I suggest moving to a more elegant way to track such data, after you complete the baseline. Tools like LinearB will help you generate insights about team productivity. You can plug your survey results into a BI tool like Google Data Studio, so it's easy to observe changes over time. These tools will also help you slice and dice the data so you can narrow down your observations.

STAGE 3: AGREE ON THE FUNDAMENTALS

To go async, we must agree on a few fundamental principles. Without this agreement, it'll be impossible to work asynchronously. The first of these principles is our Ulysses pact: "Meetings are the last resort, not the first option." And to make that possible, the team must agree to two other behaviors:

• Writing becomes a primary means of communication in the team.
• The team must build comfort with reasonable lags in communication.

This can be a thorny topic for teams that are more familiar with a synchronous way of working. Allow time for people to share their hopes and concerns with the Ulysses pact. Address any objections using everything you've learned in this book. Use the Ulysses pact as a team commitment that you can refer to throughout the shift.

Next, you'll define what a "reasonable lag" is. To do so, you must list all the communication channels your team has, how you'll use them, and what response times people should expect on each of them. You'll remember the sensible default from Chapter 9. This step allows your team to begin with that sensible default and repurpose it to your context. Figure 29.5 includes the panel for this step.

Figure 29.5 Representation of agreeing to fundamentals in stage 3.

In the last step for this stage, agree on four basic meeting protocols. We've addressed these items in Chapter 7:

- No agenda, no attenda.
- People should have the safety to decline meetings where they don't get or add value.
- Most meetings should have fewer than eight attendees.
- The team will document all meetings using meeting notes.

These protocols are relatively uncontroversial, so it shouldn't take much time to agree on them. Still, set aside some space and time for the team to share their thoughts and comments. Once you've addressed everyone's thoughts, you can take these commitments to work and move to the next stage.

STAGE 4: CLEAN UP YOUR CALENDARS

With the basics out of the way, you can now focus on concrete actions. The first step is to defrag your calendars. To do so, we'll implement a few plays we've discussed in Chapter 12:

1. Move all team meetings to one half of the day, leaving the other half inviolate.

2. Create one meeting-free day each week.

3. The first two steps address the team calendar. Everyone must also align their own calendars such that they don't schedule meetings in what's meant to be a meeting-free time.

The previous three steps will not reduce the quantum of meetings. They'll only free up contiguous blocks of time for deep work. That helps you achieve one goal from stage 1. To achieve some of the other goals, you must reduce meetings. That's the next step. The ConveRel quadrants from Chapter 7 will help you decide which meetings to delete, which to shorten, and which to keep.

As a team, classify your existing meetings into the different quadrants:

- You can easily replace the quadrant 1 (conveyance/strong relationship) meetings with async communication.

- For meetings in quadrant 2 (conveyance/weak relationship) and 4 (convergence/ strong relationship), discuss if you can shorten them or if it's possible to eliminate them in some cases.

- You can leave quadrant 3 (convergence/weak relationship) meetings as they are, but be sure to limit attendance on these. Reconsider their duration as well. If some of these meetings are recurring, discuss with the team if you can replace them with more purposeful, on-demand interactions.

Use Figure 29.6 to identify the panels from stage 4. Once you're done with this stage, you'll be close to achieving three of the five basic goals from stage 1—time for deep work and reducing meeting time. You can then move to the final stage.

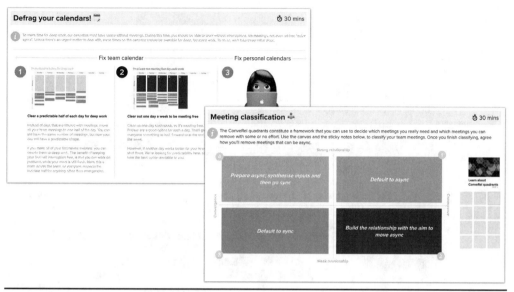

Figure 29.6 Representation of cleaning up calendars and finding ways to reduce meetings in stage 4.

STAGE 5: BUILD THE 30-DAY PROGRAM AND BEYOND

In stage 1, I proposed that you make your team handbook and collaboration charter part of your 30-day goals. Stage 5 (panels highlighted in Figure 29.7) helps you achieve that goal through light, "barn raising" activities.

> *Barn raising occurs when a community decides to come together to help achieve some specific goal.*

No one person can create a team handbook by themselves, so it makes sense to divide and conquer. As a first step, the kit provides you with a panel where you can decide which tool you'll use to host the handbook. On the same panel, you'll notice the diagram from Chapter 10, which describes various sections of the handbook. Team members can use sticky notes to sign up, so they can flesh out each of these sections. Be sure to agree on a due-by date when you can all review these initial versions.

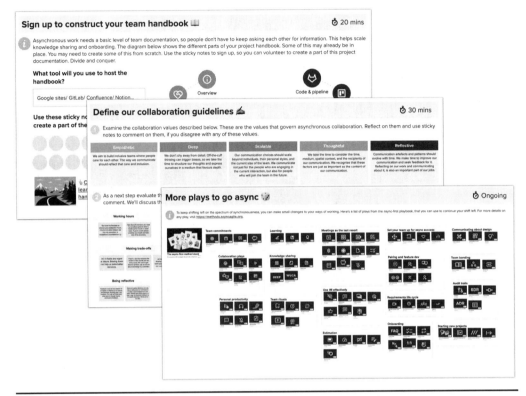

Figure 29.7 Representation of addressing more team goals in stage 5.

Next, you'll find a panel that'll help you agree on your team's collaboration guidelines. To ensure that you don't have to start from scratch, the kit already has some indicative values and guidelines in place. I expect that you may have to modify these based on the conversation you have with the team. Begin by allowing the team to internalize the values that'll drive your communication approach. Encourage your colleagues to comment on these values if they have something to share. Once everyone agrees, conduct a time-boxed, silent meeting where people examine some of the guidelines already on the board. They can comment on these guidelines, and they can even add guidelines of their own. After everyone has had a chance to comment, address any objections, suggestions, or additions. Consolidate the agreed set of guidelines into your team's collaboration charter and represent it in your team handbook.

That'll bring you to the long tail of this shift. As you've seen in this book, there are many different plays you can introduce to your team, so you shift left on the spectrum of synchronousness. However, you and your team are in the best place to decide which plays you want to implement. The last panel of the starter kit lists all the plays we've discussed in Parts II and III of this book. I've categorized them so it's easy for you to select plays for areas where you want to make an impact. From this point on, choose your own adventure!

The Whiteboard Is Not a Task Board

The starter kit aims to help you identify and agree on actions and tasks you'll complete as a team. It's not, however, an effective tracking tool. So, once you agree on an action, I suggest tracking it on your team's task board. Most task boards provide you with the functionality to filter by tags, labels, or categories. You can use those features to separate these team-improvement tasks from your regular development work.

A TEAM SHIFT, OWNED BY THE TEAM

The purpose of this starter kit is to simplify the shift to asynchronous work. This, I've found, is particularly useful for teams that follow an office-centric model, even when working remotely. And in the spirit of collective ownership, it makes sense that the team owns and drives such a shift in their ways of working.

CHAPTER SUMMARY

The async-first starter kit is a collection of tools and templates to guide your team through their shift to an async-first way of working. The kit guides you through a five-stage process.

1. In stage 1, you agree on the goals for this shift and how you'll celebrate if you achieve those goals.

2. In stage 2, you'll gather and tabulate baseline data. This may generate some insights for the team and encourage you to commit to additional goals.

3. Stage 3 focuses on some fundamental agreements, such as meetings as the last resort, how to use your team's communication channels and protocols for meetings.

4. At stage 4 you'll start acting. First, you'll defrag your calendars so you can free up contiguous blocks of time for deep work. Next, you'll identify meetings that you can delete, shorten, or modify.

5. Finally, in stage 5 you'll sign up to build different sections of your team handbook and agree on your collaboration guidelines. You'll also find a list of plays you can implement for the long tail of your async-first shift. Align on a common team purpose. In the long run, this will help you retain team cohesion and a sense of collective ownership.

Just like that, we've ended what's the penultimate chapter of this book. In the last chapter, I look ahead to the future of work as I see it while authoring this book. In the process, I want you to imagine how you, your team, and your organization can participate in this future, armed with your new ways of working. For that, just flip the page.

30

A BRAVE NEW WORLD
OF WORK

5:30 a.m. It's Tuesday morning, and it's a warm Indian summer. Nita wakes up to her alarm and pulls her curtains. Sunlight comes streaming in through the window. She freshens up and settles down to read her Kindle as she sips her morning coffee. Nita loves reading, so she makes it a point to read a few pages each morning before she gets into her routine. That routine involves waking up Abin and then getting his breakfast and lunch boxes ready, before they drive to school.

8:00 a.m. After dropping Abin, Nita stops at the gym. In recent months, she's started paying attention to her health and fitness. Today is her session with her private trainer. It is tough work, but strangely, she feels more energized than tired. She's rushing home now, though. Time to shower, cook, and get ready for work.

9:15 a.m. These days Nita begins her workday at a regular time. Her teammates have moved to an async-first way of working, so there are barely any meetings, except the ones they really need. She starts off her day looking at the team's task board.

Her business analyst has tagged her on a user story relating to a feature that needs new screen designs. She adds this to her list of tasks for the day. But first, she must finish writing that design proposal she's been working on since yesterday.

12:30 p.m. Phew! It has been an intense morning of work. The proposal was almost complete. Nita just needed to add a few fat marker sketches and add it to Confluence so her product manager in Boise, Idaho, can view it.

The new screen designs, however, were tricky. It's always tough to accommodate a new feature on an already crowded screen, so Nita had to rack her brain on this one. Thankfully, she was able to get some ideas from her client's documented design system. She's not done yet, but it's lunch time, so that break is handy.

2:40 p.m.   After lunch, Nita powers through her design work and finally gets the screens up on Invision. She tags her business analyst on the stories and links up the Invision project so they can check the screens out. It's time to pick up Abin from school.

3:15 p.m.   Nita settles in after picking up Abin. He'll manage his own homework before he heads out for cricket. She opens Slack and sees a few messages from June, the tech lead.

June asks for a quick sync to walk through the carry-over filters feature that Nita had recently designed. Nita is heading to a one-on-one with her manager at 3:30 p.m., so she points June to the feature breakdown page on Confluence that describes the functionality in some detail.

6:30 p.m.   It's time to wrap up the day. As it turns out, June didn't need a synchronous walk-through after all. The Confluence page was enough. "This is so well structured!" said June. Nita's one-on-one with her manager is also quite productive. She is able to get some feedback about her work, which she hopes to put into action right away.

Ah, just 40 minutes to sundown. Maybe it's time for an evening walk?

9:30 p.m.   Evenings are never light for a single parent. But in recent months, Nita has been glad to spend them with Abin. They cooked together today and watched an episode of *Street Food Asia* before Abin headed off to sleep. Work doesn't distract her after hours these days. She uses Freedom to block out email and instant messaging after 7:30 p.m., so try as she might, she's locked out of them until the next morning.

Nita has begun to get to sleep early as well. After all, her day starts early each day. But before she sleeps, she'll read a few pages of that book she's onto.

ANOTHER WORLD OF WORK IS POSSIBLE

Nita's new day represents an alternate reality to the one we saw in Chapter 1. It's a calm, flexible, focused way of working that balances our commitments to both work and our personal lives. I believe that the tools, methods, and approaches we've explored together in this book can help us all find our own version of Nita's new day.

The world of work is changing. Some argue that it has changed forever since the COVID-19 pandemic. As you keep Nita's day in perspective, I want to share with you how I see the future of work unfold. In that context, I want you to imagine how these asynchronous collaboration techniques can help you not just be effective at your work but also be a colleague everyone enjoys working with.

From my perspective, five key trends are likely to shape the future of work we're headed into. Let me describe them to you.

FLEXIBILITY AS A DESIRE AND A RIGHT

It's safe to say that remote work has gone from being a privilege to something that employees expect and value. In my own experience, many executives wouldn't entertain any conversations about remote work before 2020. And then of course, things changed. As I've mentioned earlier, since 2021, I've run three separate surveys with large groups of technologists. In each survey, a larger percentage of people has reported their desire to work remotely all the time.

In June 2021, only 15.47 percent people wanted to work remotely all the time. In April 2022, that percentage had doubled. In August 2022, that percentage had tripled. This is fascinating to watch even as a dispassionate observer. Apparently as people get more comfortable with remote work, they want it even more. At this rate, by mid-2024, about 90 percent of knowledge workers may want to work remotely all the time, as you see in Figure 30.1. There's also a possibility that these preferences will regress somewhat, but the fact that almost universal remote work is even a possibility seems like huge progress from just a few years back.

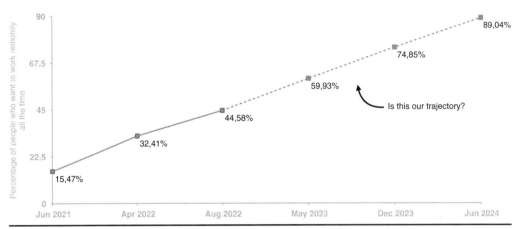

Figure 30.1 People's desire to work remotely all the time is increasing rapidly.

It's natural then that many employees would even take a pay cut to work remotely. It may seem miraculous, but people are choosing balance in their lives. Work needs to be meaningful, but it's not the only source of meaning in people's lives.

Gustavo Razetti says,

> A significant number of employees benefit from the flexibility to define not only where but also when they work. Seizing the opportunity to embrace their kids is NOT an obstacle to doing great work.

While employees want to work remotely and flexibly, there are competing regulations and legislations at play. For example, will remote work become a legal right in some countries?

On the other end of the spectrum, India, in a bid to keep their special economic zones (SEZs) relevant, first passed a law that limited remote work to only 50 percent of a company's registered employees. Then after much pushback from employees and employers alike, they've rolled back this decision until 2024. However, the tussle between people's demands, how regulation shapes up, and how employers respond remains a changing space. The question is, what bargaining chips do employees hold?

A SKILLS ECONOMY

Raj Choudhury of Harvard Business School believes that top talent shapes trends at work. For example, back in the day, only managers got laptops. Top talent asked for laptops as well, and today a work laptop is the norm. Remember the

BlackBerry? That magical device from which only managers sent and received email? Top talent asked for access to email on mobile devices, and they got that too. Professor Choudhury believes that top talent will ask for the flexibility to work from anywhere and get it. That in turn will precipitate an industry-wide trend. Even behemoths like Apple have lost some of their top talent because of inflexible policies.

On the other hand, for people who're qualified, there isn't a dearth of opportunities. Today there are dozens of job boards that target people who want to work remotely such as We Work Remotely, Remote OK, Flex Jobs, and even LinkedIn. Companies like A.Team run their projects on the idea of a builder economy, where people with skills team up to solve complex problems, and they get paid well for it.

Raphael Ouzan from A.Team says,

> The pandemic eroded many tightly held assumptions. That we need to work in an office every day. That building great companies and products means accepting the tediousness of a traditional 9 to 5. That you can make good money or make a real positive impact on the world—but not both.

At the heart of this shift is a demand for skills that are in short supply, particularly in the world of tech. Recruiters who are looking for top talent will soon have to benchmark themselves against global competitors. You can't be content being the best employer in your neighborhood. In an increasingly flatter world, people with the most sought-after skills will have the most bargaining power when it comes to work conditions. The more the industry woos top talent, the more the industry will have to listen to everyone else as well. In a skills economy, a flexible workplace is inevitable. And with flexibility come lifestyle changes.

DIGITAL NOMADISM

Before I describe this trend, I need to explain three Indianisms to you:

- **SINK.** An earning individual (single income) with no kids
- **DINK.** A working couple (double income) with no kids
- **Uncle.** A middle-aged or old man who isn't up to speed with the latest trends

And yes, I was a bit of an Indian "uncle" when it came to recognizing *digital nomadism*. My ignorance is particularly obvious when you consider the fact that even the venerable Indian newspaper, *The Hindu*, reported on this phenomenon seven years back. This is how *Forbes* defines the whole thing:

> Thanks to the pandemic, more people are choosing to embrace a location-independent, technology-enabled lifestyle that allows them to travel and work remotely. They are called digital nomads, and the trend is becoming more widespread.

I'm still going to sit on the fence with this trend, because I'm not yet sure how "widespread" it is. While I know of many digital nomad families, the trend currently seems limited mostly to the people we call SINKs and DINKs in India. What we do know is that it isn't just the Silicon Valley techie who earns $300,000 a year.

The reason that I think this trend is worth keeping in mind is because of how rapidly immigration policies are changing to accommodate this idea. At the time of publication, 58 countries have digital nomad visas of some kind. Companies have had to scramble to craft policies for international remote work so they don't violate tax regulations in any country. At the same time, this reflects a desire on the part of many knowledge workers to live their lives flexibly. After all, if all they need is a laptop and an internet connection, why should any location matter? All that matters is the employee's skill and the results they produce.

THE FOUR-DAY WORKWEEK

Speaking of results, you can't ignore the four-day workweek. The idea isn't novel. 37Signals, one of the OGs of remote work, has a benefit called "summer hours" where employees work 32 hours, or four days a week, from May to the end of August. They've always said that 40 hours is plenty, and 32 hours is enough. Rheingans, the German digital consultancy, has followed a five-hour workday since 2017. That's just 25 hours a week, and they're doing fine!

There's a good reason for that. Most of us can't do more than four hours of deep work each day. Even that takes heaps of practice. Add a bunch of hours to that for communicating about work, attending training or teaching others, and maybe some gossip and whatnot, and you still have enough time in hand to have a productive 32-hour, four-day workweek.

This isn't some niche experiment. 4-Day Week Global, the nonprofit foundation behind many such trials, had already proven the efficacy of its model with its experiments at the Perpetual Guardian, a trust company in New Zealand. The model was so successful that it improved productivity by 20 percent during the trial period, and now Perpetual Guardian has made the change permanent.

In 2022, the world saw its largest four-day workweek trial to date: 900-odd employees across 33 companies. The results are eye-popping to say the least:

- Revenue rose 8 percent over the trial and was up 37.55 percent in comparison to the same period in 2021.
- Hiring rose, absenteeism went down, and resignations declined slightly.
- People felt they were more productive and doing a better job at work with the shift to a four-day week. They were also able to exercise more control over their schedules.

It's no surprise that companies that went through this trial want to stick with the four-day week. The people who went through this trial say that they expect significant pay hikes to go back to a four-day week. The testimonials for such shifts have come not just from regular employees but also from the leadership.

Mark Howland, Charity Bank's director of marketing and communications, says this:

> With my day off I've been going on quite long bike rides, looking after myself, taking some time out, and then having the whole weekend to get things done around the house and to spend time with family. The five-day working week is a 20th century concept, which is no longer fit for the 21st century.

These trials will continue, and I suspect the clamor for a shorter workweek may get louder. The UAE has already transitioned into a four-and-a-half-day workweek.

The 40-hour workweek is an 80-year-old concept that was already a few decades late when it arrived. You see, in the industrial era, if an employee worked at a factory longer, they inevitably produced more output. Studies from 1890 showed that employees were working 100-hour workweeks! And this was several years after the famous May Day strike of 1867. In the United States, it took several years of labor struggle to finally bring the 40-hour workweek into law. Congress passed the Fair Labor Standards Act in 1938. It was initially for a 44-hour workweek, and then a couple of years later, they shortened it to 40 hours each week. Many other countries adopted this pattern around the same time, give or take a few years.

Knowledge work is different from industrial work. Spending eight hours at work doesn't always mean having two times the amount of output as compared to four hours at work. The four-day workweek recognizes that reality. I hope the struggle for meaningful work hours isn't as long and protracted as the struggle for the 40-hour workweek. We owe a more sensible workplace to the next generation of knowledge workers.

GEN Z AND THEIR SENSIBILITIES

The next generation are the latest entrants to the workplace. Call them Zoomers or Gen Z, they started entering the workplace in 2017 or thereabouts. I find this age group fascinating for more than one reason. This is a time when most of the developed world is aging. More people will leave the workforce than those that'll enter it. The United States is a prime example of this. So, we should expect an acute talent shortage in tech during the next decade or so. While we'll need young workers to enter the industry in large numbers, the developed world simply won't have enough of them. Younger, developing countries will become hotspots for talent if they aren't already.

That's why Zoomers are an important demographic to watch out for. This group is anything but homogenous. Gen Z in the West is quite different from Gen Z in the Global South. And even in the Global South, a first-generation college graduate from a small Indian town will be vastly different from a Zoomer from a more privileged background.

My own data says that Zoomers and the general population of technologists have similar work preferences. For example, 46 percent of Zoomers want to be exclusively remote as compared to 45 percent for the general population. That's an insignificant difference.

That said, people with less than two years in the industry express that their biggest struggle with remote work is their need to be around other people. I get that. These are youngsters who've been around people for most of their lives as students. It can be disorienting to then switch to a remote-first workplace. They need to figure out how to build their professional network, how to manage their own growth and learning, and how to receive mentorship. Of course, there are tools and means to do all of this, but it's unfamiliar territory.

Lastly, there are the values this group will hold dear. This varies by subgroup as well. In the West, Gen Z is very involved in social causes. Sixty-eight percent of Indian Gen Z have persuaded their employers to act on climate change, and 95 percent seek to reduce their own impact on the environment (source: Deloitte). What impact does this have on a pointless commute to the office? Or on the heavy carbon footprint of all-glass office buildings? As this demographic finds more representation in the workplace, their values and sensibilities will no doubt influence their employer's policies. We should all watch this space closely.

A SHIFT FOR AUTONOMY

With all this in context, some of us may feel a sense of uncertainty and trepidation about the future. There's one thing we can all agree on, though. For most people, where they work from, be it home, an office, or a third place, is an expression of their need for autonomy. The hours they work fulfil a similar need. No one—yes, no one—wants to give up that autonomy once they have it.

As you'll notice, I'm not trying to make too many predictions here. The concept of universal remote work would have seemed nonsensical to some people as recently as 2019. Yet here we are. Things can change rapidly with one precipitating event.

- Who knows what happens when the recession and the semiconductor shortage are behind us, when the war in Ukraine is over, and when tech is booming again?
- What if there's another wave of the pandemic?
- What happens if more big-tech firms adopt four-day workweeks?
- As legislation and regulations change, what impact will we see on the world of work?

Regardless of what the future holds, it'll be a distributed future for sure. And in that future, I hope the ability to work asynchronously serves you as a superpower.

IT'S TIME TO SIGN OFF

Oh boy! We're at the end of the book. I wanted to close this book by painting a vignette of what the future of work may look like. The idea was for you to imagine how your asynchronous collaboration skills will be handy in this future.

CHAPTER SUMMARY

In this chapter, we explored five trends that'll influence the future workplace:

- Most knowledge workers want flexibility at work, and the number of people who want to work remotely all the time is increasing. Some countries may even grant remote work as a right for employees.
- Even in a slowdown there are plenty of jobs for skilled knowledge workers. People with in-demand skills can get the work conditions they demand, and this will only get better with time.
- As people have more disposable income, they'd like to improve their life-styles. Traveling while working, i.e., digital nomadism, is no longer a fringe trend. Several countries already support such mobility.
- The 40-hour workweek may be a relic of the past for knowledge work. The four-day workweek movement is gaining steam in some parts of the world with several successful experiments to back it up.
- Gen Z will soon be a large part of the workforce. Their values and expecta-tions are already influencing corporations and will undoubtedly also shape the future of work.

As an author, I have my biases. You have seen glimpses of these biases throughout the chapters you've read thus far. Setting aside my biases, though, I see enough evidence that the workplace of the future will look nothing like the first few decades of my career.

Despite the immense loss and suffering the pandemic caused, it helped the world learn how remote work can bring a new flexibility to the way we work. It's time that we also rethink how we operate in this new virtual workplace. Think of it as a new sport. It'll need new techniques, new tools, new sensibilities. This book was my attempt to help you learn that new sport. Thank you for reading!

It's time now to say goodbye and part ways. I wish you all the best in your async-first journey. Go give your team the gift of a better way to work.

ENDNOTES

CHAPTER I

5 **"Catherine Tansey"**: Tansey, Catherine. "Asynchronous Work: What It Is and How to Make It Work for Your Team," Lattice, March 22, 2023. https://lattice.com/library/what-is-asynchronous-work-heres-everything-you-need-to-know-to-implement-it-at-your-organization. Accessed April 25, 2023.

5 **"Marcelo Lebre"**: Lebre, Marcelo. "Why You Should Be Working Asynchronously in 2023," blog, n.d. https://remote.com/blog/why-you-should-be-doing-async-work. Accessed April 25, 2023.

7 **"The Anywhere Operating System"**: Thomas, Luke and Aisha Samake. *The Anywhere Operating System*. South Portland, Maine: Friday Feedback Inc., 2021.

7 **"Future Forum's research"**: Future Forum. "Research Archive," n.d. https://futureforum.com/research/. Accessed April 25, 2023.

7 **"deep work"**: Newport, Cal. *Deep Work: Rules for Focused Success in a Distracted World*. New York: Grand Central Publishing, 2016.

7 **"Maker's Schedule, Manager's Schedule"**: Graham, Paul. "Maker's Schedule, Manager's Schedule," blog, July 2009. Accessed April 25, 2023. http://www.paulgraham.com/makersschedule.html.

8 ***"Flow: The Psychology of Optimal Experience"***: Czikszentmihaly, Mihaly. *Flow: The Psychology of Optimal Experience*. New York: Harper Perennial Modern Classics, 2008.

8 ***"Thinking, Fast and Slow"***: Kahneman, Daniel. *Thinking, Fast and Slow*. New York: Farrar, Straus and Giroux, 2013.

9 **"women's representation in IT was just 33 percent in 2022"**: Deloitte Insights. "Women in the Tech Industry: Gaining Ground, but Facing New Headwinds," December 1, 2021. https://www2.deloitte.com/us/en/insights/industry/technology/technology-media-and-telecom-predictions/2022/statistics-show-women-in-technology-are-facing-new-headwinds.html. Accessed April 25, 2023.

10   **"Marcelo Lebre"**: Lebre, Marcelo. "Why You Should Be Working Asynchronously in 2023," blog, n.d. https://remote.com/blog/why-you-should-be-doing-async-work. Accessed April 25, 2023.

11   **"he said, she said"**: Wiktionary. "He Said, She Said - Wiktionary," n.d. https://en.wiktionary.org/wiki/he_said,_she_said. Accessed April 25, 2023.

CHAPTER 2

15   **"shifting left"**: Wikipedia. "Shift-left testing," May 28, 2023. https://en.wikipedia.org/wiki/Shift-left_testing. Accessed July 15, 2023.

15   **"*Effective Remote Work*"**: Stanier, James. *Effective Remote Work: For Yourself, Your Team, and Your Company*. Raleigh, North Carolina: The Pragmatic Bookshelf, 2022.

17   **"37signals"**: "The 37signals Guide to Internal Communication," n.d. https://37signals.com/how-we-communicate/. Accessed April 26, 2023.

18   **"the value that... "**: Stanier, James. "Asynchronous Communication Is the Great Leveler in Engineering," *Shopify Engineering* (blog), May 20, 2022. https://shopify.engineering/asynchronous-communication-shopify-engineering. Accessed April 26, 2023.

18   **"*The Karate Kid*"**: IMDB. *The Karate Kid*, n.d. https://www.imdb.com/title/tt0087538/. Accessed April 26, 2023.

18   **"There's a quote…"**: YouTube. "Mr. Miyagi - Balance," November 5, 2008. https://www.youtube.com/watch?v=QsPoBXemFmg. Accessed April 26, 2023.

CHAPTER 4

30   **"a delightful summary…"**: Atlassian. "You Waste A Lot of Time at Work," n.d. http://www.atlassian.com/time-wasting-at-work-infographic. Accessed April 26, 2023.

31   **"Gonçalo Silva"**: "Gonçalo Silva on Twitter," n.d. https://twitter.com/goncalossilva. Accessed April 26, 2023.

31   **"the InfoQ podcast"**: Hastie, Shane. "Gonçalo Silva on Working Completely Asynchronously," *InfoQ* (podcast) January 8, 2021. https://www.infoq.com/podcasts/working-completely-asynchronously/. Accessed April 26, 2023.

33   **"manifesto for agile software development"**: "Manifesto for Agile Software Development," n.d. https://agilemanifesto.org/. Accessed April 26, 2023.

33 **"Sidu Ponappa"**: "Sidu Ponappa on Twitter," n.d. https://twitter.com/ponnappa. Accessed April 26, 2023.

33 **"in an early 2022 podcast"**: *The Shape of Work* (podcast). "#200: Sidu Ponappa on Why Culture Is a 'Dangerous Label', Hiring a Dream Team of Makers and Engineers, and Applying Product Thinking to Solve for Attrition," March 10, 2022. https://www.springworks.in/the-shape-of-work-podcast/episode/200-sidu-ponappa-on-why-culture-is-a-dangerous-label-hiring-a-dream-team-of-makers-and-engineers-and-applying-product-thinking-to-solve-for-attrition. Accessed April 26, 2023.

34 **"Sarvenaz Myslicki"**: DevInterrupted. "How to Fix Tech's Mentorship Problem," April 11, 2022. https://devinterrupted.com/podcast/how-to-fix-techs-mentorship-problem/. Accessed April 26, 2023.

34 **"A problem with the Agile Manifesto"**: RJD (Remote Java Dev). "A Problem with the Agile Manifesto," blog, January 5, 2020. https://remotejavadev.com/a-problem-with-the-agile-manifesto/. Accessed April 26, 2023.

35 **"the inverted pyramid of journalism"**: Wikipedia. "Inverted Pyramid (Journalism)," November 11, 2021. https://en.wikipedia.org/wiki/Inverted_pyramid_(journalism). Accessed April 26, 2023.

36 **"Tips for better writing"**: GitLab. "Communicating Effectively and Responsibly Through Text," n.d. https://about.gitlab.com/company/culture/all-remote/effective-communication/. Accessed April 26, 2023.

36 **"Technical writing courses"**: Google Developers. "Overview of Technical Writing Courses," 2022. https://developers.google.com/tech-writing/overview. Accessed April 26, 2023.

36 **"Technical writing fundamentals"**: Level Up GitLab. "GitLab Technical Writing Fundamentals," 2022. https://levelup.gitlab.com/courses/gitlab-technical-writing-fundamentals. Accessed April 26, 2023.

36 **"*Smart Brevity*"**: VandeHei, Jim, Mike Allen, and Roy Schwartz. *Smart Brevity: The Power of Saying More with Less.* New York: Workman Publishing, Co., Inc., 2022.

36 **"How to Write in Plain English"**: Plain English Campaign. "Plain English Campaign," n.d. https://plainenglish.co.uk/files/howto.pdf. Accessed April 26, 2023.

37 **"Hemingway"**: Hemingway Editor. "Hemingway Editor," n.d. https://hemingwayapp.com/. Accessed April 26, 2023.

37   **"Flesch-Kincaid reading tests"**: Wikipedia. "Flesch–Kincaid Readability Tests," July 12, 2016. https://en.wikipedia.org/wiki/Flesch%E2%80%93Kincaid_readability_tests. Accessed April 26, 2023.

CHAPTER 5

44   **"Cal Newport"**: Newport, Cal. *Deep Work: Rules for Focused Success in a Distracted World*. London: Piatkus, 2016.

44   **"Johann Hari"**: Hari, Johann. *Stolen Focus: Why You Can't Pay Attention*. New York: Crown, 2022.

44   **"Harvard University's SITN blog, 2018"**: Haynes, Trevor. "Dopamine, Smartphones & You: A Battle for Your Time - Science in the News." Harvard University *Science in the News* (blog) May 1, 2018. https://sitn.hms.harvard.edu/flash/2018/dopamine-smartphones-battle-time/. Accessed April 26, 2023.

44   **"triggers a similar rush"**: Vozza, Stephanie. "How to Cut Your Email Time in Half," *FastCompany*, January 10, 2017, https://www.fastcompany.com/3066716/how-to-cut-your-email-time-in-half. Accessed April 26, 2023.

45   **"define these as focus time"**: Google Calendar Help. "Use Focus Time in Google Calendar," n.d. https://support.google.com/calendar/answer/11190973?hl=en&co=GENIE.Platform%3DDesktop. Accessed April 26, 2023.

45   **"some delightful suggestions…"**: Team, Dropbox, Anthony Wing Kosner, and Paul Boutin. "Virtual First Toolkit: How to Communicate Effectively," blog, October 13, 2020. https://blog.dropbox.com/topics/work-culture/-virtual-first-toolkit--how-to-communicate-effectively. Accessed April 26, 2023.

45   **"Screen Time"**: Apple Support. "Use Screen Time on Your iPhone, iPad, or iPod Touch," September 12, 2022. https://support.apple.com/en-us/HT208982. Accessed April 26, 2023.

45   **"similar features"**: Android. "Digital Wellbeing | Android," n.d. https://www.android.com/intl/en_in/digital-wellbeing/. Accessed April 26, 2023

45   **"App blockers like Freedom"**: Freedom.to. "Freedom: Internet, App and Website Blocker." n.d. https://freedom.to. Accessed April 26, 2023

46   **"GitLab Handbook"**: GitLab. "Leadership," n.d. https://about.gitlab.com/handbook/leadership/. Accessed April 26, 2023.

CHAPTER 6

49   **"work execution"**: Newport, Cal. *A World Without Email: Reimagining Work in an Age of Communication Overload*. Edmonton, Alberta: Portfolio, 2021.

50   **"M&Ms – meetings and managers...**: Fried, Jason. "Why Work Doesn't Happen at Work," TED Talk, n.d. https://www.ted.com/talks/jason_fried_why_work_doesn_t_happen_at_work. Accessed April 26, 2023.

51   **"Atlassian"**: Atlassian. "Jira Software - Features | Atlassian," n.d. https://www.atlassian.com/software/jira/features. Accessed April 26, 2023.

53   **"Twist"**: Twist. "Twist: Organized Work Communication for Flexible Teams," n.d. https://twist.com/. Accessed April 29, 2023.

53   **"The average knowledge worker..."**: MacKay, Jory. "Communication Overload: Most Workers Can't Go 6 Minutes Without Checking Email." *RescueTime* (blog), July 11, 2018. https://blog.rescuetime.com/communication-multitasking-switches/. Accessed April 26, 2023.

53   **"Seth Godin calls 'thrashing'"** Godin, Seth. *Linchpin: Are You Indispensable?* Edmonton, Alberta: Portfolio, 2010.

53   **"democratic"**: thedecider.app, "Democratic Decision Making — How Do We Decide?" n.d. https://thedecider.app/democratic-decision-making. Accessed April 26, 2023.

53   **"consensus"**: thedecider.app, "Consensus Decision Making — How Do We Decide?," n.d. https://thedecider.app/consensus-decision-making. Accessed April 26, 2023.

53   **"As Aviva Pinchas..."**: Pinchas, Aviva. "287 - Async Consent Based Decision Making - Collaboration Superpowers," *Collaboration Superpowers* (podcast), September 27, 2021. https://www.collaborationsuperpowers.com/287-async-consent-based-decision-making/. Accessed April 26, 2023.

54   **"consent"**: thedecider.app, "Consent Decision Making — How Do We Decide?" n.d. https://thedecider.app/consent-decision-making. Accessed April 26, 2023.

55   **"Jeff Bezos"**: "Jeffrey P. Bezos's letter to Amazon shareholders," n.d. https://www.sec.gov/Archives/edgar/data/1018724/000119312516530910/d168744dex991.htm. Accessed April 26, 2023.

55   **"James Stanier"**: Stanier, James. "The Engineering Manager," blog, n.d. https://www.theengineeringmanager.com/. Accessed April 26, 2023.

55   **"Effective Remote Work"**: Stanier, James. *Effective Remote Work: For Yourself, Your Team, and Your Company*. Raleigh, North Carolina: The Pragmatic Bookshelf, 2022.

CHAPTER 7

59   **"productivity goes up"**: Wright, Aliah D. "Study: Teleworkers More Productive—Even When Sick." SHRM, February 13, 2015. https://www.shrm.org/resourcesandtools/hr-topics/technology/pages/teleworkers-more-productive-even-when-sick.aspx. Accessed April 29, 2023.

61   **"The Anywhere Operating System"**: Thomas, Luke and Aisha Samake. *The Anywhere Operating System*. South Portland, Maine: Friday Feedback, Inc., 2021.

63   **"Cameron Herold"**: Herold, Cameron. *Double Double: How to Double Your Revenue and Profit in 3 Years or Less*. Austin, Texas: Greenleaf Book Group LLC, 2011.

64   **"More than eight people and..."**: Axtell, Paul. "The Most Productive Meetings Have Fewer Than 8 People," *Harvard Business Review*, June 22, 2018. https://hbr.org/2018/06/the-most-productive-meetings-have-fewer-than-8-people. Accessed April 29, 2023.

64   **"silently write their points"**: Rogelberg, Steve G. and Liana Kramer. "The Case for More Silence in Meetings," *Harvard Business Review*, June 14, 2019. https://hbr.org/2019/06/the-case-for-more-silence-in-meetings. Accessed April 29, 2023.

66   **"Airbnb experience"**: Airbnb. "Online Experiences," n.d. https://www.airbnb.co.in/s/experiences/online. Accessed April 29, 2023.

CHAPTER 8

70   **"run complex workshops"**: YouTube. "[TW Converge 2020] Facilitate with Style in a Distributed, Remote Setup," August 7, 2020. https://www.youtube.com/watch?v=684OlVLazAI. Accessed April 29, 2023.

71   **"pen pals"**: Wikipedia. "Pen Pal," June 1, 2007. https://en.wikipedia.org/wiki/Pen_pal. Accessed April 29, 2023.

71 *"simcha*, a word…"*: The Rabbi Sacks Legacy. "Collective Joy," Covenant & Conversation, August 25, 2019. https://www.rabbisacks.org/covenant-conversation/reeh/collective-joy/. Accessed April 29, 2023.

72 **"Data from Gallup…**: Inc., Gallup. "Why We Need Best Friends at Work." January 15, 2018. https://www.gallup.com/workplace/236213/why-need-best-friends-work.aspx. Accessed April 29, 2023.

73 **"in many comforts"**: TechVision. "Inside Google's Massive Headquarters," YouTube, November 18, 2020. https://www.youtube.com/watch?v=Z-pT0XDYvDM. Accessed April 29, 2023.

73 **"Companies like Infosys"**: Infosys Mysore. "All About Accommodation - Infosys Mysore Campus," April 8, 2020. https://infosysmysore.in/category/accommodation/. Accessed April 29, 2023.

73 **"built its own ranch…"**: Westwood, Lauren. "Salesforce Announces Wellness Center - The Trailblazer Ranch." Salesforce Ben, February 11, 2022. https://www.salesforceben.com/salesforce-announces-wellness-center-the-trailblazer-ranch/. Accessed April 29, 2023.

73 **"there's a dollar value…"**: Fluegge-Woolf, Erin R. "Play Hard, Work Hard: Fun at Work and Job Performance," *Management Research Review* 38, no. 8 (2014): 682-705. https://www.emerald.com/insight/content/doi/10.1108/MRR-11-2012-0252/full/html. Accessed April 29, 2023.

74 **"Doist"**: Twitter. "Twitter," n.d. https://twitter.com/doist/status/976554066527641601. Accessed April 29, 2023.

74 **"Automattic"**: Automattic. "How We Work," November 18, 2020. https://automattic.com/how-we-work/. Accessed April 29, 2023.

74 **"the Cowork experience"**: The Cowork Experience | Team Offsites & Online Program for Remote Teams. "Home | The Cowork Experience," n.d. https://thecoworkexperience.com/. Accessed April 29, 2023.

74 **"two company-wide retreats…"**: Moghe, Sumeet Gayathri. "India Away Day 2016 - Highlights Reel (Final)," YouTube, October 12, 2016. https://www.youtube.com/watch?v=XvbXUE_Z6OI. Accessed April 29, 2023.

CHAPTER 9

77   **"adapt a James Clear quote"**: Clear, James. "3-2-1: On Taking Action, Changing Incentives, and Belonging," n.d. https://jamesclear.com/3-2-1/june-4-2020. Accessed April 29, 2023.

80   **"stole this one…"**: Team, Dropbox, Anthony Wing Kosner, and Paul Boutin. "Virtual First Toolkit: How to Communicate Effectively," blob, October 13, 2020. https://blog. dropbox.com/topics/work-culture/-virtual-first-toolkit--how-to-communicate-effectively. Accessed April 29, 2023.

80   **"at a cost"**: Raeburn, Alicia. "Context Switching Is Killing Your Productivity," *Asana Productivity* (blog), October 26, 2022. https://asana.com/resources/context-switching. Accessed April 29, 2023.

81   **"lead to higher stress…"**: Mark, Gloria, Daniela Gudith, and Ulrich Klocke. "The Cost of Interrupted Work: More Speed and Stress," n.d. UCI Donald Bren School of Information and Computer Sciences, n.d. https://www.ics.uci.edu/~gmark/chi08-mark.pdf. Accessed April 29, 2023.

81   **"Asana's 2022 anatomy of work"**: Asana. "Anatomy of Work 2023 - Rise of the Connected Enterprise," n.d. https://asana.com/resources/anatomy-of-work. Accessed April 29, 2023.

82   **"maker's schedule versus…"**: Graham, Paul. "Maker's Schedule, Manager's Schedule," blog, July 2009. http://www.paulgraham.com/makersschedule.html. Accessed April 29, 2023.

83   **"experimented with maker weeks…"**: Slack. "Focus Fridays and Maker Weeks at Slack," n.d. https://slack.com/intl/en-in/blog/news/focus-fridays-and-maker-weeks-at-slack. Accessed April 29, 2023.

83   **"have David Heinemeier Hanson…"**: Fried, Jason and David Heinemeier Hansson. "Less Mass," *The Rework Podcast*, February 8, 2022. https://www.rework.fm/less-mass/. Accessed April 29, 2023.

84   **"Dropbox"**: Hinds, Rebecca and Bob Sutton. "Dropbox's Secret for Saving Time in Meetings." Inc.com, May 11, 2015. https://www.inc.com/rebecca-hinds-and-bob-sutton/drop-box-secret-for-saving-time-in-meetings.html. Accessed April 29, 2023.

84   **"Asana"**: Hinds, Rebecca and Robert I. Sutton. "Meeting Overload Is a Fixable Problem," *Harvard Business Review*, October 28, 2022. https://hbr.org/2022/10/meeting-overload-is-a-fixable-problem. Accessed April 29, 2023.

84   **"Shopify"**: Bove, Tristan. "Shopify Is Axing All Meetings Involving More than Two People in a Remote Work Twist That the Company Itself Calls 'Fast and Chaotic,'" *Fortune*, January 3, 2023. https://fortune.com/2023/01/03/shopify-cutting-meetings-worker-productivity/. Accessed April 29, 2023.

CHAPTER 10

87   **"Martin Fowler"**: Fowler, Martin. "Using an Agile Software Process with OffshoreDevelopment," blog, July 18, 2006. https://martinfowler.com/articles/agileOffshore.html. Accessed April 29, 2023.

88   **"Gitlab rightly says"**: GitLab. "The Importance of a Handbook-First Approach to Documentation," n.d. https://about.gitlab.com/company/culture/all-remote/handbook-first-documentation/. Accessed April 29, 2023.

88   **"document everything about their company…"**: GitLab. "Handbook," n.d. https://about.gitlab.com/handbook/. Accessed April 29, 2023.

92   **"GitLab"**: The DevSecOps Platform | GitLab. "The DevSecOps Platform," n.d. https://about.gitlab.com/. Accessed April 29, 2023.

92   **"Confluence"**: Atlassian. "Confluence | Your Remote-Friendly Team Workspace | Atlassian," n.d. https://www.atlassian.com/software/confluence. Accessed April 29, 2023.

92   **"SharePoint"**: SharePoint, Team Collaboration Software Tools. "SharePoint, Team Collaboration Software Tools," n.d. https://www.microsoft.com/en-ww/microsoft-365/sharepoint/collaboration. Accessed April 29, 2023.

92   **"Notion"**: Notion. "Your Wiki, Docs & Projects. Together," n.d. https://www.notion.so/product. Accessed April 29, 2023.

92   **"Almanac"**: Almanac. "Almanac | The Modern Way to Collaborate," n.d. https://almanac.io/. Accessed April 29, 2023.

92   **"Mediawiki"**: MediaWiki. "MediaWiki," n.d. https://www.mediawiki.org/wiki/MediaWiki. Accessed April 29, 2023.

92   **"Qatalog"**: Qatalog. "Qatalog | Your Bespoke Operating System for Work," n.d. https://qatalog.com/. Accessed April 29, 2023.

92   **"Scribe"**: Scribe. "Scribe | Visual Step-by-Step Guides," n.d. https://scribe.how. Accessed April 29, 2023.

92   **"Glean"**: Enterprise AI Search & Knowledge Discovery | Glean. "Enterprise AI Search & Knowledge Discovery | Glean," n.d. https://www.glean.com/. Accessed April 29, 2023.

93   **"Confluence"**: Atlassian "Page History and Page Comparison Views | Confluence Data Center and Server 7.6 | Atlassian Documentation," August 12, 2020. https://confluence.atlassian.com/conf76/page-history-and-page-comparison-views-1018768888.html. Accessed April 29, 2023.

CHAPTER 11

98   **"an all-day meeting"**: 37signals. "Group Chat: The Best Way to Totally Stress Out Your Team," n.d. https://37signals.com/group-chat-problems/. Accessed May 3, 2023.

99   **"Remote Team Interactions Workbook"**: Skelton, Matthew and Manuel Pais. *Remote Team Interactions Workbook*. Portland, Oregon: Revolution Press, 2022.

100   **"Clockwise"**: Google Calendar & Slack Integration | Clockwise. "Google Calendar & Slack Integration | Clockwise," n.d. https://www.getclockwise.com/slack-app. Accessed May 3, 2023.

100   **"a 2021 survey by Cendex"**: Smith, Jayne. "Over Half of UK Employers Say Their Staff Work Additional Unpaid Hours Every Day." Workplace Insight, August 25, 2021. https://workplaceinsight.net/over-half-of-uk-employers-say-their-staff-work-additional-unpaid-hours-every-day/. Accessed May 3, 2023.

100   **"Wired Magazine"**: Carnegie, Megan. "We Finally Know the True Toll of All Those Bad Slacks." WIRED UK, September 10, 2021. https://www.wired.co.uk/article/time-wasted-slack-microsoft-teams. Accessed May 3, 2023.

104   **"Slack"**: Slack. "Use Threads to Organise Discussions." Slack Help Center, n.d. https://slack.com/intl/en-in/help/articles/115000769927-Use-threads-to-organise-discussions-. Accessed May 3, 2023.

105   **"a handy usage guide"**: EqualExperts. "GitHub - EqualExperts/Slack-Guide: The Best Damn Guide to Slack Ever. An Open Source GitHub Pages Site." GitHub, n.d. https://github.com/EqualExperts/slack-guide. Accessed May 3, 2023.

CHAPTER 12

107   **"the most famous..."**: Yip, Jason. "It's Not Just Standing Up: Patterns for Daily Standup Meetings." martinfowler.com, February 21, 2016. https://martinfowler.com/articles/itsNotJustStandingUp.html. Accessed May 3, 2023.

111   **"Dwight Eisenhower"**: Wikipedia. "Dwight D. Eisenhower," August 1, 2020. https://en.wikipedia.org/wiki/Dwight_D._Eisenhower. Accessed May 3, 2023.

113   **"IFTTT"**: IFTTT. "IFTTT - Connect Your Apps," n.d. https://ifttt.com/. Accessed May 3, 2023.

113   **"Zapier"**: Zapier. "Zapier | Automation That Moves You Forward," n.d. https://zapier.com/. Accessed May 3, 2023.

113   "try Geekbot": Geekbot. "Automate Asynchronous Standups, Retrospectives, and Surveys | Geekbot," n.d. https://geekbot.com/. Accessed May 3, 2023.

113   "Butler": Trello. "Trello Automation: Automate Your Workflow with Butler | Trello," n.d. https://trello.com/en/butler-automation. Accessed May 3, 2023.

113   "Basecamp": Basecamp. "Features," n.d. https://basecamp.com/features. Accessed May 3, 2023.

113   "Fellow": Sheehan, Hannah. "How to Automate Stand-Up Meetings and Status Updates with Fellow," Fellow.app, November 5, 2021. https://fellow.app/blog/product/how-to-automate-stand-up-meetings-and-status-updates-with-fellow/. Accessed May 3, 2023.

113   "Range": Range. "Async Daily Standups | Keep Your Team Aligned from Anywhere," n.d. https://www.range.co/for/standups. Accessed May 3, 2023.

CHAPTER 13

117   "the official scrum guide": Scrum Guides. "Scrum Guide | Scrum Guides," n.d. https://scrumguides.org/scrum-guide.html. Accessed May 3, 2023.

122   "Ryan Singer's": Singer, Ryan. "Stop Running in Circles and Ship Work That Matters," BAsecamp, 2019. https://basecamp.com/shapeup. Accessed May 3, 2023.

CHAPTER 14

133   "Mural's 'Private Mode'": MURAL Help Center. "Private Mode | MURAL Help Center," n.d. https://support.mural.co/en/articles/4427381-private-mode. Accessed May 3, 2023.

135   "Paulo Caroli": Caroli.org. "Caroli.Org: Knowledge and Agile and Lean Transformation," March 1, 2022. https://caroli.org/. Accessed May 3, 2023.

135   "terrific companion site...": SantoPixel. "FunRetrospectives | Have Fun, Learn from the Past and Prepare for the Future!" n.d. https://www.funretrospectives.com/. Accessed May 3, 2023.

135   "use the companion app": Fun Retrospectives App. "Fun Retrospectives App," n.d. http://app.funretrospectives.com. Accessed May 3, 2023.

CHAPTER 15

137   *"Effective Remote Work"*: Stanier, James. *Effective Remote Work: For Yourself, Your Team, and Your Company.* Raleigh, North Carolina: The Pragmatic Bookshelf, 2022.

138   *"Full Stack Testing"*: Mohan, Gayathri. *Full Stack Testing: A Practical Guide for Delivering High Quality Software.* Sebastopol, California: O'Reilly, 2022.

139   *"The Checklist Manifesto"*: Gawande, Atul. *The Checklist Manifesto: How to Get Things Right.* New York: Metropolitan Books, 2009.

CHAPTER 16

147   **"as the Economist described…"**: The collaboration curse. "The Collaboration Curse," n.d. https://www.economist.com/business/2016/01/23/the-collaboration-curse. Accessed May 25, 2023.

148   **"Rob Cross, Reb Rebele and Adam Grant…"**: Cross, Rob, Reb Rebele, and Adam Grant. "Collaborative Overload," *Harvard Business Review*, January 1, 2016. https://hbr.org/2016/01/collaborative-overload. Accessed May 25, 2023.

CHAPTER 17

156   **"a comprehensive article about pairing…"**: Böckeler, Birgitta and Nina Siessegger. "On Pair Programming." martinfowler.com, January 15, 2020. https://martinfowler.com/articles/on-pair-programming.html. Accessed May 25, 2023.

156   **"Martin Fowler's flippant quip"**: Fowler, Martin. "Bliki: PairProgrammingMisconceptions." martinfowler.com, October 31, 2006. https://martinfowler.com/bliki/PairProgrammingMisconceptions.html. Accessed May 25, 2023.

156   **"There are challenges…"**: Böckeler, Birgitta and Nina Siessegger. "On Pair Programming." martinfowler.com, January 15, 2020. https://martinfowler.com/articles/on-pair-programming.html. Accessed May 25, 2023.

157   **"antifragile"**: Taleb, Nassim Nicholas. *Antifragile: Things That Gain from Disorder.* New York: Penguin Books Ltd., 2012.

158   **"a hilarious video…"**: Gunjal, Digvijay. "Pair Programming Anti Patterns," YouTube, October 15, 2018. https://www.youtube.com/watch?v=McZ131y0OYU. Accessed May 25, 2023.

160   "**Andrew Montalenti**": Montalenti, Andrew "An Async Kind of Pair Programming," blog, December 14, 2015. https://amontalenti.com/2015/12/14/async-pairing. Accessed May 25, 2023.

CHAPTER 18

165   "**Confluence has a very practical template**": Atlassian. "Meeting Notes Template | Atlassian," n.d. https://www.atlassian.com/software/confluence/templates/meeting-notes. Accessed May 25, 2023.

166   "**an excellent guide...**": Henderson, Joel. "GitHub - Joelparkerhenderson/ Decision-Record: Decision Record: How to Initiate and Complete Decisions for Teams, Organizations, and Systems." GitHub, April 7, 2022. https://github.com/joelparkerhenderson/ decision-record. Accessed May 25, 2023.

166   "**built-in template**": Atlassian. "DACI: Decision Documentation | Atlassian," n.d. https:// www.atlassian.com/software/confluence/templates/decision. Accessed May 25, 2023.

166   "**by extension, simple design**": Fowler, Martin. "Is Design Dead?" martinfowler.com, May 1, 2004. https://martinfowler.com/articles/designDead.html. Accessed May 25, 2023.

166   "**last responsible moment**": Sironi, Giorgio. "Lean Tools: The Last Responsible Moment - DZone," May 9, 2012. https://dzone.com/articles/lean-tools-last-responsible. Accessed May 25, 2023.

166   "**Joel Henderson's guide to ADRs**": Henderson, Joel. "GitHub - Joelparkerhenderson/ Architecture-Decision-Record: Architecture Decision Record (ADR) Examples for Software Planning, IT Leadership, and Template Documentation." GitHub, April 29, 2023. https://github.com/joelparkerhenderson/architecture-decision-record. Accessed May 25, 2023.

166   "**Michael Nygard's original...**": Nygard, Michael. "Documenting Architecture Decisions," November 15, 2011. https://www.cognitect.com/blog/2011/11/15/documenting-architecture-decisions. Accessed May 25, 2023.

167   "**store them in source control**": npryce. "GitHub - Npryce/Adr-Tools: Command-Line Tools for Working with Architecture Decision Records." GitHub, March 30, 2020. https:// github.com/npryce/adr-tools. Accessed May 25, 2023.

167   "**ADR-manager**": adr-manager. "Adr-Manager," n.d. https://adr.github.io/adr-manager/. Accessed May 25, 2023.

167   "adr-tools": npryce. "GitHub - Npryce/Adr-Tools: Command-Line Tools for Working with Architecture Decision Records." GitHub, July 25, 2018. https://github.com/npryce/adr-tools. Accessed May 25, 2023.

168   "balance between too much…": Rachev, Preslav. "What's with the 50/72 Rule?" blog, February 21, 2015. https://preslav.me/2015/02/21/what-s-with-the-50-72-rule/. Accessed May 25, 2023.

168   "Jira integrates with…": Atlassian Support. "Integrate with Development Tools | Atlassian Support," n.d. https://support.atlassian.com/jira-cloud-administration/docs/integrate-with-development-tools/.

168   "Hoorvash Nikoo's guide": Nikoo, Hoorvash. "Writing Meaningful Commit Messages," Reflectoring.io, February 22, 2021. https://reflectoring.io/meaningful-commit-messages/. Accessed May 25, 2023.

168   "Conventional commits guide": Conventional Commits. "Conventional Commits," n.d. https://www.conventionalcommits.org/en/v1.0.0/. Accessed May 25, 2023.

169   "Commitzen": commitizen. "GitHub - Commitizen/Cz-Cli: The Commitizen Command Line Utility. #BlackLivesMatter." GitHub, February 1, 2023. https://github.com/commitizen/cz-cli. Accessed May 25, 2023.

169   "trunk-based development": Hamant, Paul. "Trunk Based Development." Introduction, n.d. https://trunkbaseddevelopment.com/. Accessed May 25, 2023.

169   "considers this latter approach…": Morris, Kief.. "Why Your Team Doesn't Need to Use Pull Requests," blog, January 2, 2021. https://infrastructure-as-code.com/book/2021/01/02/pull-requests.html. Accessed May 25, 2023.

169   "Ryan Boucher": GitHub. "Distributedlife - Overview," n.d. https://github.com/distributedlife. Accessed May 25, 2023.

169   "Dan Mutton": Thoughtworks. "Thoughtworks," n.d. https://www.thoughtworks.com/en-in/profiles/d/dan-mutton. Accessed May 25, 2023.

170   "a simple guide to writing pull requests": McMinn, Keavy. "How to Write the Perfect Pull Request, The GitHub Blog, January 22, 2015. https://github.blog/2015-01-21-how-to-write-the-perfect-pull-request/. Accessed May 25, 2023.

170   "make it easy to reference…": Atlassian Support. "Reference Issues in Your Development Work," n.d. https://support.atlassian.com/jira-software-cloud/docs/reference-issues-in-your-development-work/. Accessed May 25, 2023.

170   "**gitStream**": LinearB. "gitStream - Every Pull Request Is Unique | LinearB," n.d. https://linearb.io/platform/gitstream/. Accessed May 25, 2023.

CHAPTER 19

173   "**user story mapping**": Patton, Jeff. *User Story Mapping: Discover the Whole Story, Build the Right Product*. Edited by Peter Economy. Sebastopol, California: O'Reilly, 2014.

173   "**design sprints**": Knapp, Jake, John Zeratsky, and Braden Kowitz. *Sprint: How to Solve Big Problems and Test New Ideas in Just Five Days*. New York: Simon & Schuster, 2016.

173   "**dual track development**": "Dual Track Development Is Not Duel Track – Help Your Organization Focus on Successful Outcomes," Jeff Patton & Associates. May 10, 2017. https://www.jpattonassociates.com/dual-track-development/. Accessed May 25, 2023.

174   "**Write the Docs**": "Welcome to Our Community!" Write the Docs, n.d. https://www.writethedocs.org/. Accessed May 25, 2023.

174   "**Effective Remote Work**": Stanier, James. *Effective Remote Work: For Yourself, Your Team, and Your Company*. Raleigh, North Carolina: The Pragmatic Bookshelf, 2022.

175   "**much better than…**": Fried, Jason and David Heinemeier Hansson. *It Doesn't Have to Be Crazy at Work*. New York: HarperBusiness, 2018.

176   "**design docs**": *Industrial Empathy*. "Design Docs at Google," blog, July 6, 2020. https://www.industrialempathy.com/posts/design-docs-at-google/. Accessed May 25, 2023.

178   "**as the guide says**": *Industrial Empathy*. "Design Docs at Google," blog, July 6, 2020. https://www.industrialempathy.com/posts/design-docs-at-google. Accessed May 25, 2023.

CHAPTER 20

183   "**four key metrics**": Thoughtworks. "Four Key Metrics | Technology Radar," March 29, 2022. https://www.thoughtworks.com/en-in/radar/techniques/four-key-metrics. Accessed May 25, 2023.

183   "**a handy template…**": TeamTopologies. "GitHub - TeamTopologies/Team-API-Template: A Template for Defining a Team API - as Explained in the Team Topologies Book." GitHub, May 2, 2023. https://github.com/TeamTopologies/Team-API-template. Accessed May 25, 2023.

183   "Team Topologies": Skelton, Matthew and Manuel Pais. *Team Topologies: Organizing Business and Technology Teams for Fast Flow*. Portland, Oregon: IT Revolution Press, 2019.

184   "acknowledge that code...": Fowler, Martin. "Bliki: CodeAsDocumentation." martinfowler.com, March 22, 2005. https://martinfowler.com/bliki/CodeAsDocumentation.html. Accessed May 25, 2023.

184   "Kira's aka hackergrrl's": GitHub. "Hackergrrl - Overview," n.d. https://github.com/hackergrrl. Accessed May 25, 2023.

184   "Art of README": hackergrrl. "GitHub - Hackergrrl/Art-of-Readme: Things I've Learned about Writing Good READMEs." GitHub, August 21, 2022. https://github.com/hackergrrl/art-of-readme. Accessed May 25, 2023.

185   "Make a README": Make a README. "Make a README," n.d. https://www.makeareadme.com. Accessed May 25, 2023.

185   "Readme.so": readme.so. "Readme.So," n.d. https://readme.so/. Accessed May 25, 2023.

CHAPTER 21

189   "James Stanier says": Stanier, James. *Effective Remote Work: For Yourself, Your Team, and Your Company*. Raleigh, North Carolina: The Pragmatic Bookshelf, 2022.

191   "the impostor syndrome": Wikipedia. "Impostor Syndrome," October 1, 2021. https://en.wikipedia.org/wiki/Impostor_syndrome. Accessed May 25, 2023.

191   "Cate Huston, engineering director...": Apple Podcasts. "Dev Interrupted: Asynchronous Communication with Cate Huston of DuckDuckGo on Apple Podcasts," n.d. https://podcasts.apple.com/us/podcast/asynchronous-communication-with-cate-huston/id1537003676?i=1000499132689. Accessed May 25, 2023.

192   "Antoine de Saint-Exupery famously said": Saint-Exupéry, Antoine. *Wind, Sand and Stars*. New York: Houghton Mifflin Harcourt Publishing Company, 1967.

193   "Vagrant": Install | Vagrant | HashiCorp Developer. "Install | Vagrant | HashiCorp Developer," n.d. https://developer.hashicorp.com/vagrant/downloads. Accessed May 25, 2023.

193   "DevEnv": "Fast, Declarative, Reproducible, and Composable Developer Environments," n.d. https://devenv.sh/. Accessed May 25, 2023.

193 **"Visual Studio's dev containers"**: "Developing Inside a Container Using Visual Studio Code Remote Development," n.d. https://code.visualstudio.com/docs/devcontainers/containers. Accessed May 25, 2023.

193 **"more than 1000…"**: "development-environment. GitHub Topics." GitHub, May 23, 2023. https://github.com/topics/development-environment. Accessed May 25, 2023.

193 **"has sped up ideas…"**: Thoughtworks. "Thoughtworks NEO | Award-Winning Engineering Portal Reimagines Developer Experience and Accelerates Time to Value," n.d. https://www.thoughtworks.com/clients/thoughtworks-neo. Accessed May 25, 2023.

194 **"Backstage…"**: Backstage Software Catalog and Developer Platform. "Backstage Software Catalog and Developer Platform," n.d. https://backstage.io/. Accessed May 25, 2023.

CHAPTER 22

199 **"manage by walking…"**: O'Reilly Online Learning. "Technique: Manage by Walking Around and Listening," n.d. https://www.oreilly.com/library/view/behind-closed-doors/9781680500332/f_0082.html. Accessed May 26, 2023.

200 **"info decks"**: Fowler, Martin. "Bliki: Infodeck." martinfowler.com, November 16, 2012. https://martinfowler.com/bliki/Infodeck.html. Accessed May 26, 2023.

201 **"Oliver Sibony, Cass Sunstein and Daniel Kahneman"**: Kahneman, Daniel, Olivier Sibony, Roberta Fusaro, and Julia Sperling-Magro. "Sounding the Alarm on System Noise," *The McKinsey Quarterly*, May 18, 2021. https://www.mckinsey.com/capabilities/strategy-and-corporate-finance/our-insights/sounding-the-alarm-on-system-noise. Accessed May 26, 2023.

202 **"James Clear says this"**: Clear, James. "James Clear on Twitter." Accessed May 26, 2023. https://twitter.com/jamesclear/status/1251172346431504386. Accessed May 26, 2023.

204 **"techniques such as silent meetings"**: *Harvard Business Review.* "The Case for More Silence in Meetings," June 14, 2019. https://hbr.org/2019/06/the-case-for-more-silence-in-meetings. Accessed May 26, 2023.

205 **"Zoom fatigue"**: Rogelberg, Steven G. and Liana Kreamer. "How to Combat Zoom Fatigue," *Harvard Business Review*, April 29, 2020. https://hbr.org/2020/04/how-to-combat-zoom-fatigue. Accessed May 26, 2023.

205 **"Antifragile"**: Taleb, Nassim Nicholas. *Antifragile: Things That Gain from Disorder.* New York: Penguin Books Ltd., 2012.

CHAPTER 23

210   **"Kim Scott"**: Scott, Kim Malone. *Radical Candor: How to Get What You Want by Saying What You Mean,* Fully Revised and Updated Edition. London: Pan, 2019.

213   **"Patrick Kua"**: patkua.com. "About Patrick Kua - Patkua.Com," n.d. https://www.patkua.com/about/. Accessed May 26, 2023.

213   **"Crucial Confrontations"**: Patterson, Kerry, Joseph Grenny, Ron McMillan, and Al Switzler. *Crucial Confrontations: Tools for Resolving Broken Promises, Violated Expectations, and Bad Behavior.* New York: McGraw-Hill Professional, 2005.

213   **"Radical Candor"**: Scott, Kim Malone. *Radical Candor: How to Get What You Want by Saying What You Mean,* Fully Revised and Updated Edition. London: Pan, 2019.

CHAPTER 24

217   **"According to Wikipedia"**: Wikipedia. "Environment Variable," December 18, 2017. https://en.wikipedia.org/wiki/Environment_variable. Accessed May 26, 2023.

217   **"Upstream"**: Heath, Dan. *Upstream: The Quest to Solve Problems Before They Happen.* London: Bantam Press, 2020.

218   **"Team Topologies"**: Team Topologies. "Team Topologies," May 9, 2022. https://teamtopologies.com. Accessed May 26, 2023.

218   **"their excellent book"**: Skelton, Matthew, and Manuel Pais. *Team Topologies: Organizing Business and Technology Teams for Fast Flow.* Portland, Oregon: IT Revolution Press, 2019.

220   **"50% smaller managerial level…"**: Alder, Matt. "Ep 416: Asynchronous Working - The Recruiting Future Podcast." *The Recruiting Future Podcast,* March 6, 2022. https://recruiting-future.com/2022/03/ep-416-asynchronous-working/. Accessed May 26, 2023.

221   **"process of change"**: Virginia Satir - Wikipedia. "Virginia Satir - Wikipedia," March 6, 2015. https://en.wikipedia.org/wiki/Virginia_Satir#Process_of_Change_Model. Accessed May 26, 2023.

222   **"the SPACE framework"**: Forsgren, Nicole, Margaret-Anne Storey, Chandra Maddila, Thomas Zimmermann, Brian Houck, and Jenna Butler. "The SPACE of Developer Productivity - ACM Queue," n.d. https://queue.acm.org/detail.cfm?id=3454124. Accessed May 26, 2023.

222   "DAU/MAU": Geckoboard. "DAU/MAU Ratio | KPI Example | Geckoboard," n.d. https://www.geckoboard.com/best-practice/kpi-examples/dau-mau-ratio/. Accessed May 26, 2023.

224   "James Clear lists…": Clear, James. "Core Values List," n.d. https://jamesclear.com/core-values. Accessed May 26, 2023.

226   "Simon Sinek's TED Talk": Sinek, Simon. "How Great Leaders Inspire Action," TED Talk, September 2009. https://www.ted.com/talks/simon_sinek_how_great_leaders_inspire_action/c. Accessed May 26, 2023.

226   "Essentialism": The Disciplined Pursuit of Less": McKeown, Greg. *Essentialism: The Disciplined Pursuit of Less*. New York: Currency, 2014.

CHAPTER 25

229   "GitLab": GitLab. "Handbook," n.d. https://about.gitlab.com/handbook/. Accessed May 26, 2023.

230   "Lew Platt, former CEO of HP, says": Jantunen, Joonus. "New Technologies to Take Knowledge Management in Procurement to the Next Level," CPOstrategy. October 29, 2019. https://cpostrategy.media/blog/2019/10/29/new-technologies-to-take-knowledge-management-in-procurement-to-the-next-level/. Accessed July 31, 2023.

235   "it would take 35 years…": Farnam Street Media. "Half Life: The Decay of Knowledge and What to Do About It," blog, March 12, 2018. https://fs.blog/half-life/. Accessed May 26, 2023.

235   "The Strength of Weak Ties": Granovetter, Mark S. "The Strength of Weak Ties." *American Journal of Sociology* 78, no. 6 (May 1973): 1360–80. https://doi.org/10.1086/225469. Accessed May 26, 2023.

CHAPTER 26

245   "the lowest common denominator…": Cassiday, Laura and David Rock. "We're Calling This 'the Worst Return to Office Strategy.' Why This Hybrid Approach Won't Work." *FastCompany*, June 6, 2022. https://www.fastcompany.com/90761863/were-calling-this-the-worst-return-to-office-strategy-why-this-hybrid-approach-wont-work. Accessed May 26, 2023.

245   "industry evidence for…": Kelly, Mary. "Virtual Learning Is Better. Period." NeuroLeadership Institute, April 19, 2022. https://neuroleadership.com/your-brain-at-work/virtual-learning-is-better/. Accessed May 26, 2023.

245   "a boom in online learning": World Economic Forum. "These 3 Charts Show the Global Growth in Online Learning," n.d. https://www.weforum.org/agenda/2022/01/online-learning-courses-reskill-skills-gap/. Accessed May 26, 2023.

247   "Google's experiments with...": Wakabayashi, Daisuke. "Google's Plan for the Future of Work: Privacy Robots and Balloon Walls." *The New York Times*, April 30, 2021. https://www.nytimes.com/2021/04/30/technology/google-back-to-office-workers.html. Accessed May 26, 2023.

247   "Tulsa Remote": Tulsa Remote. "Tulsa Remote," n.d. https://tulsaremote.com. Accessed May 26, 2023.

248   "what Prithwiraj (Raj) Choudhury said...": *Freakonomics Radio*. "Will Work-from-Home Work Forever? - Freakonomics," n.d. https://freakonomics.com/podcast/will-work-from-home-work-forever-ep-464/. Accessed May 26, 2023.

248   "a disproportionate burden...": Pew Research Center. "Women More than Men Adjust Their Careers for Family Life," October 1, 2015. https://www.pewresearch.org/short-reads/2015/10/01/women-more-than-men-adjust-their-careers-for-family-life/. Accessed May 26, 2023.

248   "more sacrifices for...": IndiaSpend.com, Tish Sanghera. "How Domestic Responsibilities Are Keeping India's Women Away from Workforce, Increasing Inequality." Scroll.in, March 26, 2019. https://scroll.in/article/917767/how-domestic-responsibilities-are-keeping-indias-women-away-from-workforce-increasing-inequality. Accessed May 26, 2023.

248   "leveled the playing field...": McLaren, Samantha. "Why the Rise of Remote Work May Help Companies Become More Diverse — and More Inclusive," May 16, 2023. https://www.linkedin.com/business/talent/blog/talent-acquisition/why-remote-work-may-help-companies-become-more-diverse.

249   "it's an epic win...": Hunt, Steven T. "SAP BrandVoice: How Hybrid Remote Work Improves Diversity And Inclusion." Forbes, May 12, 2021. https://www.forbes.com/sites/sap/2021/05/12/how-hybrid-remote-work-improves-diversity-and-inclusion/. Accessed May 26, 2023.

249   "Companies that care about...": Evers, Hans-Dieter. "The Value of Diversity." *Penang Monthly*. 7. 30–33., 2012. https://www.researchgate.net/publication/259175354_The_Value_of_Diversity.

249 **"needs nuance"**: Shreedhar, Ganga, Kate Laffan, and Laura M. Giurge. "Is Remote Work Actually Better for the Environment?," *Harvard Business Review*, March 7, 2022. https://hbr.org/2022/03/is-remote-work-actually-better-for-the-environment. Accessed May 26, 2023.

249 **"Harvard Business Review cover story"**: Choudhury, Prithwiraj (Raj). "Our Work-from-Anywhere Future," *Harvard Business Review*, November 1, 2020. https://hbr.org/2020/11/our-work-from-anywhere-future. Accessed May 26, 2023.

249 **"people are more productive..."**: Apollo Technical LLC. "Surprising Working From Home Productivity Statistics (2023)," January 3, 2023. https://www.apollotechnical.com/working-from-home-productivity-statistics/. Accessed May 26, 2023.

250 **"As Raj Choudhury says"**: Ren, Henry. "Bloomberg - Are You a Robot?," n.d. https://www.bloomberg.com/news/articles/2022-02-15/in-10-years-remote-work-will-simply-be-work. Accessed May 26, 2023.

250 **"resources (in tech that's often..."**: Christensen, Clayton M. and Michael Overdorf. "Meeting the Challenge of Disruptive Change," *Harvard Business Review*, March 1, 2000. https://hbr.org/2000/03/meeting-the-challenge-of-disruptive-change. Accessed May 26, 2023.

250 **"In their book..."**: Fried, Jason and David Heinemeier Hansson. *Remote: Office Not Required*. New York: Currency, 2013.

251 **"Such a perception"**: Molla, Rani. "You're Going Back to the Office. Your Boss Isn't." Vox, October 12, 2022. https://www.vox.com/recode/2022/10/12/23400496/remote-work-from-home-office-boss-manager-hypocrisy. Accessed May 26, 2023.

252 **"James Stanier"**: Stanier, James. *Effective Remote Work: For Yourself, Your Team, and Your Company*. Raleigh, North Carolina: The Pragmatic Bookshelf, 2022.

CHAPTER 27

259 **four stages of competence"**: Wikipedia. "Four Stages of Competence," May 11, 2018. https://en.wikipedia.org/wiki/Four_stages_of_competence. Accessed May 26, 2023.

CHAPTER 28

268 **"Research from Clockwise"**: Clockwise. "Happy and Productive: The ROI of a Sustainable Work Culture," n.d. https://www.getclockwise.com/library/happy-and-productive. Accessed May 26, 2023.

268   "Abby Peel, co-lead...": Peel, Abby. "Digital Presenteeism - Digital People." October 27, 2020. https://digitalpeople.blog.gov.uk/2020/10/27/digital-presenteeism/. Accessed May 26, 2023.

270   "Stop the Meeting Madness": Perlow, Leslie A., Constance Noonan Hadley, and Eunice Eun. "Stop the Meeting Madness," *Harvard Business Review*, July 1, 2017. https://hbr.org/2017/07/stop-the-meeting-madness. Accessed May 26, 2023.

271   "A World Without Email": Newport, Cal. *A World Without Email: Reimagining Work in an Age of Communication Overload*. Edmonton, Alberta: Portfolio, 2021.

271   "Present Shock...": Rushkoff, Douglas. *Present Shock: When Everything Happens Now*. New York: Current, 2014.

CHAPTER 29

276   "Creative Commons license": Creative Commons — Attribution-NonCommercial-ShareAlike 4.0 International — CC BY-NC-SA 4.0. "Creative Commons — Attribution-NonCommercial-ShareAlike 4.0 International — CC BY-NC-SA 4.0," n.d. http://creativecommons.org/licenses/by-nc-sa/4.0/. Accessed May 26, 2023.

283   "barn raising": "Http://Meatballwiki.Org/Wiki/BarnRaising," n.d. http://meatballwiki.org/wiki/BarnRaising. Accessed May 26, 2023.

CHAPTER 30

290   "many employees would...": Korolevich, Sara. "The State of Remote Work in 2021: A Survey of the American Workforce," August 24, 2021, https://www.goodhire.com/resources/articles/state-of-remote-work-survey/. Accessed May 26, 2023.

290   "Gustavo Razetti says": Razzetti, Gustavo. "Why Malcolm Gladwell (and Many Leaders) Get Remote Work All Wrong," August 11, 2022, https://www.fearlessculture.design/blog-posts/why-malcolm-gladwell-and-many-leaders-get-remote-work-all-wrong. Accessed May 26, 2023.

290   "will remote work...": business.gov.nl. "Working from Home: Your Employees' Rights," n.d. https://business.gov.nl/running-your-business/staff/health-and-safety-at-work/working-from-home-your-employees-rights/. Accessed May 26, 2023.

290   **"limited remote work…"**: *The Hindu*. "Centre Allows 'Work from Home' for Maximum One Year in SEZ," July 20, 2022. https://www.thehindu.com/news/national/centre-allows-work-from-home-for-maximum-one-year-in-sez/article65661068.ece. Accessed May 26, 2023.

290   **"rolled back this decision…"**: "IT Units in SEZs Permitted to Allow 'work from Home' till Dec 2023, Centre Amends Rules - ET Government." ETGovernment.com, n.d. https://government.economictimes.indiatimes.com/news/governance/it-units-in-sezs-permitted-to-allow-work-from-home-till-dec-2023-centre-amends-rules/96106517. Accessed May 26, 2023.

290   **"top talent shapes trends…"**: Daisley, Bruce. "Harvard Professor: Work from Anywhere Is Our Destiny," *East Sleep Work Repeat* (blog) May 18, 2022. https://eatsleepworkrepeat.com/harvard-professor-work-from-anywhere-is-our-destiny/. Accessed May 26, 2023.

291   **"behemoths like Apple…"**: Owe, Malcom. "Apple's Director of Machine Learning Exits over Return-to-Office Policy," AppleInsider, May 7, 2022. https://appleinsider.com/articles/22/05/07/apples-director-of-machine-learning-exits-over-return-to-office-policy. Accessed May 26, 2023.

291   **"builder economy"**: Ouzan, Raphael. "Why We Raised $60M to Create the Team Economy," *Mission* (blog) May 17, 2022. https://www.a.team/mission/why-we-raised-60m-to-create-the-builder-economy. Accessed May 26, 2023.

292   **"The Hindu, reported…"**: K., Bhumika. "Say Hello to the Digital Nomads," *The Hindu*, August 21, 2015. https://www.thehindu.com/features/metroplus/say-hello-to-indias-digital-nomads/article7565751.ece. Accessed May 26, 2023.

292   **"Forbes defined the…"**: Castrillon, Caroline. "Why The Digital Nomad Lifestyle Is On The Rise." *Forbes*, July 17, 2022. https://www.forbes.com/sites/carolinecastrillon/2022/07/17/why-the-digital-nomad-lifestyle-is-on-the-rise/. Accessed May 26, 2023.

292   **"54 countries have…"**: Johnson, Tracey. "58 Countries with Digital Nomad Visas - The Ultimate List." *Nomad Girl* (blog), June 26, 2023. https://nomadgirl.co/countries-with-digital-nomad-visas/. Accessed May 26, 2023.

292   **"a five-hour workday"**: Morath, Eric. "The 5-Hour Workday Gets Put to the Test." *WSJ*, May 14, 2023. https://www.wsj.com/articles/the-5-hour-workday-gets-put-to-the-test-11571876563. Accessed May 26, 2023.

292   **"four hours of deep work…"**: Ericsson, K. Anders. "Training History, Deliberate Practice and Elite Sports Performance: An Analysis in Response to Tucker and Collins Review—What Makes Champions?" *British Journal of Sports Medicine* 47, no. 9 (October 30, 2012): 533–35. https://doi.org/10.1136/bjsports-2012-091767. Accessed May 26, 2023.

292   **"4-Day Week Global"**: "The 4 Day Week Pilot Program Results — 4 Day Week Global," n.d. https://www.4dayweek.com/us-ireland-results. Accessed May 26, 2023.

293   **"Perpetual Guardian has made…"**: Nadkarni, Anuja. "Perpetual Guardian Makes Four-Day Week Permanent." Stuff, October 1, 2018. https://www.stuff.co.nz/business/107525245/perpetual-guardian-makes-fourday-week-permanent. Accessed May 26, 2023.

293   **"The results are…"**: "The 4 Day Week Pilot Program Results — 4 Day Week Global," n.d. https://www.4dayweek.com/us-ireland-results. Accessed May 26, 2023.

293   **"Mark Howland, Charity Bank's…"**: Cooban, Anna. "How the World's Biggest Four-Day Workweek Trial Run Changed People's Lives." CNN Business, August 1, 2022. https://www.cnn.com/2022/08/01/business/4-day-work-week-uk-trial/index.html. Accessed May 26, 2023.

293   **"a four-and-a-half-day work week"**: Mansoor, Zainab. "UAE's New Workweek - How Has It Impacted the Ecosystem?" *Gulf Business*, April 2, 2022. https://gulfbusiness.com/uaes-new-workweek-how-has-it-impacted-the-ecosystem/. Accessed May 26, 2023.

293   **"The United States…"**: The Economics Daily. "Number of People 75 and Older in the Labor Force Is Expected to Grow 96.5 Percent by 2030" November 4, 2021. https://www.bls.gov/opub/ted/2021/number-of-people-75-and-older-in-the-labor-force-is-expected-to-grow-96-5-percent-by-2030.htm. Accessed May 26, 2023.

295   **"Gen Z is very involved…"**: Carnegie, Megan. "Gen Z: How Young People Are Changing Activism," BBC Worklife, August 8, 2022 https://www.bbc.com/worklife/article/20220803-gen-z-how-young-people-are-changing-activism. Accessed May 26, 2023.

295   **"Deloitte"**: Deloitte India. "Deloitte GenZ and Millennial Survey 2022," May 18, 2022. https://www2.deloitte.com/in/en/pages/about-deloitte/articles/Deloitte-GenZ-and-Millennial-Survey-2022.html. Accessed May 26, 2023.

295   **"heavy carbon footprint…"**: Tapper, James. "Experts Call for Ban on Glass Skyscrapers to Save Energy in Climate Crisis," *The Guardian*, July 28, 2019. http://www.theguardian.com/environment/2019/jul/28/ban-all-glass-skscrapers-to-save-energy-in-climate-crisis. Accessed May 26, 2023.

INDEX

A

accelerating leftward, 81–84
access control, 92
accountability partners, 161
actions, 134
    defaulting to, 9–10
    inputs, 129
    tech huddles, 150–151
    working independently, 46–47
ad hoc conversations, 152
advocacy, 265
agendas
    meetings, 63
    that need meetings, 200, 201
agents, change, 255, 256
agile approaches
    to design, 173–178
    to documentation, 181–186
agile manifestos, 33–34, 40–41, 87
agility, 17
agreeing on fundamentals, 280–281
aligning
    with common purposes, 226–227
    goals, 276–278
Allen, Tim, 250
analysis of tasks, 47
Antifragile (Taleb), 205
anti-patterns, 272
The Anywhere Operating System
    (Thomas/Samake), 61
app blockers, 45
applications, 6
architectural decision records (ADRs),
    166–167, 176, 185
artifacts
    make your own templates (MYOT), 176
    onboarding, 189–190
    writing, 189–190
artificial intelligence (AI), 158
    assistance, 231
    management, 237
assessing goals, 279. *See also* goals
assets, 91
assistance, artificial intelligence (AI), 231
assume positive intent (API), 105

async-first
    behavioral cues, 85
    definition of, 16
    goals of, 258–259
    leadership, 197 (*see also* leadership)
    method stacks, 264
    possibilities of, 289–295
    retrospective processes, 134
    schedules, 287–288
    starting, 275–285
    strategies to protect and extend, 260–261
    team ownership, 284
asynchronous audio, 38–39
asynchronous collaboration, 5–6, 8,
    10–11, 17
asynchronous communication, 18, 64–66,
    142
asynchronous mode, desk checks/kickoffs,
    138–144
asynchronous status reporting, 124
asynchronous video, 38–39
async islands
    advocacy, 265
    communities of practice, 262–263
    forces for/against change, 256–258
    goals of async-first, 258–259
    improving systems, 259–260
    influencing departments to join, 262
    organizational inertia, 255–264
    recruiting vertical slices, 261
    sharing defaults/templates/tools,
        263–264
    strategies to protect and extend
        async-first, 260–261
async work
    benefits of, 11, 13–14
    meetings and, 17
A.Team, 291
audio, asynchronous, 38–39
auditing systems, 232–234
audit trails, 163–172, 204
    architectural decision records (ADRs),
        166–167
    business decision records (BDRs), 166
    commit messages, 168–169

documentation, 171
examples of, 171
just ask patterns, 163–164
meeting notes, 164–165
pull requests (PRs), 169–170
replacing summaries, 164
automation, 220
code, 186
documentation, 181
onboarding, 193–194
tools, 113–115
autonomy, 7, 49, 295
hybrid work, 253
in teams, 148–149
avoiding busywork, 203–204
A World Without Email (Newport), 271

B

back-and-forth communication, 50
backlogs, 91, 119–120
balance
communication, 18
systems in, 17–18
Basecamp, 113
baselines, tabulating baseline data, 278–280
baton-pass pairing routines, 157
behaviors
accelerating leftward, 81–84
async-first behavioral cues, 85
encouraging productive, 82
shifting, 77–85 (*see also* shifting
behaviors)
toxicity in virtual workplaces, 267–272
benefits
of async work, 11, 13–14
of pair programming tools, 156–157
of remote work, 137 (*see also* remote
work)
of writing, 31–32
Bezos, Jeff, 55, 64
biases, 272–273
binary judgments, 14
blocking distractions, 43, 44–45
bonding, teams, 156
book clubs, 46
Boucher, Ryan, 169
brain drains, 247–248
brainstorming, 133
breakdown documents, 175–176
broadcasting commitments, 77–81
buddy systems, onboarding, 194
budgets for meetings, 74
building relationships, 66, 71–72, 74. *See
also* communication; relationships
business decision records (BDRs), 166
business intelligence (BI) tools, 278
busywork, avoiding, 203–204
Butler, 113

C

calendars. *See also* schedules
cleaning up, 281–282
free, 152
Google Calendar, 165
syncing, 82
calm, creating, 221–223
camaraderie
cost of, 72–73
on teams, 156
Campfire, 247
candor, practicing, 213–216
capabilities of systems, 231–232
capped downsides, 123
celebrating hard workers, 271–272
change, 13
agents, 255, 256
focus on value, 13–14
forces for/against, 256–258
overcoming organizational inertia,
255–264
processes, 221
systems in balance, 17–18
Ulysses pacts, 17
visualization on spectrum, 14–16
channels, 105
identifying, 55
naming, 99
charts
hill, 124
responsible, accountable, consulted,
informed (RACI), 89, 90, 91
chat status, changing, 78, 99
The Checklist Manifesto (Gawande), 139
checklists
examples, 140
onboarding, 191–192
requirement templates and, 139
Choudhury, Prithwiraj (Raj), 248, 249, 290,
291
cleaning up calendars, 281–282
Clear, James, 77, 224
code
automation, 186
documentation, 185–186
overviews, 184
repositories, 184
reviews, 156
codebases, 91, 182, 184–185
CodeSee, 186
cognitive loads, managing, 218–219
collaboration, 204, 205, 218
asynchronous, 5–6, 8, 10–11, 17
audits, 232
costs of, 70–71
curses, 147
documents, 25, 211
guidelines, 183
online, 5

protocols (*see* protocols [collaboration])
strategies, 6
synchronous, 30
tools, 24–27
whiteboards, 131
collecting inputs, 129, 130
commitments, broadcasting, 77–81
commit messages, 168–169
common purposes, aligning with, 226–227
communication, 10
asynchronous, 18, 142
back-and-forth, 50
balance, 18
email as secondary tool, 52–53
emotion, 36
EqualExpert Slack guide, 105
face-to-face, 33, 69–75 (*see also* face-to-face communication)
functional design, 173–178
idea papers, 174–175
instant messaging (IM) (*see* instant messaging [IM])
knowledge sharing, 10–11
leadership, 202
onboarding, 190 (*see also* onboarding)
parameters of, 34
practicing candor, 213–216
as a process, 204–205
progress, 47
protocols, 55
of purpose, 170
reading skills, 45–46
simplifying complexity of, 178
synchronous, 18
teams, 164
tech design, 173–178
toxicity in virtual workplaces, 269–270
urgency of, 98–99
written communication *versus* documentation, 29
communities
platforms, 236
of practice, 262–263
tacit knowledge, 229–238
competence, 259, 260
compliance, 256
complicated subsystem teams, 218
comprehension, 43
computers, 5
concentration, 7–8
Confluence, 165, 167
connectivity, internet, 5
conscious competence, 259
conscious incompetence, 259
consent-based decision-making, 54, 142
content
instant messaging (IM), 102
projects, 91–92

context
documentation, 182 (*see also* documentation)
projects, 89–91
switches, 81
in team handbooks, 89
continuous flow, 118–122
Conventional Commits guide, 168
ConveRel quadrants, 61–63, 270
convergence, 62, 129
conversations, 212. *See also* communication; instant messaging (IM)
ad hoc, 152
targeting, 102–103
threads, 104
conveyance, 62, 128
core hours, 157
core values, 224
costs
budgets for meetings, 74
of camaraderie, 72–73
of collaboration, 70–71
for stakeholders, 246–249
COVID-19 pandemic, 1, 5, 244, 289. *See also* remote work
create, read, update, delete (CRUD) applications, 6
Cross, Rob, 148
cultures
building team, 223–225
culture-building, 216
defaulting to action, 9–10
meetings, 8
onboarding, 191 (*see also* onboarding)
org culture, 258
risk-averse, 148
cycles
development, 117–126 (*see also* development cycles)
shape up, 122–125
time, 120–121
two-track approach, 124–125
use of demos, 122
Czikszentmihaly, Mihaly, 8

D

data, tracking, 280
data-driven retrospectives, 131
David Heinemeier Hansson (DHH), 72
decentralized models, 149
decision-making
architectural decision records (ADRs), 166–167, 176, 185
business decision records (BDRs), 166
consent-based, 142
meetings, 64
processes, 53–55
decisions, events, explanations, proposals (DEEP), 94, 95

deep work, 7, 8
  planning focus time, 79
  value of, 14
defaults
  to action, 9–10
  managing, 259
  sharing, 263–264
  stages of sensible, 275–284
defining development environments, 193
definition of done (DoD), 139–140
definition of ready (DoR), 139–140
defragging calendars, 281–282
delivery pressures, 257
demos, use of, 122
descriptions, projects, 184
design
  agile approach to, 173–178
  breakdown documents, 175–176
  checklists, 191–192
  functional, 173–178
  idea papers, 174–175
  inclusion, 204
  make your own templates (MYOT), 176
  mini design documents, 178
  pair programming tools, 157
  simplifying complexity of
    communication, 178
  for success skills, 217–227
  tech, 173–178
  technical design documents, 176–178
desk checks, 137–145
  definition of, 138
  maintaining practice of, 144–145
  remote native, 145
  replacing with video, 142–143
details of user stories, 141–142
dev-box tests, 138
development cycles, 117–126
  definition of ready (DoR), 139
  sprints, 117–125
  strength of processes, 125
DevEnv, 193
digital nomadism, 291–292
directly responsible individual (DRI), 149,
  159
distraction blocking, 43, 44–45
distributed standups, 108–109. See also
  standup meetings
distributed teams, 149
distributed work arrangements, 1
distribution of teams, 245–246
documentation, 29
  agile approach to, 181–186
  agile manifesto, 87
  audit trails, 171
  automation, 181
  code, 185–186
  codebases, 184–185
  handbooks, 181–186 (see also
    handbooks)

improving, 181
onboarding, 189–190
README files, 184–185
simplifying, 92
tools, 92, 165 (see also tools)
triggers, 94–95
"Write the Docs" community, 174
written communication versus, 29 (see
  also written communication)
documents
  architectural decision records (ADRs),
    176
  breakdown, 175–176
  collaboration, 211
  GitLab, 88 (see also GitLab)
  idea papers, 174–175
  meeting minutes, 165
  meetings, 64
  mini design, 178
  shared, 174
  six-page memo patterns, 64
  technical design, 176–178
  versioning systems, 93, 94
done, definition of, 139–140
dopamine, 44
doubt, strategies for, 47
dumb questions, 190–191

E

editing
  team handbooks, 93–94
  text, 37
effective meetings, 151–152, 201. See also
  meetings
Effective Remote Work (Stanier), 15, 55,
  137
efficiency, 70
  of sprint ceremonies, 122
  of teams, 193, 195
Eisenhower matrix, 111, 112
email
  as secondary tool, 52–53
  signatures, 78
emojis, 101. See also communication
emotion, communication of, 36
empowerment, 7
enabling teams, 218
encouraging productive behaviors, 82
enterprise social networks (ESNs), 235
environments
  projects, 183
  setting up retrospectives, 131–134
  variables, 217
EqualExpert Slack guide, 105
events, retrospectives as processes,
  128–130, 134–135
examples
  of audit trails, 171
  of checklists, 140

of detailed user stories, 141–142
learning from, 178
of onboarding checklists, 192
of schedules, 3–4
of survey forms, 130
expenses, operations, 247. *See also* costs
expression, means for, 232
external forces, 255, 257–258

F

face-to-face communication, 33, 69–75
building relationships, 74
cost of camaraderie, 72–73
cost of collaboration, 70–71
effectiveness of, 40
hybrid meetings, 71
onsite/offsite meetings, 73
time zones, 69–70
value of being in person, 71–72
facilitating knowledge flows, 234–238
facilitation (team mentoring), 219
fear of missing out (FOMO), 10
feature breakdown documents, 175–176
feedback, 170, 175, 212
loops, 145
practicing candor, 213–216
skills, 214–216
Fellow, 113, 165, 211
files, README, 182, 184–185
first among equals (FaE), 149, 220
flexibility, 6–7, 289–290
of pair programming tools, 157
schedules, 7, 138
flex work, 248. *See also* hybrid work
flow
audit trails, 163 (*see also* audit trails)
continuous, 118–122
facilitating, 234–238
Flow: The Psychology of Optimal Experience (Czikszentmihaly), 8
focus
building, 46 (*see also* distraction blocking)
systems, 203
transactions, 203
on value, 13–14
focus time, planning, 79
focus weeks, 83
forces for/against change, 256–258
change agents, 256
external forces, 257–258
internal forces, 256–257
formatting
architectural decision records (ADRs), 167
text, 101
forums as rituals, 128
fostering strong relationships, 195
four-day workweeks, 292–294

Fowler, Martin, 87
free calendars, 152
frequency of retrospectives, 127–130
frequently asked questions (FAQs), 175, 190–191
Fried, Jason, 50, 250, 251
functional design, 173–178
fundamentals, agreeing on, 280–281

G

Gawande, Atul, 139
Geekbot, 113
Gen Z, 294–295
GitHub, 167
GitLab, 46, 88, 115
Glean, 186
global pandemics. *See* COVID-19 pandemic
Gmail, scheduling email, 79
goals
aligning, 276–278
of async-first, 258–259
teams, 283
of teams, 219
Godin, Seth, 53
Google
Calendar, 165
Drive, 167
Jamboard, 131
Looker Studio, 278
Workspace, 165, 230, 231
Graham, Paul, 7, 82
Granovetter, Mark, 235
Grant, Adam, 148
guidelines, 105, 283, 284

H

habits, reading, 45–46
half days, 82
handbooks
agile approach to documentation, 181–186
content, 89–92
documentation, 181–186
iterations of team, 93–94
need for source of truth, 87–88
onboarding, 190–191 (*see also* onboarding)
projects, 89, 182
shared realities, 95
start with teams, 88
transactions, 204
writing team, 87–96
Hansson, David Heinemeier, 250, 251
Hari, Johann, 44
Heath, Dan, 217
helping each other, 212
Henderson, John, 166

hill charts, 124
hogging keyboards, 159
Howland, Mark, 293
huddles. *See* tech huddles
Hugo, 165
Huston, Cate, 191
hybrid meetings, 71
hybrid work, 243–254
    autonomy, 253
    brain drains, 247–248
    costs for stakeholders, 246–249
    embracing science, 249–251
    impact on the environment, 249
    inclusion, 248–249
    organizations, 244–245
    perception of asymmetry, 251
    preferences for remote work, 243–253
    team distribution, 245–246
    treating everyone as remote, 251–253

I
idea papers, 174–175
identifying channels, 55
IFTTT, 113
implementation of pull requests (PRs), 170
improving
    documentation, 181
    systems, 259–260
    written communication, 36
inclusion, 204–205
    benefits of writing, 31
    design, 204
    hybrid work, 248–249
    in workplaces, 9
incompetence, 259
indexing, 32
ineffective management, 258
inline videos, 39
in-person meetings, 71–72. *See also* face-to-face communication; meetings
in-person training, 245
inputs, 129, 130
installation, 184
instant messaging (IM), 53, 147
    content, 102
    EqualExpert Slack guide, 105
    guidelines, 105
    limiting messages, 100–101
    managing reactions, 103
    naming channels/rooms, 99
    productivity, 97–98
    statuses, 99–100
    targeting conversations, 102–103
    threads, 104
    visibility of guidelines, 105
integration, 170
interaction patterns, 218, 219
internal forces, 255, 256–257
internal structure of teams, 219–220

internet connectivity, 5
interpreting written communication, 34, 35
interruptions, 44, 80. *See also* distraction blocking
    quick syncs, 150
    rituals, 137
iterations of team handbooks, 93–94

J
Jira, 113
journalism, 35
just ask patterns, 163–164

K
Kahneman, Daniel, 8
kickoffs, 137–145
    definition of, 138
    maintaining practice of, 144–145
    meetings, 141
    remote native, 145
knowledge
    capabilities of systems, 231–232
    forms of, 230
    management, 238
    managing ecosystems of, 237
    project handbooks, 91
    sharing, 10–11, 87–88, 156
    tacit, 229–239 (*see also* tacit knowledge)
    work industry, 1
kudos, 134

L
layers of companies, supporting, 261
leadership, 197
    avoiding busywork, 203–204
    communication, 202
    culture-building, 216
    effective meetings, 201
    escaping recurring meetings, 200–201
    by example, 202–203
    inclusion, 204–205
    managing people, 209–216
    mindsets, 199–207
    misaligned, 257
    one-on-one interactions, 211–212
    practicing candor, 213–216
    reducing repetitive work, 201–202
    resiliency, 205–206
    success skills, 209–210
    time management, 206
    toxicity in virtual workplaces, 267–272
    tyranny of the way, 199–200
    vigilance of toxicity in virtual workplaces, 271–272
    workloads, 210–211
limiting messages, 100–101

LinearB, 183
links, responding with, 95
locations
    face-to-face communication, 69–70
    meetings, 64–66
logs, 168
loops, feedback, 145

M

maintaining quality with fewer meetings,
    138–145
maker weeks, 83
make your own templates (MYOT), 176
management. *See also* leadership
    artificial intelligence (AI), 237
    defaults, 259
    ineffective, 258
    knowledge, 238
    knowledge ecosystems, 237
    managing people, 209–216
    project management tools, 109–112
    reactions, 103
    stocks, 234–238
    teams, 218–219
    time, 45, 206
    toxicity in virtual workplaces, 267–272
mandatory meetings, 109. *See also* standup
    meetings
Manifesto for Agile Software Development,
    33–34, 40–41
Markdown, 185
Martin, Liam, 220
matrices, Eisenhower matrix, 111, 112
McMinn, Keavy, 170
meaningful synchrony, 270–271
measurements
    progress, 124
    scope, 124
    sprints as denominator of, 121
    throughput, 120–121
meetings
    agendas, 63
    async work and, 17
    best practices for, 143–144
    building relationships, 66, 74
    ConveRel quadrants, 61–63
    cost of camaraderie, 72–73
    cultures, 8
    decision-making processes, 64
    documents, 64
    dollars wasted because of, 60
    effective, 151–152, 201
    face-to-face communication, 69–70 (*see
        also* face-to-face communication)
    hybrid, 71
    kickoffs, 141 (*see also* kickoffs)
    as last resorts, 57–67, 77
    length of, 63–64
    maintaining quality with fewer, 138–145

mandatory, 109 (*see also* standup
    meetings)
minutes, 165
no-meeting Fridays, 82–83
notes, 164–165
onsite/offsite, 73
planning, 74
predictability of, 82
productivity and, 59–61
purging recurring, 83–84
recurring, 200–201
retrospectives, 131 (*see also*
    retrospectives)
schedules, 82–83 (*see also* schedules)
standup, 107–116 (*see also* standup
    meetings)
summaries, 165
time zones, 64–66
value of being in person, 71–72
as waste of time, 30
and written communication, 30
mentoring, 156
merge requests (MRs), 169
messages. *See also* communication; email;
    instant messaging (IM)
    commit, 168–169
    content, 101
    limiting, 100–101
    schedules, 78–79
metrics, 279
    cycle time, 121
    tracking, 183
Microsoft
    Office 365, 165
    Teams, 113, 158
    Word, 37
mindsets
    change, 13 (*see also* change mindsets)
    leadership, 199–207
mini design documents, 178
Miro, 131
misaligned leadership, 257
mix pairing, 160–161
models, distributed teams, 149
momentum, gaining internal, 257
Montalenti, Andrew, 160
Morris, Kief, 169
Mullenweg, Matt, 105
Mural, 131, 133, 225
Mutton, Dan, 169, 170

N

naming channels/rooms, 99
Newport, Cal, 7, 44, 49, 50, 271
new ways to work
    benefits of async work, 11
    collaboration strategies, 6
    concentration, 7–8
    defaulting to action, 9–10

flexibility, 6–7
inclusive workplaces, 9
knowledge sharing, 10–11
software development, 5
Nikoo, Hoorvash, 168
no-meeting Fridays, 82–83
notes, 164–165. *See also* documents
Nygard, Michael, 166

O

off-boarding, 92
Office 365, 165
office spaces, 246
onboarding, 92, 189–196
automation, 193–194
buddy systems, 194
checklists, 191–192
fostering strong relationships, 195
frequently asked questions (FAQs),
190–191
reliability, 193–194
team efficiency, 195
team handbooks, 182–183
writing artifacts, 189–190
one-on-one interactions, 211–212
online collaboration, 5
online learning, 245
onsite/offsite meetings, 73
operations
expenses, 247
project handbooks, 91
optimizing systems, 120–121
organizational inertia, 255–264
organizations, hybrid work, 244–245
org culture, 258
Otter, 165
outcomes of retrospectives, 127–130
Outlook, 165
Ouzan, Raphael, 291
overheads, communication, 190

P

page owners, 94
pair programming tools, 155–161
accountability partners, 160
benefits of, 156–157
flexibility of, 157
Microsoft Teams, 158
mix pairing/solo work, 160–161
personal discipline, 158–159
viewpoints about, 155
Zoom, 158
Pais, Manuel, 99, 218
pandemics. *See* COVID-19 pandemic
Parabol, 53, 131
parameters of communication, 34
partner inertia, 257
passive pairing, 159

patterns
anti-patterns, 272
interaction, 218, 219
just ask, 163–164
reputation, 231
Peel, Abby, 268
performance, 81, 209–216, 256
Perpetual Guardian (New Zealand), 292,
293
personal discipline, 158–159
personal productivity, 47
personal well-being, 212
philosophizing, 159
physical standup meetings, 108. *See also*
standup meetings
Pinchas, Aviva, 53
pipelines, 91
pitfalls, navigating, 241
planning
focus time, 79
meetings, 74
scrum ceremonies, 118
platforms, 165, 236. *See also* tools
platform teams, 218
Platt, Lew, 230
pods, 149
pointless synchrony, 30
Polaris, 183
porous walls, creating, 230–234
possibilities of async-first, 289–295
autonomy, 295
digital nomadism, 291–292
flexibility, 289–290
four-day workweeks, 292–294
Gen Z, 294–295
skills economies, 290–291
practice
communities of, 262–263
definition of, 29
predictability of meetings, 82
preferences for remote work, 243–253
*Present Shock: When Everything Happens
Now* (Rushkoff), 271
prioritization, 119–120
backlogs, 119, 122
inputs, 129
processes
change, 221
communication as, 204, 205 (*see also*
communication)
onboarding (*see* onboarding)
retrospectives as, 128–130, 134–135
strength of, 125
teams, 144
two-track approach, 124–125
productivity, 6, 70, 204. *See also*
asynchronous collaboration
instant messaging (IM), 97–98
meetings and, 59–61
personal, 47

remote work, 249–250
teams, 47
tech huddles, 151–152
tools, 26
products, definition of, 29
progress
    communicating, 47
    on expectations, 212
    measuring, 124
    team communication and, 52
    updating, 110
projects
    content, 91–92
    context, 89–91
    environments, 183
    handbooks, 89, 182
    management tools, 109–112
    problems with, 6
    tracking metrics, 183
protocols (collaboration), 49
    decision-making processes, 53–55
    email as secondary tool, 52–53
    identifying channels, 55
    response times, 55
    statuses/transitions (workflow), 50–52
    work execution, 49–50
    workflow, 49–50
proximity bias, 272–273
pull requests (PRs), 115, 169–170
purging recurring meetings, 83–84
purpose, communication of, 170

Q

quality, maintaining with fewer meetings,
    138–145
questions
    dumb, 190–191
    frequently asked questions (FAQs), 175,
        190–191
    just ask patterns, 163–164
quick syncs
    replacing, 80–81
    tech huddles, 150

R

radical candor, 214, 215
Radical Candor (Scott), 213
Range, 113
rationing distractions, 45
Razetti, Gustavo, 290
reactions, management, 103
reading, 43, 45–46
README files, 182, 184–185
ready, definition of, 139–140
reasonable lag, defining, 280
Rebele, Reb, 148
recordings, 38–39

records, 91. *See also* documents
    architectural decision records (ADRs),
        166–167, 176, 185
    business decision records (BDRs), 166
recruiting vertical slices, 261
recurring meetings, 83–84, 200–201. *See
    also* meetings
reducing pressure, 221–223
reducing repetitive work, 201–202
relationships, 62
    building, 66, 71–72
    face-to-face communication, 74
    fostering strong, 195
    strong, 62
    weak, 62
relevance, maintaining, 115
reliability, onboarding, 193–194
remote.com, 9
remote native, 145
Remote: Office Not Required (Hansson/
    Fried), 250, 251
Remote Team Interactions Workbook
    (Skelton/Pais), 99
remote teams, 50
remote work, 1
    desire for, 289–290
    organizations, 244–245
    preferences for, 243–253
    productivity, 249–250
    remote feature of, 137
    secret sauce, 250–251
    serendipity, 250
    shift to, 5
    statistics, 59, 60
    team distribution, 245–246
repetitive work, reducing, 201–202
replacing
    desk checks with video, 142–143
    quick syncs, 80–81
    summaries, 164
reporting asynchronous status, 124
reputation patterns, 231
requirements, 138, 139
resiliency, 205–206
resources, written communication, 36
responding with links, 95
responsible, accountable, consulted,
    informed (RACI), 89, 90, 91
retrospectives, 127
    convergence and, 129
    data-driven, 131
    frequency of, 127–130
    as processes, 128–130, 134–135
    scrum ceremonies, 135
    setting up environments, 131–134
    templates, 132
    timelines, 129
    voting asynchronously, 131
risk-averse cultures, 148

rituals
    forums, 128
    interruptions, 137 (*see also* desk checks; kickoffs)
    sprints, 117 (*see also* sprints)
roadmaps, 91
roles, 89, 90, 91
rooms, naming, 99
Rushkoff, Douglas, 271

S

Sack, Jonathon, 71
safety checks, 132–133
Samake, Aisha, 61, 62
Satir change curve, 221
schedules, 3–4, 287–288
    flexibility, 7, 138
    focus weeks, 83
    half days, 82
    maker weeks, 83
    messages, 78–79
    no-meeting Fridays, 82–83
    pair programming tools, 157
    retrospectives, 127–130
    tech huddles, 152–153
scope
    measuring, 124
    quantifying change, 139
    sprints, 119–120
score calculators, 278
Scott, Kim, 213, 214, 215
scrum ceremonies, 118, 135
searches, 32
secrets, 91
secret sauce, remote work, 250–251
self-organizing teams, 49
self-sign-up, 47
sensible defaults. *See* defaults
serendipitous discovery, 231
serendipity, remote work, 250
setting up retrospective environments, 131–134
shape up cycles, 122–125
sharing
    defaults, 263–264
    development environments, 193
    documents, 174
    knowledge, 156
    realities, 95
    templates, 263–264
    tools, 263–264
shifting behaviors, 77–85
    accelerating leftward, 81–84
    async-first behavioral cues, 85
    broadcasting commitments, 77–81
signatures, email, 78
Silva, Gonçalo, 31–32

simplifying
    complexity of communication, 178
    documentation, 92
Singer, Ryan, 123
sizes of teams, 164
Skelton, Matthew, 99, 218
skills economies, 290–291
Slack, 105, 113
slowing things down, 31–32, 80
social batteries, 72
social media, dopamine and, 44
software development
    Manifesto for Agile Software Development, 33–34
    new ways to work, 5
    surveys, 6, 7
    workflow, 50
solo work, 160–161
SonarQube, 183
SPACE framework, 222
special economic zones (SEZs), 290
spectrum
    of synchronousness, 15, 17
    visualization of, 14–16
speed, 204
sprints
    continuous flow, 118–122
    development cycles, 117–125
    scope, 119–120
stages of sensible defaults, 275–284. *See also* defaults
    stage 1: aligning goals, 276–278
    stage 2: tabulating baseline data, 278–280
    stage 3: agreeing on fundamentals, 280–281
    stage 4: cleaning up calendars, 281–282
    stage 5: building 30-day programs, 283–284
stages of workflow, 52
stakeholders, costs for, 246–249
standup meetings, 107–116
    automation tools, 113–115
    distributed standups, 108–109
    lag, 115–116
    length of, 108
    maintaining relevance, 115
    project management tools, 109–112
    Zoom with video off, 108
Stanier, James, 15, 16, 55, 137, 174
starting async-first, 275–285
statistics
    readability, 37
    remote work, 59, 60
#status channel, 113
statuses
    asynchronous status reporting, 124
    instant messaging (IM), 99–100
    workflow, 50–52

StepSize, 186
stocks, managing, 234–238
stories, 138
    details of, 140–141
    queuing up in advance, 141–142
    user, 138
strategies
    collaboration, 6
    for ConveRel quadrants, 61–63
    decision-making processes, 53–55
    distraction blocking, 43, 44–45
    doubt, 47
    to protect and extend async-first,
        260–261
    reading, 45–46
    shifting behaviors, 77–85
    statuses/transitions (workflow), 50–52
    Ulysses pacts, 17
    working independently, 46–47
stream-aligned teams, 218
streamlining decision-making processes,
    53–55
"The Strength of Weak Ties" (Granovetter),
    235
strong relationships, 62
structure
    after the fact, 232
    of text, 32
success skills, 209–210, 217–228
    aligning with common purposes,
        226–227
    building team cultures, 223–225
    creating calm, 221–223
    design for, 217–227
    internal structure of teams, 219–220
    reducing pressure, 221–223
    team management, 218–219
summaries
    changes to handbooks, 93
    meetings, 165
    replacing, 164
supporting scale, 10–11
survey forms, 130
surveys
    maturity, 279
    software development, 6, 7
synchronous collaboration, 30
synchronous communication, 18
synchronousness, spectrum of, 15, 17
synthesizing inputs, 129
System 1, 8
systems
    audits, 232–234
    in balance, 17–18
    capabilities of, 231–232
    focus, 203
    improving, 259–260
    optimizing, 120–121

T
tabulating baseline data, 278–280
tacit knowledge, 229–239. See also
    knowledge
    adding managers, 237–238
    capabilities of systems, 231–232
    communities, 229–238
    creating porous walls, 230–234
    facilitating flows, 234–238
    knowledge management, 238
Taleb, Nassim, 205
targeting conversations, 102–103
task boards, 52, 53, 144. See also
    communication
    updating statuses, 110
    whiteboards as, 284
tasks
    analysis, 47
    project management tools, 109–112
Team APIs, writing, 183, 262
team handbooks. See also handbooks
    content, 89–92
    documentation triggers, 94–95
    iterations of, 93–94
    need for source of truth, 87–88
    onboarding, 182–183
    shared realities, 95
    start with teams, 88
    tools, 92
    versioning systems, 93, 94
    writing, 87–96
teams
    autonomy in, 148–149
    bonding, 156
    broadcasting commitments, 77–81
    clarifying norms, 145
    collaboration, 230 (see also
        collaboration)
    communication, 164 (see also
        commitments)
    creating documentation, 30 (see also
        documentation)
    culture-building, 216
    cultures, 223–225
    defining values, 223
    distributed, 149
    distribution, 245–246
    efficiency, 193, 195
    goals, 283
    hubs, 26
    identifying values, 224
    internal structure of, 219–220
    management, 218–219
    managing, 209–216
    meetings, 66 (see also meetings)
    Microsoft Teams, 113
    off-boarding, 92
    onboarding, 92 (see also onboarding)
    ownership, 284

processes, 144
productivity, 47
remote, 50
retrospectives, 127 (*see also* retrospectives)
self-organizing teams, 49
sizes of, 164
stages of sensible defaults (*see* stages of sensible defaults)
standup meetings, 107–116
success skills, 217–228 (*see also* success skills)
tech huddles, 147 (*see also* tech huddles)
templates for team values, 225
topologies, 219, 262
treating everyone as remote, 251–253
workflow, 51
tech design, communication, 173–178
tech huddles, 147–153
    actions, 150–151
    autonomy in teams, 148–149
    effective meetings, 151–152
    overview of, 148
    quick syncs, 150
    schedules, 152–153
technical design documents, 176–178
templates, 165
    make your own templates (MYOT), 176
    requirements, 139
    retrospectives, 132
    sharing, 263–264
    team values, 225
    Team Values Discovery, 225
tests, dev-box, 138
text
    changing, 32
    communication, 30 (*see also* written communication)
    formatting, 101
    interacting with, 32
    structure of, 32
Thinking Fast and Slow (Kahneman), 8
30-day programs, building, 283–284
37signals, 72
Thomas, Luke, 61, 62
thrashing, 53
threads, topics, 104
throughput, 120–121
ties, types of, 236
time
    cycles, 120–121
    management, 45, 206
    pair programming tools, 157
    recurring meetings, 83–84, 200, 201
    response times, 55
timelines
    retrospectives, 129
    scrum ceremonies, 118
time zones
    face-to-face communication, 69–70
    meetings, 64–66

titles, 184
tl;dv, 165
tools, 23
    automation, 113–115
    business intelligence (BI), 278
    code automation, 186
    collaboration, 24–25
    defining development environments, 193
    documentation, 165
    EqualExpert Slack guide, 105
    feature breakdown documents, 175–176
    gaps in capabilities of, 258
    instant messaging, 53
    maintaining, 92
    Manifesto for Agile Software Development, 33–34, 40–41
    Microsoft Word, 37
    pair programming, 26, 155–161 (*see also* pair programming tools)
    productivity, 26
    project management, 109–112
    README files, 185
    sharing, 263–264
    with specific context, 26–27
    task boards, 51, 52
    team handbooks, 92
    text editors, 37
    tracking metrics, 183
    whiteboards, 131
topics, threads, 104
topologies, teams, 218–219, 262
toxicity in virtual workplaces, 267–272
    communication, 269–270
    growth of, 267–271
    leadership vigilance of, 271–272
    meaningful synchrony, 270–271
tracking
    data, 280
    metrics, 183
training
    in-person, 245
    online learning, 245
transactions, 203
transitions, workflow, 50–52
Trello, 113
triggers, documentation, 94–95
trust, 7, 214
truth, need for source of, 87–88
Tulsa Remote project, 247
2 × 2 matrix, 233–234
two-track approach, 124–125

U

Ulysses pacts, 17, 77
unconscious competence, 260
unconscious incompetence, 259
updating statuses, 110
Upstream (Heath), 217
usage, 184
user stories, 138, 141–142

V

Vagrant, 193
values
  alignment, 223
  asynchronous communication, 18
  of being in person, 71–72
  core, 224
  of deep work, 14 (see also deep work)
  focus on, 13–14
  identifying, 224
  synchronous communication, 18
  Team Values Discovery, 225
  of tools, 23
variables, environments, 217
versioning systems, 93, 94
vertical slices, recruiting, 261
video
  asynchronous, 38–39
  desk checks, 142–143 (see also desk checks)
  inline, 39
  replacing desk checks with, 142–143
  Zoom with video off, 108
videoconferencing, 70, 147. See also Zoom
virtual workplaces, configuring, 227
virtual workplaces, toxicity in, 267–272
visibility bias, 272–273
visualization on spectrum, 14–16
visuals, overviews, 184
Visual Studio, 193

W

weak relationships, 62
weak ties, 235
well-being, 212
whiteboards
  collaboration, 131
  as task boards, 284
wiki pages, 174
work environments, improving, 11
work execution, 49–50
workflow, 49–50
  representing practices for, 144
  software development, 51
  statuses, 50–52
  transitions, 50–52
work-from-anywhere setups, 246. See also remote work
working independently, 43, 46–47

work-life balance, 5–6
workloads, 210–211
workplaces
  inclusive, 9
  toxicity in virtual, 267–272
Workspace (Google), 230, 231
"Write the Docs" community, 174
writing. See also communication
  architectural decision records (ADRs), 166–167
  artifacts, 189–190
  asynchronous audio, 38–39
  asynchronous video, 38–39
  benefits of writing, 31–32
  checklists, 191–192
  commit messages, 168–169
  content for team handbooks, 89–92
  versus documentation, 29
  effectiveness of face-to-face communication, 40
  improving, 36
  inline videos, 39
  interpreting, 34, 35
  iterations of team handbooks, 93–94
  journalism, 35
  Manifesto for Agile Software Development, 33–34, 40–41
  meetings and, 30
  need for source of truth, 87–88
  notes (meetings), 164–165
  reading skills, 45–46
  README files, 185
  responding with links, 95
  shared realities, 95
  start handbooks with teams, 88
  Team APIs, 183
  team handbooks, 87–96
  text editors, 37

X–Y–Z

x as service, 219
Yip, Jason, 107, 108
Zapier, 113
Zoom, 69. See also face-to-face communication
  pair programming tools, 158
  with video off, 108
Zoomers, 294–295

Register Your Product at informit.com/register

Access additional benefits and save up to 65%* on your next purchase

- Automatically receive a coupon for 35% off books, eBooks, and web editions and 65% off video courses, valid for 30 days. Look for your code in your InformIT cart or the Manage Codes section of your account page.
- Download available product updates.
- Access bonus material if available.**
- Check the box to hear from us and receive exclusive offers on new editions and related products.

InformIT—The Trusted Technology Learning Source

InformIT is the online home of information technology brands at Pearson, the world's leading learning company. At informit.com, you can

- Shop our books, eBooks, and video training. Most eBooks are DRM-Free and include PDF and EPUB files.
- Take advantage of our special offers and promotions (informit.com/promotions).
- Sign up for special offers and content newsletter (informit.com/newsletters).
- Access thousands of free chapters and video lessons.
- Enjoy free ground shipping on U.S. orders.*

* Offers subject to change.
** Registration benefits vary by product. Benefits will be listed on your account page under Registered Products.

Connect with InformIT—Visit informit.com/community

 twitter.com/informit

Pearson

Addison-Wesley • Adobe Press • Cisco Press • Microsoft Press • Oracle Press • Peachpit Press • Pearson IT Certification • Que